THE RABBI MICHAEL J ELJARRAT LEARNING PROGRAMME

Fundamentals of Judaism

Written by Rabbi Michael J Eljarrat

© Copyright holder Rabbi Michael J Eljarrat

ALL RIGHTS RESERVED.

Including but not limited to: The text, format, translations, layout, artwork, graphics, content and style.

No part of this class or course thereof may be reproduced IN ANY FORM- PHOTOCOPY, OR OTHERWISE- Even for personal use without WRITTEN permission from the copyright holder.

Legal Notice:
THE CONTENTS OF THIS WORK INVOLVED EXTENSIVE RESEARCH AND COSTS AND THE RIGHTS OF THE COPYRIGHT HOLDER WILL BE STRICLY ENFORCED.

The copyright holder can be contacted:
By e-mail eljarrat@mweb.co.za
Telephone 00 27 11 485 1731

BEEJEWISH © is part of the Michael J Eljarrat education foundation
www.beejewish.org

TABLE OF CONTENTS

Introduction iv

Part 1: Fundamentals of Faith

Part 1.1

1. Class one: Proof of G-ds existence 1
2. Class two: Human Suffering 4
3. Class three: Reward & Punishment 7
4. Class four: Your Personal Contribution 10

Part 1.2

5. Class five: The 13 Principles of faith # 1-3 13
6. Class six: The 13 Principles of faith # 4-6 16
7. Class seven: The 13 Principles of faith # 7-9 20
8. Class eight: The 13 Principles of faith # 10-13 23

Part 1.3

9. Class nine: Ethics: Loving your fellow Man 26
10. Class ten: Ethics: Evil Speech 29
11. Class eleven: Ethics: Charity 33
12. Class twelve: Ethics: Modesty 36
13. Class thirteen: Ethics: Kindness 40
14. Class fourteen: Ethics: Business Ethics 44
15. Class fifteen: Ethics: Medical Ethics 47

Part 1.4

16. Class sixteen: Life Cycle: Circumcision 50
17. Class seventeen: Life Cycle: Bar Mitzvah 53
18. Class eighteen: Life Cycle: Engagement & Marriage 56
19. Class nineteen: Life Cycle: Death & Burial Part 1 59
20. Class twenty: Life Cycle: Death & Burial Part 2 62

Part 2: Fundamentals of Observance

Part 2.1

21. Class twenty one: Introduction to Shabbos/ Preparation for Shabbos ... 65
22. Class twenty two: Receiving Shabbos 68
23. Class twenty three: Kiddush 71

Part 2.2

24. Class twenty four: The 39 Works of Shabbos an Application of Laws 75
25. Class twenty five: The 39 Works of Shabbos - Order of Bread 79
26. Class twenty six: The 39 Works of Shabbos - Order of Fabrics 84
27. Class twenty seven: The 39 Works of Shabbos - Order of Hides ... 88
28. Class twenty eight: The 39 Works of Shabbos - Order of Building Part 1 ... 91
29. Class twenty nine: The 39 Works of Shabbos - Order of Building Part 2 ... 94

Part 2.3

30. Class thirty: The laws of "Muktzah"	98
31. Class thirty one: The laws of "Borer"	102
32. Class thirty two: Personal Grooming on Shabbos	105
33. Class thirty three: Shabbos Behavior and the Prohibitions of Isaiah	108
34. Class thirty four: Electricity On Shabbos	111

Part 2.4

35. Class thirty five: Cooking & Reheating Part 1	113
36. Class thirty six: Cooking & Reheating Part 2	116
37. Class thirty seven: Cooking & Reheating Part 3	119
38. Class thirty eight: Cooking & Reheating Part 4	123
39. Class thirty nine: Cooking & Reheating Part 5	126

Part 2.5

40. Class forty: The Laws of Eruv	128
41. Class forty one: Emergencies On Shabbos	132
42. Class forty two: The Laws of Havdalah	135

Part 2.6

43. Class forty three: Introduction to Kosher/ Philosophy	138
44. Class forty four: The Slaughtering/ Salting Process	141
45. Class forty five: Meat & milk/ Forbidden Mixtures	144
46. Class forty six: Checking Vegetables	147
47. Class forty seven: Sifting Flour & Checking Eggs	150
48. Class forty eight Kashering Utensils & Immersing New Utensils	153
49. Class forty nine: Mistakes In the Kitchen	156
50. Class fifty: Manufactured Products & Traveling	159
51. Class fifty one: Taking Challah	163
52. Class fifty two: Chalav Yisroel & Pas Yisroel	166

Part 3: Fundamentals of Prayer & Torah

Part 3.1

53. Class fifty three: Modeh Ani & Morning Brochos	169
54. Class fifty four: Pesukay De'Zimrah	172
55. Class fifty five: Shemah & its Brochos	175
56. Class fifty six: The Amidah Shemona Esray	178
57. Class fifty seven: Tachnoon & conclusion of Morning service	181
58. Class fifty eight: Mincha & Mariv	184
59. Class fifty nine: Friday Night Service & Zemiros	187
60. Class sixty: Shabbos Morning/ Musaf & Mincha	189
61. Class sixty one: Rosh Chodesh & Hallel	192
62. Class sixty two: Pasach/Shavuos/ Succos	197
63. Class sixty three: Rosh HaShana	199
64. Class sixty four: Yom Kippur	201
65. Class sixty five: Chanuka & Purim	203
66. Class sixty six: Brochos On Foods & Events	205

Part 3.2

67. Class sixty seven: The Written & Oral Torah	208
68. Class sixty eight: The Importance of Learning Torah /Fixing time	213
69. Class sixty nine: How Halachah is Decided	216
70. Class seventy: Defining a Talmid chacham & Ben Torah	219

71.	Class seventy one: The Torah Readings & procedure	222
72.	Class seventy two: 613 Mitzvos A look at Teffilin & Mezuzah	225
73.	Class seventy three: The need To Study mussar/A Torah Life style	228
74.	Class seventy four: Rabbinical Rulings & contemporary Halachah	232
75.	Class seventy five: Kabbalah & Mysticisim	236

Part 4: Fundamentals of Jewish History

Part 4.1

76.	Class seventy six: Introduction: From Creation To Avraham	239
77.	Class seventy seven: The Patriarachs	244
78.	Class seventy eight: From Moshe To King David	248
79.	Class seventy nine: From Tanayim to Geonim	252
80.	Class eighty: From Rishonim to Late Achronim	255

Part 4.2

81.	Class eighty one: Israel & Jerusalem	259
82.	Class eighty two: Mitzvos Of Israel	263
83.	Class eighty three: Current Situation/ Biblical References	266
84.	Class eighty four: The South African community & communities around the world	269
85.	Class eighty five: The difference between Judaism & other Religions	272
86.	Class eighty six: Different Philosophical Approaches	275

Part 5: Fundamentals of the Jewish calendar

87.	Class eighty seven: Rosh Hashana Laws & Significance Part 1	278
88.	Class eighty eight: Rosh Hashana Laws & Significance Part 2	281
89.	Class eighty nine: Yom Kippur Laws & Significance Part 1	283
90.	Class ninety: Yom Kippur Laws & Significance Part 2	286
91.	Class ninety one: Succos Laws & Significance Part 1	288
92.	Class ninety two: Succos Laws & Significance Part 2	293
93.	Class ninety three: Chanukah Laws & Significance Part 1	296
94.	Class ninety four: Chanukah Laws & Significance Part 2	299
95.	Class ninety five: Purim Laws & Significance Part 1	302
96.	Class ninety six: Purim Laws & Significance Part 2	305
97.	Class ninety seven: Pesach Laws & Significance Part 1	307
98.	Class ninety eight: Pesach Laws & Significance Part 2	311
99.	Class ninety nine: Pesach Laws & Significance Part 3	314
100.	Class one hundred: Shavuos Laws & Significance	318

Introduction

With praise and gratitude to Hashem

For several years I have had the opportunity to engage, interact and teach people from all walks of life. The one common theme which emerged time and time again; was that the average layman had a vast array of misconceptions about Judaism in general, as well as the lack of a clear and concise text outlining the fundamental concepts of Judaism.

Although there are literally thousands upon thousands of Jewish texts available, these texts are often out of reach for the new-comer to Judaism, due to a lack of learning skills and proper guidance. What this book aims to achieve is, the development of the very first building block in the life long process of Torah study. Thus this book can be seen as a supplementary text, opening the path way to the next level of learning.

For anyone wanting to understand Judaism and what it entails, Fundamentals of Judaism is an introductory text dealing with the key aspects and core philosophical approaches to Judaism.

This text provides insight and guidance to those wishing to learn about Judaism at the most basic level of comprehension.

This book was originally written as a course set work for Non-Jews in the process of converting to Judaism, and has been adapted to form a clear and concise user manual to navigate through the complexities of Judaism.

The book contains 100 classes divided into sections dealing with:

1. Fundamentals of Jewish Faith
2. Fundamentals of Observance (Kosher and Shabbos)
3. Fundamentals of Prayer & Torah
4. Fundamentals of Jewish History
5. Fundamentals of the Jewish calendar

This book is a great starting point for anyone wanting to understand Judaism and Jewish culture. Online resource material is available at www.beejewish.org where this book is available in a weekly class format with supplementary audio and visual tools.

This book is dedicated in Honour of my father's 70th Birthday with the deepest love and gratitude from the entire family.

I would like to take this opportunity to thank all those individuals who have attended my classes over the years, and have given me great insight and inspiration.

In particular I would like to thank my father who has been a shining example to me, of upholding the virtues of humility, honesty and integrity under the most difficult of circumstances. May he live to 120 with strength, happiness and success... I would like to thank my mother for all her support and encouragement, as well and my brother Ray, and sister Debbie and their respective families for being by my side during turbulent times. I would also like to thank my Grandmother "Granny Rivka" for her many words of wisdom, and insight.
Last but not least my wife and Aishes Chyil Chaya Zelda, who has stood by my side and has given me strength and encouragement throughout my endeavours.

A special thank you to: Avraham, Sarah, Jaco and Laurika du Preez for all their help and support.

Lastly I would like to thank the many generous contributors who have made this work possible:

The course work in this book is dedicated in memory of the following individuals:

יצחק בן מרדכי זצ"ל
נתן בן פרץ   זצ"ל
חיה טויבא סגרסקי זצ"ל
אליעזר מאיר בן צבי
Rabbi Yakov Scherer
Sonia Levine

May we soon merit serving Hashem in the new בית המקדש
ובא לציון גואל

Kindly note that this work is not intended for final Halachic rulings. Please consult a competent Rabbi in your area regarding any practical questions.

THE RABBI MICHAEL J ELJARRAT LEARNING PROGRAMME -CLASS ONE

CLASS 1   FAITH AND DOUBT
PROOF OF G-D'S EXISTENCE

The question of G-d's existence seems entwined into the essence of every religion – no less so in Judaism. This class is designed to answer some of the questions surrounding this issue:
- What is the difference between faith and knowledge?
- Can we prove G-d's existence?
- Why do we need proof – isn't blind faith good enough?
- How do we know we heard G-d at Mt. Sinai?
- How can belief be a commandment?

Faith vs. Knowledge

faith n. firm belief, esp. without logical proof.

knowledge n. a theoretical or practical understanding of a subject, language etc.[1]

"Every Jew should know and believe in G-d."[2]

Faith is the result of emotional response and desire – in certain situations, our logic may be giving us one message, but our need to believe the opposite is so great that we ignore the evidence in front of us and go with our feelings instead. Faith expresses what we wish is true, not what is actually true.

On the other hand, from facts, evidence and details, we acquire knowledge. It is rational.

 Which of these two approaches would it be best to base our lives upon? Should we select one over the other? Does belief in G-d come from the head or the heart?

The interaction between emotion and logic

Emotions are fluid, changeable, easily influenced. Should our belief in G-d stem solely from our emotions, it is likely that at the first challenge to our faith, it would waver and eventually disappear. On the other hand, a purely intellectual understanding of G-d would not encompass the aspects of G-d that are beyond human understanding.

Is the solution therefore just to combine emotion and logic? Unfortunately, our heads and hearts are not always ideal team-mates. Our *yetzer hara* (evil inclination) can tempt us away from our logical understanding of G-d, resulting in doubt and ways to deny G-d. After all, this is arguably easier, allowing us greater freedoms and less responsibility.[3] While this may sound dramatic,

---
1 The Concise Oxford English Dictionary
2 Derech Hashem by Rabbi Moshe Chaim Luzzato, chapter 1
3 Kovetz Maamarim by Rabbi Elchonon Wasserman

even our greatest efforts are not sufficient to avoid the temptation of our evil inclination, just as even the smallest bribe can cloud the perception of a judge. Modern thought terms this inner conflict between our emotion and logic cognitive dissonance.[4]

Judaism teaches that belief in G-d must have a rational basis:

"You shall know this day and take to your heart that Hashem, He Is the G d in heaven above and on the earth below – there is none other."[5]

However, we are not expected to ignore the emotions that in part characterise us as human beings. In fact, belief in G-d must come from a combination of faith and knowledge – allowing what we know in our minds to enter our hearts. In order to believe in G-d, we need to be emotionally prepared to accept the logic and "consequences" of that belief.

> CONCEPT IN ACTION: *Tefillin* are comprised of two parts, one fitting on the forehead and one on the bicep, close the heart. This is a daily reminder that emotional connection and intellectual understanding are necessary to fulfil the *mitzvah* of believing in G-d.

> WISDOM IN HEBREW: The story of Creation begins with the letter *beis* (ב), which has a numerical value of two – opposites can work together to form a perfect whole.

From the verse quoted above, it appears that Judaism commands us to belief in G-d – how can we be commanded to think and feel in a certain way? The Sages teach that belief in G-d is a quality inherent in every human being. If this is true, why do we still need to be commanded to believe in G-d? The *Shema* says the following:

"…and not explore after your heart and after your eyes after which you stray…"[6]

From this we learn that we are in fact commanded to guard against our eyes being clouded by our evil inclination, which will enable us to fulfil the commandment and continuously build our relationship with G-d.

The greatest of Jewish philosophers have disagreed as to which proof of G-d's existence is the strongest – but not that there is one. Proof can be found in both Jewish philosophy and history.

Philosophical proof of G-d's existence

Imagine entering a room and noticing a piece of paper lying on the floor, the lines filled with elegant handwriting. Would you assume that a pot of ink had fallen next to the page, the ink streaming over the page and supernaturally forming into letters, words and paragraphs on its own? Or, would you assume that someone had written on the page, which had later fallen on the floor? What do you think a friend's reaction would be if you pointed out a building and proceeded

---

4 This theory was first proposed by Leon Festinger in 1957
5 The Artscroll Chumash. Deuteronomy 4:39.
6 The Artscroll Chumash. Numbers 15:39

to explain that it miraculously formed overnight? Is it just coincidence that in nature, repeating ratios can be found, that the cells and atoms that form every living thing operate in harmony?

The very complexity of creation itself is proof of G-d's existence and of His on-going involvement with His creation.

Historical proof of G-d's existence

Many religions trace their history from a revelation being received by a single individual, who then shared it with his community, claiming that it was given to him by G-d. Only Judaism asserts that the revelation given at Mt. Sinai was given to an entire nation by G-d Himself, a nation who has then maintained its traditions, in an unbroken chain – father to son, for more than three millennia. Is it possible that in excess 600,000 souls would agree to a common concept of G-d, pretend to have seen Him and then preserve that story for 3,000 years?

The fact that this nation did indeed share in this event, man, woman and child and that their descendents are teaching their own children about that revelation today, is historical proof that G-d exists, and once showed Himself to His people.

In summary

Having discussed the basis of belief in G-d, and what it means to sustain that belief, two proofs of G-d's existence have been presented. Many people are only ready to accept those proofs once they have already established a relationship with G-d, just as most people only recognise their soul mate as such after they have already committed to the relationship. Our journey towards belief in G-d may be just that, a journey, but the destination may be found within our own souls.

Learning outcomes - by the end of the lesson, students should:

1. Be able to differentiate between faith and knowledge
2. Understand the working proofs of G-d's existence
3. Understand and be able to practise the commandment of belief in G-d

Review questions

1. What is faith? (2)
2. Why is it important to have logical proof, isn't it good enough just to feel it? (3)
3. Discuss two possible ways with which we can we prove G-d's existence (15)

Additional reading

1. *Derech Hashem* – Rabbi Moshe Chaim Luzzato
2. *Kovetz Maamarim* – Rabbi Elchonon Wasserman

THE RABBI MICHAEL J ELJARRAT LEARNING PROGRAMME – CLASS TWO

CLASS 2 FAITH AND DOUBT
HUMAN SUFFERING

After understanding the need to have tangible proof of G-d's existence, the next step is to understand the question which very often leads to doubt. All to often we see tragedy in our own lives and in the life's of others, and the issue of human suffering manifests itself in questions such as -"where was G-d when?.- Or - "how could, G-d let this happen?"
Why do the good suffer and the bad prosper? – Why do good people die young?

When approaching the question of why do bad things happen to good people? We need to ask ourselves 2 important questions, which will be the basis of our discussion.
1. Why do things happen at all?
2. How well do we understand the definition of a Good & Bad Person?

"Make your way known to me."[1]

We find an interesting portion in the Torah, where the Jewish people had sinned with the Golden Calf. In an intimate conversation Moses asks G-d make your way known to me, to which G-d replies amongst other things "no man can see my face and live."
G-d promises Moses that He will indeed show Himself however since it would be impossible for Moses to see the face of G-d, G-d says that He will show Moses the back of His head. When one reads this portion in the Torah one is puzzled with the many seemingly strange events which took place. After understanding this portion in the Torah we will see that this short passage contains the answers to unlocking the mystery surrounding human suffering.

The Talmud[2] explains that after the sin of the Golden Calf, G-d wanted to destroy the Jewish Nation and start a new Jewish Nation from Moses and his decedents. At that point Moses prayed for the salvation of the Jewish Nation and asked G-d "make your way known to me" meaning why do we have righteous people suffering and wicked people prospering. The Talmud relates 2 possibilities to what G-d replied to Moses, one possibility is that a completely righteous person will not suffer however an incomplete righteous person will suffer, a completely wicked person will suffer and a not complete wicked person will prosper. The second opinion in the Talmud is that G-d did not answer Mosses' question as the verse says "no man can see my face and live", however G-d did show Moses the back of His head, namely the knot of his Teffilin of the head.

---

1. Exodus 33:13
2. Brochos 7a

THE RABBI MICHAEL J ELJARRAT LEARNING PROGRAMME – CLASS TWO

Where as this passage of Talmud addresses our issue, a great deal of explanation is still needed. To (examine) and explain this piece of Talmud we will need to examine several terms used in the Talmud in order to appreciate the answer given by G-d. Simply speaking the term "Rosha" – wicked person and the term "Tzadik" – righteous person refers to the sum total of person's deeds, a person with mostly good deeds can be classified as a "tzadik" where as a person with mostly bad deeds can be classified as a "Rosha" – wicked person. The table below summarizes:

CLASS OF PERSON	PERCENTAGE OF GOOD DEEDS	QUALITY OF LIFE
TZADIK GAMUR COMPLETELY RIGHTEOUS	100% GOOD DEEDS	NO SUFFERING
TZADIK SHE- ANO GAMUR NON COMPLETE TZADIK	51% GOOD DEEDS	SUFFERING
ROSHA SHE- ANO GAMUR NON COMPLETE ROSHA	51% BAD DEEDS	NO SUFFERING
ROSHA GAMUR COMPLETE ROSHA	100% BAD DEEDS	SUFFERING

What would seem apparent is that the quality of life of an individual depends on his deeds. We find a support to this concept from the commentary of the Malbim on the verse "G-d is the shadow under your right hand."[3]

The Malbim explains that G-d acts towards us in the same fashion that we act towards others i.e. G-d mimics our behavior in the same way as a shadow mimics the object causing its reflection. Therefore we can understand why the completely righteous do not suffer where as the completely wicked do suffer.

However the question still remains why should the non- complete tzadik suffer and the non-complete Rosha, prosper? To understand this we will examine the following verse "He will sit smelting and purifying silver ect"[4] The commentaries explain[5] that the silver purification process requires several key aspects in order to remove all it's impurities. Firstly the raw silver needs to be placed in the hottest place within the purifying chamber. Secondly the raw silver has to remain there until all of its impurities have been removed and finally the silver has to be removed the instant it has become pure. If the silver remains in the heat once it has been purified, this will cause the impurities to be re-absorbed into the silver, after which it can never be re-purified, and how does one know when the silver is pure?, when one can see one's reflection in the silver. Based on this we can understand that G-d purifies us like silver; G-d places us in the "heat" (Intense suffering) until the point that we are pure, and how does G-d know when we are pure? When G-d sees His reflection in us, when we are G-D like in our behaviour.

---

3. Tehillim -Psalms 1
4. Malachi -Chapter 3 verse 3
5. Rav Alter- Chicago

THE RABBI MICHAEL J ELJARRAT LEARNING PROGRAMME – CLASS TWO

Therefore the underlying concept, is that in Jewish thought suffering is not viewed as a "coincidence" but rather G-d out of His love for us, wants us to reach our potential which often remains dormant, until prompted by hardship and suffering. In the Talmud cited above regarding the conversation between G-d and Moses, the second opinion holds that G-d replied to Moses you can not know my ways this is what is meant by the verse "no man can see my face and live", however G-d showed Moses the back of His head.[6] The commentaries explain that what G-d was showing Moses was that although from the front it would appear that the 2 straps of the head Teffilin are un-related and disconnected much like the seeming contradicting mercy and anger of G-d, never the less on closer inspection it all comes from the same place.

"May the omnipresent console you among the other mourners of Zion & Jerusalem"

The above statement is said to one who has G-d forbid lost a close relative as a consolation. When one inspects the statement it would seem hard to find any such consolation. Just what exactly is the point of saying this statement to one who is in tremendous grieving? The commentaries explain that out of the many names used to describe G-d[7]. One specific name appears in the above statement that of "Hamokom" – the Omnipresent, the meaning of the mourners statement is to reinforce the fact that G-d is Omnipresent literally the word "Hamokom" means "the place" meaning that G-d is in everyplace at every time, the point which the mourners statement makes is that although when tragedy strikes we often ask "where was G-d?,"[8] as if to say, this event took place without G-d's knowledge, if G-d were here, G-d would never have let this happen. Therefore the response to this is that G-d is Omnipresent, i.e. not only was G-d there, but it was G-d who made this happen.

In summary, our life on earth has a purpose and intern we have a "job" to do with our life's. When G-d sees our great potential and our under utilization of this great potential, G-d gives us a "wake up call" to help us get back on track, these alerts are because G-d loves us, and whatever difficulty or pain that we experience G-d feels the pain and suffers with us as the verse says

"I am with you in your suffering"[9]

---

6. The knot of the head Teffilin
7. Discussion point: the names of G-d such as "Shakai" on a mezuzah, the limitation of eye sight not to see daemons
8. Discussion point: Story with Rabbi Eliezer Silver regarding the rental of a Siddur in a concentration camp
9. Psalms 91

THE RABBI MICHAEL J ELJARRAT LEARNING PROGRAMME – CLASS THREE

CLASS 3
FAITH AND DOUBT
REWARD & PUNISHMENT

The concept of reward of punishment seems to be an integral part of every religion. After seeing in class 2 that our actions can have consequences on our life, we will now examine reward and punishment within Jewish thought. This class is designed to answer such questions as: Why is there reward and punishment? - What exactly is the reward? – When do we see and receive the reward? Why is there a need for punishment? – What is the world to come?

The Talmud states [1] these are the precepts whose fruits a person enjoys in this world, but whose principal remains intact for him in the world to come. They are the honor due to father and mother, acts of kindness, early attendance in the house of study morning and evening, hospitality to guests, visiting the sick, providing for a bride, escorting the dead, absorption in prayer, bringing peace between man and his fellow – and the study of Torah is equivalent to them all.

Where as for the most part we all understand that being kind and generous to others is good and noble, however we sometimes fail to ask a deeper and perhaps a more meaningful question namely "what is the purpose of creation?" We have seen previously that G-d did in fact create the world, but the question remains "What was the reason G-d created the world?" The answer to this question will help us to understand some of the concepts behind reward and punishment.

The Sefer Ha Yoshor explains that G-d created the world in order to give us pleasure, and not because G-d needs our service. The proof to this is the fact that G-d existed before the world was created; therefore G-d is not depended on this world (this concept will be further discussed in later lessons). If G-d does not need us or the world then what prompted G-d to create the world? The Sefer Ha Yoshor explains that the creation was therefore an act of kindness from G-d.

The Ramchal explains[2] that G-d wanted to give man the ultimate pleasure possible namely closeness to G-d. The assumption that closeness to G-d, being the ultimate pleasure needs to be understood:

- Why would closeness to G-d bring us the ultimate satisfaction?
- How is it possible to become close to G-d?
- Furthermore if G-d's desire is to give us the ultimate pleasure of closeness, why do we need to "earn it" why can't we just receive it?

These 3 questions will now be answered.

---

1. Shabbos 127a
2. Derech Hashem

PAGE 1

THE RABBI MICHAEL J ELJARRAT LEARNING PROGRAMME – CLASS THREE

A. THE ULTIMATE PLEASURE:

What is the ultimate experience possible for a human being to feel? We all enjoy good food, great holidays, luxury cars and accommodation. But where is the best restaurant in the world? Where is the ultimate holiday location? If we are searching for pleasure surely we should seek out the best that the world has to offer. It would make sense to say that if one would want the best Chinese food one would have to go to China, as getting something from the source would always yields the best results.

It is easily understood that there is more to man than just flesh & bone. Humans by nature are complex beings consisting of a body, mind & soul; this is reflected by our various drives and desires. When we closely examine pleasure we will see that pleasure can be divided into 1 of 5 categories. Each category of pleasure is totally unique and cannot be traded for another- for example if you were starving would you trade a good meal for a view of a great sunset?[3]

- The lowest level of pleasure is physical & material pleasure
  Examples: good food, nice clothes, comfortable home etc (Anything that involves the 5 senses)

- But what is worth more than all the money in the world?

- The next level up is love[4]; real love cannot be traded for any amount of money we see this demonstrated by parents who will give up everything to have their kidnapped child returned.

- But what is so important that would cause someone to give up the love of their lives?

- The next level up is the drive to make a difference in the world, we see this demonstrated by people who work 24/7 leaving behind their family at home, all for the sake of reaching a goal.

- But for what outcome would people give up their personal goals?

- The next greatest pleasure is the feeling of power, the true pleasure of power is the power to create the feeling of turning ideas into reality – this can be demonstrated by the mere fact that we would rather be the boss than the worker; the boss can create and control.

- But what would be missing if we had it all, an abundance of money, a loving spouse and family, meaning in life, and the power to create?

- The next and highest level of pleasure is an encounter with G-d. After all our physical desires have been taken care of and our emotional world has been satisfied the soul still craves and can only be satisfied with closeness to G-d.

B. HOW DOES ONE GET CLOSE TO G-D?:

For the believer the answer to this question is critical, and without an accurate answer the believer is left wondering and guessing. The Orchas Tzadikim says there are two groups of searchers that never get to where they want to go. The first is one who is searching but does not know what he is searching for. For example if one is searching in a crowd of people for a person that is not known by the searcher, since the searcher does not know who he/she is looking for, he/she will continue to search

---

[3]. See Rabbi Weinberg 5 levels of pleasure – website aishhatorah.com
[4]. Love comes from focusing on the virtues of another. Lust comes from focusing only on the physical virtues. Love is long lasting where as lust is transient.

THE RABBI MICHAEL J ELJARRAT LEARNING PROGRAMME – CLASS THREE

forever without any results. The second is one who knows who he/she is searching for, but does not know where to find them. For that searcher frustration awaits since all the searching effort may be directed in the wrong area all together. Like wise a person who does not recognize G-d will not find G-d, and one who does recognize G-d, but does not know where to look, will find him/her self frustrated with the lack of results.

This leads us to the all important question "Where is G-d?"

Surely if we know where G-d is, we would travel to that location and be close to G-d? This is a mistake made by many searching for G-d, however this is not the case, getting close to G-d cannot be measured in physical terms, since G-d is not physical. The only way to become close to G-d is through spiritual terms.

Closeness in spiritual terms is measured not in physical proximity but in similarity. The more similar we are to G-d, the closer we will become to G-d. It is for this reason that we spend our lives perfecting ourselves in an attempt to be similar to G-d who is perfect.

C. WHY THE NEED TO EARN?

Since G-d created mankind to reward them with the greatest pleasure, by nature reward is only feasible when earned. The difference between earnings and a gift is that earnings are deserved. The reason why G-d wants us to deserve the reward, and not just simply receive it as a gift is because the enjoyment of earnings is far greater than the enjoyment of a gift.

Since G-d's intention is to give mankind the most enjoyable pleasure, the system was set up in a way which would generate such pleasure.

For further reading see:
"Life is full of pleasures " – Other topics.

THE RABBI MICHAEL J ELJARRAT LEARNING PROGRAMME – CLASS FOUR

CLASS 4   FAITH AND DOUBT
YOUR PESONAL CONTRIBUTION

After seeing (in class 1) that G-d does in fact exist, and after understanding that our actions have consequences in our lives, the next logical step is to ask:

- "What is my individual role in the greater scheme of things?"
- "If G-d created me then surely I have a part to play?" For G-d did not create anything which has no purpose.

This lesson will address such issues as destiny and coincidence, as well as giving some useful pointers in determining your individual role to play within society.

Have you ever wondered what makes people different from animals? There are many differences but probably the biggest difference between man and beast is, man's greater intellectual abilities. Human beings are the most intelligent out of all the species created. This is demonstrated in man's occupation of planet earth. No other species of animal has drastically changed the natural environment as much as human beings. Man's greater intelligence leads him to ask complex questions, make sophisticated choices and build dynamic structures to suite his needs.

Another characteristic which is found only in man is his appearance. This means to say that no two human beings look alike, even identical twins have subtle differences which set them apart. There are no two human beings on planet earth with an identical face. By contrast animals are far more similar to one another and can appear to look almost identical. The face of any two animals is almost identical, for example two sheep, two cows or two goats will look so similar that it is almost impossible to tell them apart.

The reason why each human face is so unique is owing to the fact that "the face is a window to the soul." The face shows all the signs and expressions of human emotion, there is no body part, which allows us to view a person's inner most feelings more than the face.

Since each human being has a totally unique face, it stands to reason that each and every human being has a totally unique soul. Each and every soul that comes to planet earth has a unique purpose. This is clearly demonstrated within creation itself. When G-d created the world, G-d made only one man and not an entire species, as was the case with all the other animals. This is to show the point that each person is totally unique and as King Solomon once said each person is a world unto itself.

PAGE 1

THE RABBI MICHAEL J ELJARRAT LEARNING PROGRAMME – CLASS FOUR

Shortly after the great flood in the time of Noah, the people of Babel began building a huge tower which would ascend to heaven. Their intention was to fortify the heavens in order to prevent another great flood, as was experienced in the days of Noah.

The commentaries explain that never in the history of mankind were people as united as they were in the days of the great tower of Babel: We know from the Torah that G-d was being angered by the construction of the tower, and eventually destroyed the tower, dispersed the people and confused the people so that they were no longer able to communicate with one another.

The question is obvious, why was G-d so angry? Surely the unity of mankind is a great and noble accomplishment?

The commentaries answer that, it was not unity of mankind which angered G-d, rather the lack of uniqueness found within mankind at that time. Since each and every person living at that time dedicated his/her life to building the tower, they lost their individuality and their uniqueness as human beings, as we described above.

For this reason, G-d split up the people in order for them to find their own sense of self and their own personality, because G-d created human beings to be different from one another, unlike the other homogeneous species of animals.

The Midrash says[1], that before a soul enters the world G-d decides the destiny of that soul, will it be male or female, strong or weak, rich or poor, tall or short, good looking or ugly and so too G-d decrees exactly what will happen to this person during his/her life time. We clearly see from this Midrash that absolutely everything that happens to us has been predetermined along time before we are even born. Thus our unique role on earth has been decided, and our soul is clearly aware of what our purpose is on earth. However since we may not be in touch with our soul, our unique purpose may seem a mystery to us, but if we were to be in touch with our souls, we would have a clear vision as to why G-d put us on earth.

Unfortunately due to the influence of the nation "AMALEK" we attribute all of our life events to "COINCIDENCE" and not to divine destiny. In fact we are so stooped in this way of thinking that the word "DESTINY" sounds foreign and the word "COINCIDENCE" sounds familiar.

However this was not always the case. In days gone by people thought quite the opposite, in fact the word "COINCIDENCE" was unheard of except to one nation in the world, the nation of "AMALEK." The Torah tells us that when the Jews left Egypt, not a single nation wanted to harm the Jews, because they all saw the great wonders and miracles which took place, and they realized that G-d was protecting the Jews.

The nation of "AMAMLEK" however, was of the opinion that all the "miracles" were merely "COINCIDENCE" and therefore they decided to attack the Jews whilst they were in the dessert.

We find no greater commandment to destroy, more than what is written with regards to the nation of "AMALEK." Nowhere else in the Torah are we commanded to destroy men, woman and children; however with the nation of "AMALEK" we are told to destroy everyone.

The reason being that:

---

1. Midrash Tanchuma Parshas Pikudei

THE RABBI MICHAEL J ELJARRAT LEARNING PROGRAMME – CLASS FOUR

No nation causes more misery to the world, more than the nation who lives by "COINCIDENCE".

When we loose sight of destiny and start believing in "COINCIDENCE" we find ourselves wondering around planet earth with a pointless existence.

The Mishna in Ovos says[2] who is wise? - One who learns from everyone, who is strong? - One who subdues his personal inclination, who is rich? - He who is happy with his lot, who is honored? - One who honors others. It is these qualities which represent true greatness and uniqueness in mankind. However owing to the fact that so many of us have abandoned true values and continue with a pointless existence, we try and look for self value in meaningless activities.

The corruption in the moral fiber of society has caused us to think: Who is rich?-one with a lot of money, who is wise? - One who can undermine his competition, who is strong? - One who can prey on the weak, and who is honored? - One with status. All of these false values lead to bitter disappointment.

Although we may sometimes feel as if G-d has abandoned us in this world, and that our purpose is not special and unique, this is not true. We find in the Meggilas Esther that G-ds' name does not appear once, but it is clear for all to see that G-d was actively involved in every event. So too in our personal lives if we take a step back and look at destiny and we let go of the word "COINCINDENCE" `we will see the hand of G-d in our lives, and we will notice the signs along the way. Our soul already knows exactly what we are on earth to do, we just have to keep silent and listen to what the soul has to say.

There was once a black smith who felt very depressed everyday he would ask "Why am I on earth, what is my special purpose?" Feeling hopeless he went to see the "BAL SHEM TOV" the great Kabalist who was known for answering such questions. The trip was long and treacherous, after traveling for a day the black smith encountered a group of 9 men who pleaded with him "please help us make a Minyan so that we can say Kadish". The black smith refused. On the 3rd day the black smith finally reached the home of the "BAL SHEM TOV" and with tears in his eyes he asked "please tell me why did G-d put me on earth?" The "BAL SHEM TOV" looked at him and then exclaimed "One day you will come across a group of 9 men and ONLY YOU will be able to make the Minyan!!"

---

[2]. Chapter 4 Mishna 1

THE RABBI MICHAEL J ELJARRAT LEARNING PROGRAMME – CLASS FIVE

CLASS 5
THE 13 PRINCIPLES OF FAITH
PRINCIPLES 1-3

The thirteen principles of faith, written by Maimonides are at the core of Jewish belief. Before creating these principles, Maimonides went through the entire length & breath of Jewish literature to find that which was fundamental to Jewish thought. Rabbi Moshe/Moses Maimonides often referred to as the RAMBAM (an acronym) was a world renowned philosopher, his greatness was so wide spread that his exact moment of birth was recorded in history: Born on the 30th of March in the year 1135[1] in the city of Cordova, Spain.

The RAMBAM was forced into exile from an early age and finally settled in Fez, Morocco in 1160. It was during these early years of wondering that Maimonides began his work commentating on the Mishna.

By the age of 33 Maimonides was already a well known author and was appointed as chief Rabbi of Cairo. Apart from building a reputation as a great Rabbi, Maimonides also had a reputation of being an excellent physician.

The most famous work of Maimonides was the Mishna-Torah consisting of 14 volumes and the "Moreh Nevuchim" (guide to the perplexed). His fame spread across the world even to England where Richard the lion hearted invited him to become his personal physician; however Maimonides chose to remain in Egypt.

Approximately 100 years after Maimonides death, Rabbi Daniel bar Yehudah of Rome made the thirteen principles into a song, it is known as "Yigdal" which can be found in almost every Siddur in the world[2]. The next several classes will deal in some detail with the 13 principles of faith along side the song of "Yigdal".

1."I believe with perfect faith that G-d is the creator and ruler of all things. He alone has made, does make, and will make all things."

From Yigdal: "GREAT IS THE LIVING G-D, AND PRAISED HE EXISITS, YET HIS EXISTANCE HAS NO TIME."

The 13 principles of faith are in essence an insight into knowing G-d. When thinking about G-d we often fall into the thinking pattern that G-d is an old man with a long white beard, perhaps dressed in white. It is sometimes this thinking itself that gets us confused and doubtful. Understanding G-d in His true essence is not possible, however understanding some of the basic facts is possible and will greatly enhance our relationship with G-d.

---
1. On Saturday at 1pm
2. Artscroll siddur page 12

PAGE 1

THE RABBI MICHAEL J ELJARRAT LEARNING PROGRAMME – CLASS FIVE

Today, the emphasis of our studies is directed towards, the physical sciences. We examine and try to understand the world around us. On closer inspection we will find that man can study 1 of 2 subjects, either the created or the creator, this is a study of the latter.

The Derech Hashem writes that the human mind is only capable of understanding by comparison, i.e.: When we talk of the color green we can picture trees and foliage, however a person who was born blind will never understand the difference between the color red & green purely because there is no reference in his mind, with which to compare. Keeping this in mind we can now understand why studying the Creator is so difficult, since there is but one Creator by default we have none other with which to compare. Studying the Creator involves broadening ones mind to except that some of the answers and topics are beyond human comprehension.

To illustrate this point, let us examine the following question. "What color is the number 3?" On the surface this appears to be a valid question with a subject and query, however upon closer examination we can clearly see that there is no correct answer to this question since the question itself is invalid. So to when we ask "What gender is G-d?" there is no correct answer as the question itself is invalid, even though we feel we have a strong question. We therefore need to methodologically study our creator keeping in mind, our own limitations & abilities.

 The first principle involves belief in G-d, and secondly a belief that G-d created everything and continues to create at all times. The word "create" means making something out of nothing; this means that G-d created something from nothing. Unlike man who can only form new objects from pre-existing materials, G-d brought about the creation of the world with no pre-existing materials. The difference between man's creations is that when man creates something the creation is totally independent from the one who has created it, for example: a house may stand for many years after the builder has died. G-d's creations on the other hand require G-d's energy to flow in order for the creation to exist at all times.

 2. "I believe with perfect faith that G-d is one. There is no unity that is in any way like His. He alone is our G-d. He was, He is and He will be."

From Yigdal: HE IS ONE, NO UNITY IS LIKE HIS, HE IS HIDDEN, HIS UNITY HAS NO END.

 The second principal involves believing in the oneness and unity of G-d. Everything physical can be divided an infinite number of times; G-d however is the only being, which has absolute oneness. This is the meaning of "G-d is one" as we say in the shema.

As stated above, since G-d is unique we cannot comprehend G-d, as the Ramchal says our mind can only comprehend something which we have seen before. God's uniqueness means that nothing is comparable to G-d, therefore our mind can never fully comprehend G-d.

 God was, is, and always will be: This means that G-d is not bound by time in anyway. The way to understand this is to comprehend the fact that time is a creation of G-d, before G-d made time, time did not exist. Therefore G-d always was and always will be.

THE RABBI MICHAEL J ELJARRAT LEARNING PROGRAMME – CLASS FIVE

3. "I believe with perfect faith that G-d does not have a body. Physical concepts do not apply to Him. There is nothing whatsoever that resembles Him at all."

From Yigdal: HE DOES NOT HAVE BODILY FORM, HE IS NOT A BODY, HE IS BEYOND COMPARE IN HIS HOLINESS.

The third principle involves, believing that G-d is not physical. Since G-d is infinite G-d cannot be contained within a body, since a body has to be bigger than the person inside, in the same way that a container has to be bigger than the contents contained within the container.

Therefore if G-d were to have a body, it would have to be larger than infinity in order to contain G-d, which would mean that G-d is not infinite rather infinite less one, which of course is not true, we can also see this from the fact that G-d is omnipresent, a physical body cannot be in two places at one time.

Recommended Reading:

Maimonides Principles of Faith **AYREH KAPLAN**
NYCS/OU

THE RABBI MICHAEL J ELJARRAT LEARNING PROGRAMME – CLASS SIX

CLASS 6
THE 13 PRINCIPLES OF FAITH
PRINCIPLES 4-6

4. "I believe with perfect faith that G-d is first and last."

From Yigdal: "HE PRECEDED ALL THINGS THAT WERE CREATED, HE IS FIRST, YET WITHOUT BEGINNING."

As was said previously in principle 1 and 2, G-d is above time, and is not affected by the world. This principle stresses the fact that G-d does not need this world in order to exist. G-d was first and therefore existed without this world, and G-d will be last, if/when this world is destroyed. Therefore no physical catastrophe can affect G-d in any way.

The Sefer Ha Yosher says in the first chapter[1]

"the creator has no beginning & no end, where as everything which was created has a beginning and has an end, since anything which is depended can be said to be lacking, that which the depending surrounds."

We can understand this statement by looking at the following example: A human being needs several things in order to survive, for example food, air, shelter, to name but a few. In other words for a human being to be complete, or sustainable he/she will need these things which are essential to living.

Hence: (In the following equation)

- HUMAN BEING
- + AIR / FOOD / SHELTER ETC.
- = COMPLETE/ SUSTAINABLE HUMAN BEING

Therefore since it is impossible for a person to exist without air, for example, we could say as follows:

"In order for a person to exist, he/she must co-exist together with air".

It can therefore be said that human beings are not comploto or self sustaining, since humans depend on air, should air cease to exist in the world humans will also cease to exist.

G-d on the other hand is totally independent and is totally self sustaining, for this reason G-d could exist before the world, and after the world, since G-d is not depended on the world in any way.

---

[1] Sod Breas HA-OLAM

THE RABBI MICHAEL J ELJARRAT LEARNING PROGRAMME – CLASS SIX

Therefore G-d is not affected by any physical phenomena. This leads to the question "If G-d does not need or depend on the world, why then did G-d create the world?" this question is discussed in the Sefer Ha Yosher and the answer is given that the reason G-d created the world was purely as an act of loving kindness, this can be proven from the verse[2] "And G-d sat them in the firmament of the heaven to give light upon the earth" the verse doesn't say to give light in the heaven, but rather to give light upon the earth, hence the creations were made not to benefit G-d, but to benefit mankind and the inhabitants of earth.

5. "I believe with perfect faith that it is only proper to pray to G-d. One may not pray to anyone or anything else."

From Yigdal: "HE IS THE LORD OF THE WORLD, AND ALL THINGS CREATED, DISPLAY HIS GREATNESS AND HIS MAJESTY."

It is only fitting to pray to G-d and not to anything/anyone else. Based on principles 1-4 we see that G-d is in ultimate control over everything. Therefore if we want or need something the only "person" with the authority to change events or grant wishes is G-d Himself. For this reason praying to any intermediary is a waste of time, since the intermediary has no authorization.

The concept can be best understood with the saying:

"Speak to the head not to the tail"

Meaning when one is looking for results, or if one is trying to implement change, the only way to do so is by speaking to the one with the authority to implement that change. For example if one wishes to do business with a large company, and one does all the necessary requirements in order to put a contract in place, and then takes the contract (to the large company) for signing, but instead of getting the signature of the CEO he gets the signature of the janitor/tea lady, he has wasted his time and his contract is worthless. So too when we pray, we need to pray to the "CEO" of the universe, the one with the final say namely G-d the master of the universe.

6. "I believe with perfect faith that all the words of the prophets are true."

From Yigdal: "HE HAS GRANTED THE BOUNTY OF HIS PROPHECY TO THE MEN OF HIS CHOICE AND GLORY"

This principle involves believing that the words of the prophets are true. Since a prophecy is a revelation from G-d, which is only granted to very special & unique individuals, the words of the prophets must by default be true. All the prophets were tested to insure that they were not false. Any prophet who was proven to be a false prophet was put to death.

---

2 Genesis 1:17

THE RABBI MICHAEL J ELJARRAT LEARNING PROGRAMME – CLASS SIX

To understand this concept fully we need to examine 2 concepts.

- What is prophecy?
- Who is able to receive a prophecy?

A. WHAT IS PROPHECY?

When speaking of prophecy, many of us conjure ideas of fortune telling and glimpsing into the future, but what exactly is prophecy? The Derech Hashem[3] by the Ramchal writes that G-d placed in mankind the ability to learn & understand. This ability is called intellect, before we explain further it is necessary to understand several terms used by the Torah and our sages with regards to human intellect.

1. "Chochmah"/חכמה: This reflects to man's knowledge of the various sciences, the ability is primarily based on memory and intellect.

2. "Binah"/בינה: From the root "boneh" which means to build, this refers to man's ability to understand new concepts based on previous knowledge: I.e.: building & developing a concept.

3. "Da'as"/ דעת: This refers to man's ability to "weigh up" concepts i.e.: the ability to make decisions & judgment based on knowledge.

4. "Tevunah" / תבונה: This refers to mans ability to integrate knowledge into practical applications an example will be learning to drive a car.

5. "Saychel"/ שכל: This refers to the speed at which man is able to process new information; this is often referred to as intellect, intelligence, or IQ.

Since man has several abilities with regard to learning & understanding, it is possible for a person to be aware of something before it has happened without any supernatural powers, just by utilizing the natural human abilities. However man is limited in his ability to understand, and therefore by nature certain things will be beyond the reach of human intellect.

For this reason G-d created the concept of RUACH – HAKODESH/ רוח הקודש (lit. the Holy Spirit). Ruach Ha–Kodesh is a gift given by G-d to certain saintly individuals, which enables these individuals to have knowledge and understanding greater than what is naturally possible.

However prophecy is a level higher, prophecy is a supernatural event, whereby a persons' soul is attached to G-d. The information gained during a prophecy leaves no room for doubt. Prophecy is not a level of understanding but an event whereby the soul detaches itself from the body. We will discuss prophecy in greater detail in the next class.

3.Chapter 1.3.3

B. WHO CAN RECEIVE PROPHECY?

We must realize that prophecy is only granted to very lofty & spiritual individuals. Besides for being strongly connected to G-d, a prophet also had to have certain physical qualities, such as power, good looks and wealth. Hence a prophet was one who was exceptionally unique.

The Rambam lists several qualities needed to attain prophecy:

- Exceptionally great intelligence
- Strong character
- Not overcome by his impulses in any way
- He/She must have complete control over his/her emotions
- He/She must have a broad & firm outlook
- Be able to separate him/her self from common people.

It is therefore clear why we believe that all the words of the prophets are true, since prophecy is a very special and precise tool granted by G-d himself. The concept of prophecy will be dealt with again in the next class.

THE RABBI MICHAEL J ELJARRAT LEARNING PROGRAMME – CLASS SEVEN

CLASS 7
THE 13 PRINCIPLES OF FAITH
PRINCIPLES 7-9

7. "I believe with perfect faith that the prophecy of Moses is absolutely true. He was the chief of all prophets, both before and after him."

From Yigdal:"THERE HAS NOT ARISEN ANOTHER LIKE MOSES, A PROPHET WHO LOOKED UPON HIS IMAGE."

This principle revolves around believing firstly that Moses was a true prophet and secondly that Moses was unlike any other prophet that ever was or will be. To understand this concept fully, we need to explore exactly how prophecy works and then we need to examine the differences between Moses and the other prophets.

We have already seen in principle 6 that prophecy is unlike any natural phenomenon. The Ramchal explains[1] that prophecy is more than just a vision or an enlightened state of awareness, prophecy at its essence is the soul detaching itself from the body and ascending to spiritual heights, at which point a clear message is given to the lofty soul from heaven.

The commentaries describe the events which took place when a prophet would receive a prophecy. First the prophet would either fall asleep or would enter into a trance, at which point the body of the prophet would start convulsing, something which would look similar to an epileptic fit. The higher parts of the prophets soul would separate from the prophet's body and an intense energy would stream towards the prophet. The prophet would then be exposed to a deep awareness and an exposure to G-d. Depending on the level of spiritual greatness of the prophet, would determine the clarity of the exposure to G-d, at the moment of exposure to G-d, the prophet would begin understanding the message that G-d was telling.

It is in the following ways that Moses was different to all other prophets:

1. Moses could be awake for a prophecy unlike the other prophets who would only receive a prophecy while in a dream or in a trance.

2. Moses was not weakened by the prophecy unlike all the other prophets who would experience physical side effects from the traumatic experience.

---

1. Derech Hashem 3:3

3. Moses would receive a prophecy whenever he desired, unlike the other prophets who could only receive a prophecy when chosen by G-d. For this reason Moses is called the servant of G-d[2], because Moses could appear before G-d at anytime like a servant before his master.
4. Moses could receive his prophecy directly from G-d unlike the other prophets who would need a "lens" (an angel to convey God's message).

8. "I believe with perfect faith that the entire Torah that we now have is that which was given to Moses."

From Yigdal: "GOD GAVE A TRUE TORAH TO HIS PEOPLE, THROUGH HIS PROPHET, TRUSTED IN ALL HIS HOUSE."

This principle involves the belief that the Torah was given to us by Moses which originated from G-d. This principle follows on from the previous principle. Since Moses was the greatest prophet, no one has the power to change anything in the Torah, which was given to Moses, since everyone after Moses is less competent. Therefore the Torah, which we have today, has not been changed since it was given.

The Rambam on his commentary on the Mishna writes that the worst non believer is one who says that the Torah is not from heaven, this includes the belief that all the verses of the Torah are of equal importance as this is part of the core believe that the entire Torah is from G-d, and every verse is of equal importance.

The belief that the Torah has never been changed since the time it was given to us by G-d, has allowed the Jewish people to continue for many generations, each generation doing the same Mitzvos that the previous generation did. That is to say the Lulav, Tzitzis, Succah that Moses used, would be the same today and in the future. Thus every generation could learn from the previous generation and so the tradition was passed down from father to son, with an unbroken chain.

9. "I believe with perfect faith that the Torah will not be changed, and that there will never be another Torah given by G-d."

From Yigdal: "G-D WILL NOT REPLACE NOR CHANGE HIS LAW FOR ALL TIME, FOR ANYTHING ELSE."

This principle involves believing that the Torah will never be changed, nothing will ever be added nor will anything be subtracted.

The message in this principle is that the Torah as we have it today is totally complete as the Talmud teaches.[3] "I have created the "Yetzer Ha Rah" and I have created the Torah as the antidote says G-d". The Torah is the prescription given to us by G-d, it contains all

---

2. "Yismach Moshe" Amidah Shabbos morning
3. Kedushin 30b

THE RABBI MICHAEL J ELJARRAT LEARNING PROGRAMME – CLASS SEVEN

that is necessary to cure man from his ailments. By adding or subtracting from G-d's prescription we are destroying the remedy. Just as a doctor writes a script with specific medicines for a particular patient and changing the script could have devastating results so too G-d's Torah will not to be swopped or changed.

One of the flaws with altered forms of Judaism is that the changes made to be more liberal and accommodating in actual fact become limiting and constricting. The idea that the Torah needs to "change with the times" is a flaw in the fundamentals of belief. It is true that times do change, but the Torah has incorporated these changes and it is up to us to study deeper.

For this reason any prophet who claims that G-d told him to change the Torah, is immediately deemed a false prophet, since a change in the Torah can only lead to furthering the follower away from G-d. This can clearly be seen today, that any altered form of Judaism has led to the destruction of the Jewish nation.

The Talmud[4] says that at the time G-d gave the Torah, G-d held Mount Sinai over the Jewish nation and proclaimed if you accept the Torah, good, and if not- over "there" will be your burial place.

The commentaries explain that the reason the word "there" is used as apposed to "here", is coming to teach us, that if one leaves the Torah, and looks for alternative ways of life, then over "there" in the place away from Torah, with that very lifestyle found "there" that will ultimately destroy the person, hence "there will be your burial place."

---

4. Shabbos 88a

PAGE 3

CLASS 8
THE 13 PRINCIPLES OF FAITH
PRINCIPLES 10 - 13

10. "I believe with perfect faith that G-d knows all of man's deeds and thoughts. It is thus written (Psalm 33:15) "He has molded every heart together; He understands what each one does."

From Yigdal: "HE SEES, HE KNOWS OUR SECRETS, HE SEES EACH THINGS END AT ITS VERY BEGINNING."

The tenth principle involves believing that G-d knows everything. The first concept one needs to understand when examining this principle is that unlike man, G-d's knowledge is not external from Himself.

As was discussed in principle 6, man can obtain knowledge through the various methods available to him. That means to say, man's life and knowledge are two separate entities. A person can be alive and choose whether or not to study, if a person chooses not to study this has no bearing on the person's life, in the sense that his decision not to study will not affect his status of being alive.

Mans knowledge is a collection of thoughts and ideas stored in the mind. G-d's knowledge on the other hand does not come from studying; G-d's knowledge comes from G-d knowing Himself.

G-d's knowledge and G-d are one in the same, since G-d is the absolute form of oneness. This concept however is difficult to understand, since we have no point of reference for which to base this concept. However we can understand that since G-d is complete His knowledge therefore is also complete. Since G-d and His knowledge are one.

11. "I believe with perfect faith that G-d rewards those who keep His commandments, and punishes those who transgress His commandments."

From Yigdal: "HE REWARDS MAN WITH LOVE, AS HIS DEEDS DESERVE, HE GIVES THE WICKED EVIL ACCORDING TO THEIR WRONG."

The eleventh principle is, believing that G-d rewards those who keep His commandments, and punishing those who transgress His commandments.

THE RABBI MICHAEL J ELJARRAT LEARNING PROGRAMME – CLASS EIGHT

Since G-d created this world for man in order for him to obtain his reward it is obvious that G-d will reward those who keep the Mitzvos since that is what the world was created for.

Another point to note is what is written by the Ramchal, that reward & punishment are built into the very fabric of creation, meaning that our actions create our destiny, doing good results in reward where as doing bad results in punishment.

There is no way to escape the consequences, denying reward & punishment would be as if to deny the laws of gravity, just like we have to except gravity as part of the fabric of creation so too we need to except that reward & punishment are part and parcel of creation itself. The concept of reward and punishment has been discussed in class 3.

12. "I believe with perfect faith in the coming of the Messiah. No matter how long it takes, I will await his coming day."

From Yigdal: "HE WILL SEND OUR MESSIAH AT THE END OF DAYS, TO REDEEM THOSE WHO AWAIT HIS FINAL SALVATION."

The twelfth principle of faith is, believing in the coming of the Moshiach. Mosiach will come at the right time. The right time means the right situation not the right calendar date. Therefore it is impossible to calculate when Moshiach will come.

The messianic age will begin with the war of "Gog & Magog", but prior to this a prophet will arise to prepare the Jewish people. After the war of "Gog & magog" Eliyahu the prophet will come then Moshiach will come.

- Moshiach will become great & famous world wide more than King Solmon.
- Moshiach will be a great King and will bring about peace on earth.
- Moshiach will not be crushed or fail until he has set the world straight.
- The world will be the same when Moshiach comes, there will still be people working, rich, poor, strong, weak etc.
However it will be easier to make a living with a little effort one could accomplish a lot. All good things will be plenty like dust of the earth.
- Moshiach will bring people back to Torah and Jews will be able to fulfill all the commandments of the Torah as they were intended.
- Wisdom will increase in the world, and the main occupation of humanity will be to know G-d. People will obey the Torah without neglect or laziness.
- Mans life time will be vastly extended because there will be less trouble in the world.
- After Moshiach dies, his son will take his place and his son after him.
- Moshiachs reign will be for 1000years.

THE RABBI MICHAEL J ELJARRAT LEARNING PROGRAMME – CLASS EIGHT

We will know who the Moshiach is:

- If he comes from the house of David.
- He does not change any detail of the religion
- He is immersed in Torah and Mitzvos.
- He follows both oral and written Torah.
- Leads the Jews back to Torah.
- Strengthens the observance of the laws.
- Fights G-d's battles.

If he does all of the above we can assume that he is Moshiach. If however

- He also builds the third temple.
- Gathers the Jews from all over the world.

Then we can be certain that he is the Moshiach.

13. "I believe with perfect faith that the dead will be brought back to life when G-d wills it to happen."

From Yigdal: "GOD WILL BRING THE DEAD TO LIFE WITH GREAT LOVE, MAY HIS GLORIOUS NAME BE BLESSED FOR ALL TIME."

The thirteenth principle of faith involves believing in the resurrection of the dead. Since the time of Adams first sin, mans body has become contaminated with impurity, and the only way for mans body to become pure and reunite with the soul is for mans body to decompose.

G-d has created many cycles in nature, day and night; summer, winter, autumn and spring. A person who sees a bare tree in the middle of winter will still believe that the tree will blossom again in spring since he is aware of the cycle. Mans life is also a cycle which begins with birth then death and then resurrection.

Death is not the final sage in the cycle of mans life. Just as a seed is planted in the ground and from there a sprout comes forth, so too we don't bury our dead we only plant them.

Recommended reading:
MAIMONIDES' PRINCIPLES – THE FUNDEMENTALS OF JEWISH FAITH – ARYEH KAPLAN
PUBLISHED BY: NCSY/ORTHODOX UNION
ISBN 1-879016-04-14

THE RABBI MICHAEL J ELJARRAT LEARNING PROGRAMME – CLASS NINE

CLASS 9 ETHICS
LOVING YOUR FELLOW MAN

The concept of loving your fellow man seems rather simplistic at first, but after further examination we will see that loving your fellow man could perhaps be one of the most complex concepts.

This lesson will try and address some of the following questions:
- What is love?
- To what extent must we love another?
- When is one obliged to love another?

In our complex society we find a very broad range of people from all walks of life. In an almost natural way we find ourselves drawn to certain individuals and yet repulsed by other individuals. The mechanics behind how we as people form our relationships is a topic of discussion in its own right; however for our purposes we will try and explore just the emotion of love.

For many individuals the emotion of love comes very easily. For these individuals love requires no effort what so ever, it's as natural to them as breathing, sleeping and eating. These individuals often enjoy happy relationships; however these individuals also find themselves amidst the hardest of heartaches, as their love knows no boundaries or limits.

For other individuals the emotion of love is a totally foreign concept. For these individuals loving another requires great effort. These individuals struggle with meaningful relationships and struggle to be emotionally connected; these individuals may even struggle with loving themselves.

> The Torah states[1] "you shall love your fellow as yourself"

Keeping in mind the broad spectrum of people discussed above, this simple dictum needs clarification.
- Firstly for some, loving another is a great challenge, how does the Torah except these people to follow this commandment?
- Secondly when the Torah says "your fellow" who is this referring to?
- Thirdly, the most obvious question is, how can the Torah command us to love? If love is just an emotion that we feel, then we either feel it or we don't it is not in our control?

Another point which could be asked by those individuals that find it easy to love others is; this commandment is obvious, why do I need the Torah to command me?

---

[1] Vayikra / Leviticus 19:18

THE RABBI MICHAEL J ELJARRAT LEARNING PROGRAMME – CLASS NINE

 With all of the above questions, it is rather obvious to see that this commandment cannot be understood on a simplistic level.

What is love?

Love can be described as seeing only the virtues of another individual. The word in Hebrew for love is "AHAVAH" the root of this word is "AHAV" spelt "ALEF,HAY,BEIS". We know in Hebrew that the meaning of a word comes from its root. We also know that every letter of the Hebrew alphabet has both a numerical value and a meaning. Therefore on closer inspection the word love means as follows:

ALEF = 1 (א)

HAY = 5/to give (ה)

BES = 2 (ב)

Love in Hebrew means 1 (an individual) gives to 2 (another individual). Thus the Torah is teaching that this emotion of love is generated by giving to others. When one individual gives to another, that individual will feel the emotion of love towards the recipient of his/her giving. Therefore we can chose who we want to love, by choosing to whom we want to give.

Therefore the commandment to "love your fellow" starts with giving to your fellow, for once a person begins giving the love will then follow. The question which is often asked is, why do we feel a natural inclination to give to some and not to others?

This can be understood from the words of the "Orchas Tzadikim" and Rabbi Eliyahu Dessler.

The Orchas Tzadikim writes[2] that there are 7 categories of love.

1. The love one feels for his/her children
2. The love one has for money
3. The love one has for women (applicable to men)
4. The love one feels for relatives
5. The love one feels towards life and longevity
6. The love of honor.
7. The love of enjoyment and physical pleasures

We can clearly see from the above that although we would classify all of the above categories as "love" each category is a unique feeling of its own. We love our children and we love money and yet the feeling is different for each category.

The reason why we love our children unconditionally is because we give them so much. The reason we love money is because we invest so much of ourselves trying to attain it.

---

2. Ways of Tzadikim- Gate of love

THE RABBI MICHAEL J ELJARRAT LEARNING PROGRAMME – CLASS NINE

But what prompts us to give our all to our children? Rabbi Dessler explains that by nature man is a selfish creature, wanting only to take and not to give.

It is this very selfish nature which also causes a person to love. When a person gives a gift to a friend for example, the friend is now holding onto a small part of the giver, the giver then attaches him/her self to that small part of themselves and then begins loving the aspect of "Themselves" found within the other individual.

Hence the more of "yourself" there is in another individual; the more you will love that particular individual. This is seen very clearly with the parent-child relationship, since a child contains such a high ratio of the parent, the parent automatically loves the child, hence the unconditional love.

This concept can be seen in the title of the first chapter of "Mesilas Yesharim"[3] The chapter is entitled "Duties of man in **His** world". It is not duties of man in the world rather "His" world.

That means to say that each person has their own world which they live in. Our personal world comprises only of things closest to us. In a sense we draw a "circle of closeness" at the very centre we place ourselves; we then place those people most important to us within that circle such as family and close friends, everybody else will then fall outside of this "circle of closeness". It is within this "circle of closeness" that each person lives, this is "his" world as referrer to by the Ramchal.

Our duty therefore is to expand this circle of closeness, until we can feel a genuine love for everybody. As it says in Ovos[4] "love people and bring them close to Torah."

G-d desires us to be genuine as people; false acts of love are meaningless. This is the meaning when the Torah says "you shall love your fellow as yourself." The Torah is giving us a guideline. First we need to love ourselves, then we need to expand our "circle of closeness" to love those within the circle as much as we love ourselves, this is no easy feat and therefore one who genuinely loves others as much as him/her self is truly a great person.

---

3. Path of the just- Rabbi Moshe Chaim Luzzato
4. Chapter 1 Mishna 12

THE RABBI MICHAEL J ELJARRAT LEARNING PROGRAMME – CLASS TEN

CLASS 10   ETHICS
LOSHON HA-RAH (HORAH)

The verse in Psalms[1] says "Who is the man who desires life and loves days that he may see the good? Guard your tongue from evil and your lips from speaking deceit."

Loshon Horah, evil speech is stated as one of the most grievous sins. In the book "Chofetz Chaim"[2] 17 negative commandments are brought in association with Loshon Horah, as well as 14 positive commandments and 3 curses.

Clearly the sin of Loshon horah is serious and the laws numerous. In this lesson we will try and look at the various categories of "evil speech" as well as the root core of this problem.

Evil/Bad speech can be classified into 3 different groups.

- Loshon horah
- Recheelos
- Motzei shem rah

We will now give a broad definition for each of the 3 categories as well as an example, it is important to note that the 3 categories mentioned above are not the only types of forbidden speech, there are other categories such as "Sheker" (the prohibition "Do not lie") and "Avak Loshon Horah" (a category of Loshon Horah which is prohibited by Rabbinical law), which will not be covered in this lesson. It is important to note that the laws of forbidden speech apply to all forms of communication, such as writing etc.

Loshon Horah

As mentioned above there are numerous sources in the Torah which forbid the speaking of Loshon Horah. In essence Loshon Horah is any speech which is degrading or hurtful which is spoken about a 3rd party.

For example it is forbidden for Steven to tell his friend Jonny "Adam always comes to work late." Such a comment can be hurtful to Adam and may even result in direct damage. The laws relating to Loshon Horah are very numerous, and in certain circumstances one may tell his friend certain things about a 3rd party however in the vast majority of instances it would be forbidden.

---

1. 34:13-14
2. Authored by Rabbi Yisroel Meir Kagan Also known as the "Chofetz Chaim"

It is important to note that in the above statement "Adam always comes to work late" is only classified as Loshon Horah if the statement is true. If however the statement is false this is classified as "Motzei shem rah" (which will be discussed shortly).

Very often people are under the misconception that if the statement is true, that it is permissible to say it. This of course is not the case, even if the statement is true it is still forbidden to say it. It is only when the statement is true that we can classify the statement as Loshon Horah.

Recheelos

Similar to Loshon Horah, Recheelos is the term used for a report that someone has spoken or acted against the listener.

For example Steven and Adam both work for Russell, Russell reprimands Adam for coming late to work with reference to Steven. It is then forbidden for Adam to go tell his friend Steven; "do you know what happened at work today?" "Russell reprimanded us for coming late." Recheelos in essence is a form of tale bearing I.e. speaking about others.

The word "Recheelos" comes from the word "Rochel" which means a peddler or door to door salesman. As if to say, a person who speaks Recheelos is going from place to place "selling" the story. The category of Recheelos also applies if the information is **true**. In some ways Recheelos is worse than loshon Horah, as one who speaks Recheelos clearly has a character flaw, which motivates this behavior, where as Loson Horoh although forbidden may not be the result of a serious character flaw.

Motzei Shem Rah

Motzei shem rah can be classified as any case of Loshon Horah or Recheelos, where the statement being made is **not true**. For example in the above situations if Adam does not come to work late and Steven says to Jonny "Adam always comes late." That would be classified as Motzei shem rah, so too if a person were to tell his/her friend "Mr. X said this about you." And in actual fact Mr. X did not make any such comment, this would be classified as Motzei shem rah.

Understanding the reason why speech is so powerful:

The commentaries explain that every organ in the body which is one, such as the brain, the heart etc has a very big role to play within and without the human body, This is also true with regards to the mouth. We only have one mouth and the power of speech is so great, that with it we can either build or destroy.

The mouth is a very powerful instrument, with words we can both build, and motivate others or we can destroy and rundown others.

THE RABBI MICHAEL J ELJARRAT LEARNING PROGRAMME – CLASS TEN

The Mishna asks a question; what is worse? Being attacked with a sword? Or being attacked with a bow and arrow? We would think that being attacked with a sword is far worse, but the Mishna says that this is not the case. When one is attacked with a sword, the victim has the opportunity to negotiate with his/her attacker, and perhaps win over the heart of the attacker.

However when one is attacked with a bow and arrow, once the attacker releases the arrow there is no turning back, it's too late and the arrow has already been shot.

 So too is the power of speech once the word have left the mouth of the speaker there is no turning back, the words have been spoken and can no longer be returned.

Another point to keep in mind is that the commentaries say. We only have a limited number of words to say in our life time. We therefore need to choose how we wish to spend our word allowance.

Combating Loshon Horah is job of the mind more so than a job of the mouth. Meaning if one wants to control what one says, one has to control what one thinks. If a person has hatred in his/her heart then controlling speech is almost impossible. It is therefore necessary to remove any feelings of hatred in our heart before we can attempt to successfully control our speech.

 Our sages say that when a person speaks Loshon Horah he causes a transfer of Mitzvos & Averos to take place. The transfer causes the speaker of the loshon Horah to loose his Mitzvos and for the victim of the Loshon Horah to receive the Mitzvos of the speaker. This difficult concept can be understood as follows: As we saw previously (in class 9) when a person loves another individual, they place this individual within their "circle of closeness" and as a result one can often reap the benefit from the people within ones "circle of closeness."

For example if I help someone, and as a result that someone can in turn help a third person, the merit of that kindness can therefore be attributed to me, since the goodness came into the world as a result of my initial action.

These additional merits can only be earned while the "some one" is within the "circle of closeness." However once a person speaks Loshon Horah about that "some one" that "some one" leaves the circle of closeness and all the additional merits are lost hence a transfer takes place.

If we look throughout history, we will see that many great calamities occurred as the result of Loshon Horah, some examples include:

- The sin of Adam in the Garden of Eden, which ultimately brought death into the world.

- The sale of Yosef, which ultimately led to the slavery of the Jewish people in Egypt

- The spies who reported about the land of Israel, which kept the Jews wandering 40 years in the dessert

THE RABBI MICHAEL J ELJARRAT LEARNING PROGRAMME – CLASS TEN

- Nov the city of KOHAVIM, where thousands were killed
- The destruction of the Beis hamikidash

Although refraining from Loshon Horah can be difficult, the rewards are extremely great as the VILNA GAON writes in his letter, for every second that a person refrains from speaking (ill about other), G-d gives that person a reward so great that no creature even an angel can comprehend. If one refrains from speaking ill about others the prosecuting angels in heaven remain silent about him (Chofetz Chaim- Shmiras ha loshon)

Recommended reading:

GUARD YOUR TONGUE – BASED ON CHOFETZ CHAIM – BY ZELIG PLISKIN

AISH HA TORAH PUBLICATIONS

THE RABBI MICHAEL J ELJARRAT LEARNING PROGRAMME – CLASS ELEVEN

CLASS 11   ETHICS   CHARITY

This lesson will explore some of the laws of charity/TZEDAKAH, as well as some of the important concepts associated with the Mitzvah.

Before we begin dealing with the concept of charity, we will need to understand something very basic, and yet so fundamental.

If we go back in time, right to the very beginning when G-d created the world, but before "man" took his first steps on planet earth, we would see a very different world to what we see today. Before Adam could enter the world the situation had to be perfect, the world had to be conducive to man's existence, the world had to contain sufficient resources to sustain mans physical existence.

However man was not created merely for a physical existence, man was created to become the loftiest of all creations which would roam on planet earth. For this reason the elements essential for spiritual growth also had to be in place. These elements had to provide adequate challenge as well as balanced choices. Therefore for man to grow in the element of truth, falsehood also had to be provided to challenge man as well as giving him a balanced alternative. Only then could an honest man claim credit for his choices in life.

In order for man to become the ultimate spiritual being, man had to perfect himself through his choices, building positive character traits and eliminating negative traits. The perfect man would need to possess traits such as humility, honesty, kindness & mercy to name but a few.

However before "man" could be introduced, elements had to be in play. If G-d were to test mans ability to be kind & merciful there had to be someone or something that needed kindness and mercy.

THE RABBI MICHAEL J ELJARRAT LEARNING PROGRAMME – CLASS ELEVEN

Therefore G-d saw it fit that in the world there should be two groups of people, those that were rich and those that were poor. For the rich, their test would be in the area of mercy and kindness. For the poor their test would be in the area of honesty and humility. Every so often the people within these two test groups would change their role, in order to be tested in all traits needed. Therefore as long as "man" is being tested in this world, the need exists for both rich and poor.

 The word TZEDAKAH has its roots in the word TZEDEK which means justice. One of the understandings behind this is the concept mentioned above. The only reason why poor people exist is to create the opportunity for kindness and mercy to be demonstrated; if not for that there would be no need for poverty in the world. Hence the poor man suffers an injustice, since his poverty is mainly there to test others. When one gives TZEDAKAH one is in actual fact performing an act of TZEDEK, since one is restoring the justice and balance in the world, one is restoring the poor man to his rightful position.

Maimonides in Mishna Torah[1] writes that there are 8 levels of charity, these are as follows:

(In descending order)

1. To save another's dignity by offering them a job or business opportunity.
2. To give charity and neither party are aware of each other.[2]
3. To give charity whereby the giver knows the recipient but the recipient does not know.
4. To give charity whereby the receiver knows the giver, but the giver does not know.
5. To give charity directly, but before one is asked.
6. To give charity after being asked, but giving a suitable amount
7. To give charity less than a suitable amount, but with a pleasant face.
8. To give charity begrudgingly (with an unpleasant face).

The Rambam also adds some of the following laws and ideas:

- It is better to help family before strangers,
- It is better for a person too struggle a little than being dependant on the community, even if that means working at a job below ones accustomed dignity.
- Anyone who deceives the public and takes charity, where it is not needed is guaranteed to become poor before they die.
- Anyone who needs desperately and does not take bears the responsibility for his actions. Anyone who is not desperate but needy, and does not take charity is guaranteed that he will not die until he is in a position to sustain others.

---

1. Hilchos Matnas Aneeyim 10:7
2. Similar to at the temple

THE RABBI MICHAEL J ELJARRAT LEARNING PROGRAMME – CLASS ELEVEN

The concept of giving without making the receiver lose face can be seen in the Hebrew alphabet. The Talmud explains that the letters "Gimmel" & "Daled" face away from one another. The "Gimmel" standing for "Gomel" and the "Daled" for "Dalim" which can be read as "Gomel Dalim," give to the poor. When one gives to the poor one should "face away" i.e. not cause embarrassment.

The Rambam writes that one should be exceptionally careful not to hurt the feelings of someone who is downcast and depressed, because Hashem is close to those people, and should they cry as a result of you Hashem will take up their cause.

In Hebrew the word for money is "Damim" this is clearly related to the word "Dam" which means blood.

The same way as blood is the life force of the physical body, so too money is the life force of the emotional mind. This can be seen in the Talmud which states "A poor man is considered as dead". A person who is poor not only feels dead, but he lacks the ability to put his thoughts and goals into practice, much like a dead person.

Give and you will receive.
In Hebrew the root of the word "give" is "natan" spelt "Nun"(נ), "Tav (ת), "Nun" (נ) the word can be spelt both forward and backwards, the idea being that when you give, you will receive. All too often we think with a small mind set that "the more I give away the less there is for me." Like children fighting over a pizza, but in reality our wealth and possessions come from G-d, G-d can give a lot to all parties concerned. As when we hold a lit candle, we can light another candle and still retain our original flame, so too with giving charity we will not loose.

TZEDAKAH saves from death.
The Talmud[3] relates a story: Rebbe Akiva was once told by soothsayer that his daughter will die on the day of her wedding. The morning after her wedding when she awoke she found a dead poisonous snake, which she had killed by "chance" by putting a hair pin in the wall.

Unbeknown to her the snake was hidden in the wall and when she put her hair pin in the wall she killed the snake. When Rebbe Akiva asked his daughter why a miracle was performed for her, she replied; at the wedding there were some poor people who she invited in to eat, and in the merit of her TZEDAKAH she was saved from death.

---

3. Shabbos 156b

THE RABBI MICHAEL J ELJARRAT LEARNING PROGRAMME – CLASS TWELVE

CLASS 12   ETHICS MODESTY

In Judaism, modesty plays an important role in attaining spiritual greatness. As we will soon see, the trait of modesty plays a greater role from within, more so then any external acts or behaviors. Modesty is a mind set which lends itself to various actions and behaviors.

Although the dictionary defines modesty as a reservation in speech, dress and behavior as well as a lack of pretentiousness, this definition only focuses on external behaviors such as speech and dress. If we examine the Jewish definition of modesty we will see that modesty stems from humility, self respect and dignity. For the purpose of this class we will define modesty as "THE PRESERVATION OF HUMILITY". With this new definition in mind, many of the complex laws will become understandable.

In Hebrew the word for Modesty is "TZNIUS". One of the earliest scriptural sources for this word can be found in the verse "What does Hashem require of you but to do Justice, to love kindness and to walk humbly with your G-d."[1] From this verse we see that the word "HATZNAYAH" the word which defines modesty "TZNIUS" is characterized by humility. The Talmud in Sukkah (49b) describes this verse as referring to good deeds which are done with "TZNIUS". Rashi (ibid) explains that doing a good deed with "TZNIUS" means, performing a good deed without informing others. Thus "TZNIUS" can also be defined as "BEING DISCREET."

With the above definitions in place, it is interesting to note that the majority of the laws regarding Modesty/TZNIUS pertain to the dress code set for woman, (as well as the laws pertaining to hair coverings for married woman). In the classical works of Jewish law, technical detail is given regarding how much skin may be exposed, how much hair a married woman may reveal and under what circumstances may a man hear the voice of a woman.

---

1. Michah 6:8

THE RABBI MICHAEL J ELJARRAT LEARNING PROGRAMME – CLASS TWELVE

On the surface the laws of TZNIUS seem to be placed on a woman, restricting her conduct within a public setting. If not properly understood the laws of TZNIUS are not only difficult to understand but extremely difficult to maintain. In order to achieve a greater understanding of this subject, we will need to examine the concept of "clothing" as well as the sexual tendencies of both men and woman.

 When we think about clothing we would hardly define it as a "concept" and yet clothing plays a major role on our life. Let us take a closer look at the clothes we wear. Clothing has two primary purposes namely:

- Physical protection
- Identity

Physical protection is easy to understand, clothing offers a barrier between the external elements and our bodies. This is best demonstrated with shoes which protect our feet.

However when it comes to identity we will need further explanation.

To illustrate this concept, let us look at the various uniforms found in everyday context, and try and picture what personality comes to mind when thinking about these uniforms:

- Policeman
- Doctor
- Paramedic
- Traffic police
- Fireman
- Pilot
- Postman
- Motor Mechanic
- Airhostess
- Pharmacist

It is quite clear that when we think about the above professions or when we see these professionals in society, we quickly form an image associated with the role of that particular profession. We have come to expect certain normality's within society, for example we would expect our lawyer or accountant to be wearing a suit & tie. These images are so fixed within our mind, that if we were to see a policeman wearing a suit & tie, we would no longer associate that individual with police work. It is based on this premise that policemen can go "under cover" simply by removing their uniform.

Thus we can see that what we wear forms the shape of our identity in terms of how the world views us. In Russia, there are billionaires who pay money to a particular company, which dresses these billionaires in rags in order for them to experience the "poor" feeling. When these people are dressed in rags, society treats them in an extremely different way, from how they would, sitting in a suit and tie.

THE RABBI MICHAEL J ELJARRAT LEARNING PROGRAMME – CLASS TWELVE

Therefore it is quite clear, that in order to protect our own dignity and identity we need to dress in a way which is appropriate. When one understands that ones identity is carried within ones clothes, one will have a different view of clothing in general.

MATURE CONTENT

There is however, another purpose of clothing which we have not yet discussed, that of sexuality. When Adam and Eve were first place in the Garden of Eden, they were naked. It was only after they ate from the tree of knowledge that they felt a sense of embarrassment and G-d made clothes for them.

One of the primary differences between Men & Women is the senses involved with regard to sensual arousal. For Man the primary sense is sight, where as for Woman the primary sense is hearing, as well as the other senses.

SENSE	MEN	WOMEN
• SEEING	YES	NO
• TOUCHING	YES	YES
• SMELLING	YES	YES
• TASTING	-	-
• HEARING	NO	YES

Since the sense of sight is so important for men, and owing to the fact that "Adam & Eve" went from being naked to be clothed. It is the contrast of seeing the difference between clothed and naked which is responsible for sexual arousal in men.

It is for the above reason that the laws of TZNIUS are very applicable to women and particularly with regards to clothing. This is one of the reasons why Jewish women that are married, cover their hair, in order to savor themselves for their husbands.

Although it is forbidden for a Man to hear a woman singing, many commentaries explain that this law applies only when the woman can be seen by the man, since sight is of such primary importance.

LOYALTY

One of the blessings we give a newly married couple is "Gladden the beloved companions as you gladdened your creature in the Garden of Eden." The basic translation of the blessing is that we bless the newly married couple to be as happy as Adam & Eve were in the Garden of Eden. The question is what made Adam & Eve so happy in the Garden of Eden? The answer is both Adam & Eve knew with absolute certainty that they had the best spouse in the world, Adam knew that Eve was the best woman in the world since by default there was no other woman. On the other hand Eve also knew that she had the best Man in the world since by default there was no other man.

Loyalty to one's spouse is of primary importance, a marriage without trust is not a marriage, and this is what we say to a couple "you should build a trustworthy home." Modesty begins with absolute loyalty to ones spouse. Although modesty has many physical aspects, it is not these aspects which determine the extent of ones modesty. A woman can dress covered top to toe and yet still be immodest, if the mindset of loyalty is not in place.

PHYSICAL SEPERATION

Based on the ideas mentioned above, Orthodox Jews practice a separation between Men & Women in many contexts. The understanding being, that both men and women have very distinctive roles to play within society. It is through these roles that both Men and Women reach their full potential.

For this reason it is forbidden for Men to wear women's clothing and for Women to wear men's clothing, since this causes a clouding of the definition of Man and Woman, which leads to Women acting like Men and Men acting like Women.

Maimonides explains that when clear distinctions' are not made in society between Men and Women the lack of distinction leads to a 3 stage moral decline within society, as was evident with the biblical cities of Sodom & Gomorrah, which were eventually destroyed.

The three stages are:

- Sexual promiscuity (unfaithfulness)
- Homosexuality (same sex relationships)
- Bestiality (relationships between man & animal)

It is for this reason that the laws of Modesty have to be preserved for they are the foundation of Morality in society.

THE RABBI MICHAEL J ELJARRAT LEARNING PROGRAMME – CLASS THIRTEEN

CLASS 13   ETHICS KINDNESS

The Mishna in Ovos[1] says

"The world depends on three things – On Torah Study, on the service of G-d and on kind deeds."

This Mishna teaches us that without these 3 elements the world as we know it would cease to exist. Without kindness the world could not function, not just on a spiritual level but on a very practical level, let us see why:

For the world to function properly and for society to maintain itself, several community services need to be in place. As society has developed so too have these community services both developed and increased.

Some of these services include:

- Hospitals,
- Fire departments
- Police stations
- Schools

By nature human beings are complex unlike other animals, human beings form complex social communities, not merely herds or flocks like their animal counterparts.

What is an act of kindness?

Of course an act of kindness is an act which is friendly, helpful and considerate, however an act of kindness can best be described as an act which is done out of selflessness. Kindness is an act done not for personal gain or gratification but rather for the sake of another individual. If an act is done purely for personal gain or gratification this would be a selfish act not a selfless act of kindness.

This can be seen from the acts of kindness demonstrated by G-d Himself; such acts include:

- Creating the universe
- Making clothes for Adam & Eve
- Saving Noah and his family from the great flood

---

[1]. Chapter 1 Mishna 2

THE RABBI MICHAEL J ELJARRAT LEARNING PROGRAMME – CLASS THIRTEEN

All of the above acts done by G-d were not for personal gain, but rather to benefit the recipient thereof.

Now imagine a world in which people would only act for personal gain or gratification such a society would soon cease to exist.

- What would compel a doctor to treat a patient without adequate healthcare?
- What would compel a nurse to come to the aid of a dying patient at 2am?

If money was the sole motive then these services would rapidly disappear, since we cannot possibly compensate these services. What should a policeman get paid to risk his life daily to protect others? It is therefore an act of kindness that the world depends on. We will look at the state of the world today further in this lesson.

How can we do acts of kindness?

Given our definition above, all acts of kindness are not just acts of helping others, but rather acts, solely for the benefit of others, if so we must ask: How can we get to the level where our actions are pure?

Avraham the patriarch was exceptional at the trait of kindness; from Avraham we can learn how to perform acts of kindness. The Torah relates[2] that on the 3rd day after Avraham had his circumcision; Avraham was very bothered that he had no guests to invite. As we know Avraham would always invite guests over to his home, however on the 3rd day after his circumcision, G-d performed a miracle and made it an exceptionally hot day, in order that people would stay in doors and not walk in the open. The reason G-d did this was to give Avraham a rest and time to heal, the 3rd day being the most painful. However Avraham was still bothered, despite his immense pain, he still wanted to have guests, but there was no one to be seen.

The Torah relates further that G-d performed another miracle and made angels appear to Avraham, in the form of human beings, so that Avraham could invite them in and perform acts of kindness.

The commentaries ask: Why did G-d have to perform 2 miracles? (Making the day exceptionally hot and making angels appear) surely G-d could have just returned the weather to normal then people would have roamed the streets once again?

The commentaries answer that G-d was showing Avraham a lesson that acts of kindness are solely for the benefit of the recipient. If G-d had made regular people appear, Avraham may have taken personal gratification, with the knowledge that because of his actions, hungry people ate. However with angels, there was no gain by Avrahams actions, it was pure act of kindness.

When we feel proud of ourselves, for doing an act of kindness, and we think "If not for me, that person would…" We taint that act of kindness since we are merely the

---

2. Genesis 18.1

THE RABBI MICHAEL J ELJARRAT LEARNING PROGRAMME – CLASS THIRTEEN

messenger from G-d. The recipient will get what's coming to him/her if not from you, then from someone else. A pure act of kindness contains no personal gratification.

Kindness motivated by selflessness.

The following factious story illustrates the point of selfish kindness:
There was once a poor old woman who lived next door to a young couple. The young couple had some old leftovers in their fridge, which was beginning to smell. As an ac of kindness they gave the rotten food to the old woman, the woman ate the food and became very ill. The young couple went to visit the old woman in hospital, she later died and the young couple attended her funeral. The young couple felt very proud because with their act of kindness they were able to accomplish 3 Mitzvos (1. giving to the poor. 2. Visiting the sick. 3. Attending a funeral.)

Sometimes we hear people saying "Do kindness, it's a mitzvah", but true kindness is not done to collect merits off others. To the discerning eye it is clear to distinguish genuine acts of kindness, from selfish acts of kindness. Genuine acts of kindness come from the heart with the thought "What would I want, if I were in his/her position?" Selfish acts of kindness come from arrogance with the thought "If not for me that person would…."

Kindness falls into the category of Mitzvos between man & man. As with all mitzvos that are between man & man, simple performance is not enough. The Mitzvos between man & man are there to change our character; we do not complete the Mitzvah until we become one with the Mitzvah. Therefore to complete the Mitzvah of kindness, one needs to become a naturally kind person, who has the desire to be kind.

The Torah relates [3] that G-d tested Avraham with the greatest test of all. After waiting many years, Avraham had a child from his wife Sarah; G-d promised Avraham that his son (Yitzchak) would be the continuation of the Jewish people. When Yitzchak was 38 years old, G-d commanded Avraham to slaughter his son Yitzchak as a sacrifice to which Avraham obeyed.

As Avraham was about to slaughter his son, an angel appeared from heaven and said: "Do not slaughter the boy for now I know that you fear G-d!" The Vilna Goan and other commentaries ask why is it only now that we know that Avraham fears G-d? Surely he had proven himself beforehand?

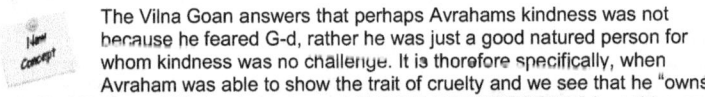

The Vilna Goan answers that perhaps Avrahams kindness was not because he feared G-d, rather he was just a good natured person for whom kindness was no challenge. It is therefore specifically, when Avraham was able to show the trait of cruelty and we see that he "owns" the trait of kindness. This is what is termed "**DEVAR VE HEPOOCHA**" (one thing and opposite) the character traits are only "owned" by the individual when that individual can be in control and display the full spectrum of the emotion. If a person can only display a one sided emotion, i.e., if he is always kind, then the emotion "owns" the person, meaning that person is controlled by his/her emotions and not the other way around.

---

3. Genesis 22:1

PAGE 3

THE RABBI MICHAEL J ELJARRAT LEARNING PROGRAMME – CLASS THIRTEEN

Until what point must kindness be shown?

 The word in Hebrew for kindness is CHESED often referred to as "GEMILUS CHASODIM" the word "GEMILUS" comes from the word "LE-HIGOMEL" which means to nurse. The reason why a mother will nurse her young baby is because the young child is unable to feed itself, however once the child matures it would no longer be appropriate for the mother to nurse the child. This is also true of the Mitzvah of Chesed, we should help others until the point that they can sustain themselves, but not to the point where an unhealthy dependence develops.

In the Amida we say that G-d is "GOMEL CHASADIM TOVIM" (he does good acts of kindness).The question which is asked is why does it say "good acts of kindness" surely all acts of kindness are 'good'?

The commentaries answer that G-d unlike man only performs "good act of kindness", man however sometimes performs acts of kindness which are not "good" for example kindness which leads to an unhealthy dependence of the recipient thereof, or kindness which causes damage, such as buying alcohol for an alcoholic or drugs for a drug addict. Although these acts are in fact kind, but the damage caused deems this kindness to be "bad". From this it is clear that whenever G-d is kind to us, all the possible outcomes are always good.

THE RABBI MICHAEL J ELJARRAT LEARNING PROGRAMME – CLASS FOURTEEN

CLASS 14   ETHICS
BUSINESS ETHICS

The concept of business ethics is far reaching and applicable to everyone. Whether a person is an employer or an employee, a business owner or a factory worker, self employed or even unemployed, everyone has a role to play within the context of business ethics.

In a broad sense business ethics deals with all concepts related to the fairness of monetary transactions. Since we all use money in one form or another, we all need to be aware of the
Torah laws related to the handling of money.

For example:

- When may one pay salaries and wages late?
- What responsibilities do I have to my employer?
- May I use stationary belonging to the business for personal use?
- How honest do I need to be with my tax returns?
- May I change interest on loans?

The answer to all of the above questions is not just a simple yes or no, but rather a complex answer which, would require a thorough knowledge of Torah laws. For this reason this lesson will not go into detail regarding all the various scenarios, but will briefly outline some of the fundamental concepts relating business ethics.

The Talmud writes that one of the questions a person is asked after his/her death is

"Were you honest in business"?

Or more literally "Did you trade in faith" There are numerous commentaries explaining the Talmud, one of which elaborates on the term "faith" used by the Talmud.

One of the principles of faith is that G-d created everything and hence G-d is the owner of all that exists. The Talmud states[1] that all of a persons earnings are decided in the period between Rosh Ha Shona & Yom kippur. That means to say that G-d has predetermined our earnings long before we have earned them.

---

1. Beitza 16a

THE RABBI MICHAEL J ELJARRAT LEARNING PROGRAMME – CLASS FOURTEEN

Very often a person thinks to themselves that the ends justify the means, its ok to be dishonest now, because the profits I make will go towards a good cause. This is not so G-d is the one who determines earnings, and disobeying a Torah law will not add to ones earnings, hence the question did you trade with "faith?"

What is Business ethics?

The question which should first be dealt with is what are ethics? Ethics can be described as the "flavor" behind ones actions. For example in a business transaction, one may have acted in accordance with the "law" but what was the "flavor" behind the action? When ones motives are to be dishonest and steal, when one has in mind from the very onset of a business transaction to lie and cheat, then even the best contract set in place, will not prevent an abomination from taking place. It's this "flavor" or motive behind ones action which determines the outcomes to one's actions. Ethics in a nutshell incorporates the principle "what you find hurtful to yourself, do not do to others."

The need for business ethics

As we have seen throughout history, without honesty there can be no socioeconomic stability. The commentaries explain that during the time preceding the great flood in the time of Noah, society fell to a low moral standard. We know from Jewish law that in order to be liable in terms of the prohibition "do not steal" one has to steal a minimums amount called a "**Shaveh Pruta**" (the value of a Pruta = just a few units). If one would steal less than that amount, one could not be prosecuted by law. In the time prior to Noah people would steal small increments less than a "Shaveh Pruta", but consistently & continuously. This caused people to lose considerable amounts of money, with no recourse whatsoever. Once again we can clearly see that the law "do not steal" is not enough to keep society from collapse, the correct attitude and ethic needs to be firmly in place, in order for a strong moral conscious to exist.

Truth & falsehood

The Talmud[2] states that from the Alef-bet we can learn how to behave. We see that the position of the letters within the Alef-bet, shows us numerous principles.

In Hebrew the word for truth is "EMES" spelt "ALEF", "MEM","TAV"

These letters are found in the Alef-bet in the following position:

- Alef is the first letter, (א)
- Mem is the middle letter (מ) and
- Tav is the last letter (ת).

---

2. Shabbos 114

THE RABBI MICHAEL J ELJARRAT LEARNING PROGRAMME – CLASS FOURTEEN

By contrast the word in Hebrew for falsehood is "SHEKER" spelt "SHIN", "KUF", "REISH" These letters are found in the Alef-bet in the following position:

- Shin (ש) is the second to last letter,
- Kuf (ק) is the fourth to last letter and
- Reish (ר) is the third to last letter.

If we pay close attention to the positions of the letters we will see, that truth is spread far apart where as falsehood is all grouped together, the Talmud tells us that the reason for this pattern is to teach us that "TRUTH" is uncommon in the world hence one has to look all over to find it. A little in the beginning, a little in the end and a little in the middle.

Where as falsehood is very common, you can find it in one glance. On a deeper level "TRUTH" is spread apart, meaning in order to understand the truth behind an idea, one needs to have a holistic view, one needs to look at the beginning, the middle and the end, to see the full picture. When one only looks at one place and then passes judgment by default, one can only see falsehood.

The Talmud also tells us that the letters for truth (ALEF,MEM, TAV) all stand on two legs, where as the letters for falsehood (SHIN,KUF,REISH) all stand on one leg. The message behind this is that truth is stable and consistent; truth can stand on its own two feet. Whereas falsehood is unstable and inconsistent. Falsehood has to always balance itself on one leg and will eventually fall. Falsehood in all its forms can only last so long until the truth eventually comes out.

Balancing ourselves

The Orchas Tzadikem writes[3] that a person has two "jobs" to do in this world. One job is to earn money to live; the other is to earn merits for the world to come. One has to balance these two jobs in such a way that one job does not detract from another. Meaning, one should not compromise on his earning of merits, for the sake of earning money, and one should not compromise on his earning money for the sake of earning merits. The balanced person does the opposite, he/she uses the two jobs to compliment one another, in such a way that his/her earnings enable the earnings of merits, and his/her earning of merits, enables the earning of money. When a person is balanced he/she can reap the full benefits that the world has to offer.

This was message that G-d thought the Jewish people in the dessert for 40 years. The commentaries explain that during the time the Jews were in the dessert, all their physical needs were taken care of. They didn't worry about food, shelter and clothing. For this reason they were reluctant to enter the land of Israel, because they knew that once they enter the land, life would return to normal and they would once again need to occupy themselves with earning a livelihood. They feared that spiritual growth is attainable only when physical concern is not an issue, for this reason G-d only gave them enough food to last for one day at a time, in order to build their trust in G-d. This is one of the fundamental aspects of Judaism that we are physical and we need to accomplish in both "jobs" in order to become balanced.

---

3. Gate 7 Gate of Happiness

THE RABBI MICHAEL J ELJARRAT LEARNING PROGRAMME – CLASS FIFTEEN

CLASS 15
ETHICS
MEDICAL ETHICS

The Gemorah in Shabbos[1] says, "One who has taken ill and is bed ridden, should consider himself as if he has been placed on the stand to be judged[2]; if he has advocates he will be saved and if not he will not be saved. These are the advocates for a person repentance and good deeds. Even if there are nine hundred and ninety nine advocating against him and just one advocating for him, he will be saved.[3]

The view adopted with regard to the perseveration of life is greatly dependant on the view adopted to the value of life itself. In Jewish thought, life is a precious gift from G-d to be valued and appreciated. Sickness is not viewed as a coincidental event, but rather a meaningful situation placed upon a person. Just as sudden as sickness can set in so too in an instant full health can be restored. For this reason the Torah views a terminally ill patient, who is on the verge of death, as a living person in almost all regards.

As we have seen previously, ethics is more than just a legal requirement, ethics is the moral fiber which covers all the unspoken, and is obviously most important in matters of life and death. Medical ethics span across a wide rage of topics everything from day to day treatments to complex life threatening situations. The following questions are some of the complex situations which arise, that need an ethical input in order to answer:

- Defining the point of death
- Palliative health care
- Organ donation and transplant
- Abortions
- Caring for the elderly

Today we have been blessed with advancement in medial technology. We have equipment and medications which would almost seem impossible in previous centuries. However with the advancement, also came more complex Halachic doubt. For this reason many of the Halachic decisions are based primarily on the works of contemporary scholars, and cannot be directly sourced to the classic sources of Jewish law.

---

1. 32a
2. One who is placed on the stand is in mortal danger (Rashi ibid)
3. Rashi explains that a persons deeds create angels; Good deeds create angels which advocate on his behalf in heaven and if there is but one angel advocating for him/her to be saved, he/ she will be saved.

THE RABBI MICHAEL J ELJARRAT LEARNING PROGRAMME – CLASS FIFTEEN

For the purposes of this lesson we will not go into detail with any one topic, but rather discuss some of the ethical situations, and the questions to ponder relating to the topics mentioned above.

Defining the point of death:

At what point is a person considered to be dead? Some of the practical implications include:

- A person on a respirator is usually in the ICU and beds in the ICU are a scarce commodity not only in monetary terms, but in terms of allocation. If we allocate a bed to a person who is technically dead, we could be causing the death of another patient awaiting a bed in the ICU.
- Regarding Organ donation, from what point may organs be harvested. Taking organs from an individual who is technically alive, is tantamount to murder.

Palliative healthcare:

Caring for a terminally ill patient has many moral and ethical issues which include:

- Can a patient who is suffering tremendously refuse to continue treatment, in order to hasten death, or is a person obligated to continue living despite all forms of suffering? Moreover if a person can refuse treatment, may one proactively take steps to hasten death, such as doctor assisted suicide?
- Very often a person who is terminally ill is no longer capable of making their own decisions either from a lack of consciousness or due to mental decline. May family members make decisions on behalf of the patient?

Organ donations and transplants:

Where as the benefits are very clear, the moral dilemmas include:

- Apart from the cornea, most organs are only viable in the period between brain death and cardiac death; based on the dilemma above regarding the definition of death, the question arises; May one remove organs from a "living" individual?
- A Halachic question is also posed regarding the donation of organs, since one has to bury an individual with all his limbs, removal of organs may be in violation of this Halachic ruling.

THE RABBI MICHAEL J ELJARRAT LEARNING PROGRAMME – CLASS FIFTEEN

Abortions:

Often a great political debate, but also an ethical dilemma, one of which include:

- If a woman is raped and falls pregnant may she have an abortion according to Jewish law? Clearly the pregnancy is unwanted. A similar question can be asked if brain damage occurs during pregnancy either to the mother or fetus, leaving the "baby to be" with a compromised quality of life, would it be ethical to terminate the pregnancy?
- If abortion is forbidden what would be the Jewish law, in a case where the pregnancy is endangering the mother's life, which life takes precedence? Similarly what would be the law, if an expecting mother cannot cope psychologically with having a baby would that be a valid reason to abort a pregnancy?

Caring for the elderly:

The elderly are sometimes given secondary priority, when it comes to healthcare; some ethical questions arise such as:

- May a doctor refuse to do a procedure, with the rational that the elderly person concerned will only live for a short time after the procedure? According to Jewish law does an old person have fewer rights than a younger person? This can be understood in the following situation. If both a 30 year old and an 80 year need a heart/liver transplant and there is only 1 heart/liver available, does the 30 year have priority based on the fact that he/ she has longer to live?
- Due to the increased risk factor, may an elderly person subject him/her self to treatment which may be unsuccessful due to their age? Or does everybody have the right to preserve their own life?

The answers to these questions would involve a great deal of study both with regards to medical concepts, as well as Torah law. These are just some of the issues that face the observant Jew.

Needless to say that one of the strongest ethical themes relates to the treatment of patients as human beings, not merely as a "number". Human beings have emotions and feelings, despite their illness, this concept should always be considered whenever dealing with ethical issues.

THE RABBI MICHAEL J ELJARRAT LEARNING PROGRAMME – CLASS SIXTEEN

CLASS 16   LIFE CYCLE
BRIS MILAH (CIRCUMCISION)

Although the subject of life after death is fundamental to Jewish thought, and is extremely fascinating, it is the period life before death that we will be exploring in our next section. In the next few classes we will take a closer look at the short time period in man's existence lasting usually no more than several decades, this time period is the "life cycle."

Starting with birth and ending with death, we will explore some of the mile-stones in the Jewish life cycle.

The verse says "Avraham circumcised his son Isaac at the age of eight days as G-d had commanded him"[1] After a miraculous birth, Avraham circumcised his son as commanded so by G-d. This was the ritual circumcision which, served as a "contract" binding Isaac to the Jewish faith. From that time and onwards all Jewish males are circumcised at the age of eight days old, and thus enter into the binding contract of Jewish faith. This is indicated in the blessing which we make at the circumcision "Who has commanded us to bring him into the covenant of Avraham, our forefather."

The first mile-stone reached by a Jewish male is at the age of eight days old, it is on this day that he becomes a real Jew in all respects. This mysterious contract contains within it several fundamental aspects of Judaism; it contains a message which will set the trend for a Jewish life.

After the circumcision has taken place the congregation says: "Amen. Just as he has entered into the covenant, so may he enter into the Torah, the marriage canopy, and good deeds." On a superficial level this blessing can be summarized as "Just as he has reached this mile-stone, so too may he reach many more mile-stones." However on a deeper level we are saying: "In the same way as he has entered this contract, so too may he enter other contracts, with a similar intention." This means to say that the message carried within circumcision, is the same message carried within, Torah (study), marriage, and good deeds in general. This leads us onto the question:

WHAT IS THE MESSAGE BEHIND BRIS MILAH?

The word BRIS means covenant and the word MILAH mean to cut/fill. It is the word MILAH which needs examination. It would almost seem paradoxical that the word "cut" would also mean to "fill." The commentaries explain that it is precisely through this "cutting" and removing the foreskin. That one is able to "fill" oneself and become a complete person.

---

1. Genesis 21:4

THE RABBI MICHAEL J ELJARRAT LEARNING PROGRAMME – CLASS SIXTEEN

The message behind BRIS MILAH is that we are not born perfect; we need to make adjustments and corrections to ourselves in order to become perfect. This is illustrated in the removal of the foreskin, and hence the "cutting" in order to "fill." We can now understand how this concept applies to the many commitments we make in life.

In marriage for example we need to realize that we are not perfect, and that adjustments and corrections need to be made. In Torah study too we must realize that there is an infinite amount of knowledge to be obtained. If one would study with the attitude "I already know this", then ones mind would become closed to learning new ideas. Thus the message which must be carried throughout ones life time is "we are not perfect, we are born to change."

WHY EIGHT DAYS OLD?

According to the commentaries, numbers have great significance. The number six represents the ultimate form of physicality thus the world was created in six days. The number seven represents spirituality hence Shabbos is on the seventh day. The number eight represents all that is above the form of natural creation which took place within seven days. Hence on the 8th day, we remove that which forms the natural form of creation, and we go above nature for the reason mentioned above.

The Mishna in Ovos says[2] "A Five year old begins Scripture… A hundred year old is as if he was dead, passed away and ceased from the world." The value of a human being is depended on his contribution to others. A person who is one hundred years old can no longer contribute to others. The Mishna above sets mile-stones to be attained at various ages in ones life. The self value of a person is dependent on his goals and achievements. So long as a person has a goal and what to achieve he/she will feel alive. Where a person reaches a stage where he/she feels that there is nothing left to accomplish, it is as if he/she has passed away and ceased from the world. This point is once again shown with the idea mentioned above "we are born to change".

THE NAMING OF THE CHILD

After the circumcision is done, the parents name the infant boy. It is with this name that he will now be called in heaven. This is the name that will be used in all ritual services, such as marriage and divorce, even when being called up to the Torah. In Jewish thought a name is far more than a "calling label" a name signifies the character of the person, and plays a role in the life he/she will lead. Thus for example the name NATHAN which means to give, will influence its name sake to be a giving person.[3] The commentaries explain that the only form of divine inspiration granted to unworthy individuals, is the one that is given to parents regarding naming of their child.

---

2. Chapter 5 Mishna 25
3. For further reading about names, read: "WHATS IN A NAME?" Author. RABBI M.GLAZERSON.

THE RABBI MICHAEL J ELJARRAT LEARNING PROGRAMME – CLASS SIXTEEN

WHO DOES WHAT AT THE BRIS?

There are 4 primary people involved in the circumcision:

- THE MOHEL – The one who performs the circumcision
- THE SUNDECK – The one who holds the baby during the circumcision.
- THE FATHER – The father of the child recites some of the blessings
- THE BABY – Is the one, on whom the circumcision is performed.

The laws pertaining to circumcision are numerous, for this reason as expert MOHEL is always sought after. There is a custom to say a special personal prayer upon hearing the baby crying, as this is a great time of mercy in heaven.

After the Bris is complete the baby is returned to the mother, and a festive meal takes place in celebration of the event which has taken place. The source for this is from Avraham who made a great feast after he had circumcised his son Isaac.

THE RABBI MICHAEL J ELJARRAT LEARNING PROGRAMME – CLASS SEVENTEEN

CLASS 17   LIFE CYCLE BAR-MITZVAH

The next mile-stone celebrated in the Jewish life cycle is that of coming of age. For Jewish boys this age is 13 and for Jewish girls this age is 12. It is at this age that the Bar Mitzvah and Bat Mitzvah are celebrated by Jewish boys and girls respectively.

The Bar Mitzvah, which literally means "son of Mitzvah", is a celebration of the fact that this Jewish boy or girl is no longer considered a child, but rather a fully responsible adult. Thus the term Bar/Bat Mitzvah. (Lit "Son/Daughter of Mitzvah") is an indication that this individual is no longer a volunteer with regards to Mitzvos, but rather an obligated adult, hence the term "son of Mitzvah."

If we ask the question:"What act is considered nobler?"

- A. An act done voluntarily or
- B. An act done out of an obligation?

It would seem that an act done voluntarily is surely far nobler. For example one who volunteers to help others, is far more caring than one who is told to help others. The one who volunteers is doing so out of the goodness of his/her heart, where as the one which is told to do so, may have no real compassion.

Thus the obvious question can be asked. "Why do we celebrate the Bar/Bat Mitzvah?' Surely up until this point the individual who was performing Mitzvos was doing so as a "volunteer" with no real obligation. However after the age of Bar/Bat Mitzvah this individual is obligated to perform Mitzvos. Therefore according to the logic presented above that the actions of a "volunteer" are greater than those of the "obligated". Surely the status of the individual has dropped, which begs the question what is there to celebrate? On the contrary the dropping of status would be reason to mourn.

The Talmud tells us, that contrary to popular belief, the actions of the "obligated" are in actual fact greater than the actions of the "volunteer". "Greater is the one who is obligated and does from one who is not obligated and does." This concept needs to be explained further.
The commentaries give several explanations, why this should be so. Two of which we will now look at.

THE RABBI MICHAEL J ELJARRAT LEARNING PROGRAMME – CLASS SEVENTEEN

A: RESPONSIBILITY vs. FREEDOM

One explanation of why the actions of the "obligated" are greater is owing to the fact that one who is obligated to perform a task, has various responsibilities concerning that task. For example one who is hired to carry out a particular task or job is responsible to see that, that task or job is complete, meets various requirements and specifications etc. The one who is hired cannot simply pass on this responsibility to another individual, nor dos he/she have the freedom to act negligently. By contrast one who is merely a volunteer, has no responsibility to the parties concerned. He/She can always pass on this responsibility to another individual with the claim "Well I'm only trying to help." A volunteer is not accountable for the completion of the task, and cannot be accused when acting negligently. Therefore since the actions of the "obligated" carry more weight, and are bound by contract, the merit associated with them is far greater than those of the volunteer.

B: OUR WILL vs. THE WILL OF G-D

One of the more frustrating situations for a person is when whilst one is in the middle of doing something, someone tells us to do that very thing. For example, If a child decides one day to clean up his/her room without being asked, but just because he/she has realized it's the right thing to do; However in the middle of tiding up, the mother walks in and shouts "clean up your room", that child will feel a great amount of frustration. In the above situation the child's immediate reaction will be "I don't' want to", even though that prior to the mother walking in, the child was more than happy to do the task, in fact the task was already in progress. However, nobody likes to be told what to do, especially when already doing the very thing told. This concept also holds true with regards to Mitzvos, when one is a volunteer, one has a sense of pride and bolstered ego. However when one is commanded, one's natural reaction is to refrain and rebel. Therefore the actions of the "obligated" are more refined and mature, and hence carry a greater reward.

BAR MITZVAH – BECOMING AN ADULT

In Hebrew the word for 'adult' is "GODOL" which literally means "BIG". There is wonderful story which was told by Avraham ben Avraham, who was an exceptionally pious convert that lived in the times of the great Vilna Goan. Avraham ben Araham was the son of a very wealthy man, who had many workers. When Avraham was executed for his conversion, his executors made a nasty remark, something to the effect of where is your G-d now? To which Avraham replied: "You can kill my body it's only a clay soldier." He went on to explain: When Avraham was a young boy, he would play everyday with the children of his father's workers. However one day, there was an enormous amount of work to do and even the children went out to work that day. Avraham being bored and lonely spent the entire day making toy soldiers for himself out of clay. Avraham was so proud of his "clay soldiers" that he lined them up at the

entrance of his home for all the children to see, when they returned. However when the children returned home later that day, they were so tired and hungry, that they never saw the clay soldiers at the entrance of the house, and they trampled over them and destroyed them. Avraham was so angry that he went to his father and said, you have to fire all your workers; they have destroyed my clay soldiers.
To which his father replied, my son they are only clay "soldiers".

At that point Avraham learned an important life lesson, namely; "Small people worry about small things, and big people worry about big things". Being an adult means being "BIG" and being big means becoming a broad and expansive individual, that does not get caught up in meaningless trivial activities, but rather in meaning full activities, and pursuits. Being "BIG" means seeing the bigger picture in life.

CUSTOMS:

There are many customs relating to the Bar Mitzvah, some of which include being called up to the Torah for the first time an "ALIYA" (being called up to the Torah) is an honor only given to male adults, and as a sign of maturity, the Bar Mitzvah boy is called up to the Torah.

There are various customs relating to the reading of the Torah, in some communities the Bar mitzvah boy reads only the blessings, in other communities the Bar Mitzvah boy is called to the Torah on the Shabbos following his 13th birthday and the entire portion of the week together with the Haftorah is read by the Bar Mitzvah boy.

It is a Mitzvah to have a ceremonial meal on the day of the 13th birthday. Nowadays many other traditions also follow in celebration of the Bar Mitzvah, such as having a special function with friends and family, the Bar Mitzvah boy making a speech and various customs with regards to wearing the Tallis (Prayer Shawl).

Care should be taken when calculating the date of the Bar Mitzvah and the appropriate Torah portion, with regards to the exact date of the birthday. The 13th birthday is calculated by first checking what Hebrew date the boy was born and then finding the same Hebrew date 13years later. Therefore if a boy is born on the 1st of the Jewish month Nissan, his Bar Mitzvah will be on the 1st of Nissan 13 years later, and his Bar Mitzvah portion will be the Torah portion of the Shabbos following the 1st of Nissan.

THE RABBI MICHAEL J ELJARRAT LEARNING PROGRAMME – CLASS EIGHTEEN

CLASS 18 — LIFE CYCLE ENGAGMENT AND MARRIAGE

The Mishna in Ovos[1] says "Any love that depends on a specific cause, when that cause is gone, the love is gone, but if it does not depend on a specific cause, it will never cease", keeping this Mishna in mind we will now explore the next mile-stone in the life cycle namely engagement and marriage.

What is marriage?

Let us first take a look at some common perceptions, and then contrast that with the Torah view. This will lead us to uncovering some of the mysteries behind relationship as well as the similarities and differences between men and woman.

*Reference:[2] "**Marriage**, legally and socially sanctioned union, usually between a man and a woman, that is regulated by laws, rules, customs, beliefs and attitudes that prescribe the rights and duties of the partners and accords status to their offspring (if any). The universality of marriage is attributed to the many basic social and personal functions it performs, such as procreation, regulation of social behavior, care of children and their education and socialization, regulation of lines of decent, division of labor between the sexes, economic production and consumption, and satisfaction of personal needs for social status, affection and companionship".*

In Judaism, Marriage is more than just a legally and socially sanctioned union. Marriage is a uniting of souls placed together to achieve a common goal. The Talmud[3] says "They (the heavenly) pair a woman to a man for marriage only in accordance with his deeds as it is stated: For the rod of wickedness shall not rest upon the lot of the righteous. Rabbah bar, bar Chanah said in the name of R'Yochanan: And it is as difficult for the Omnipresent to match up a man and woman for marriage as it was to accomplish the splitting of the Reed Sea, as it is stated, G-d gathers individuals to a house, He release prisoners at suitable moments. Is it really so? But R'Yehudah has said in the name of Rav: Forty days before the formation of an embryo a Heavenly voice issues forth and proclaims: "The daughter of so and so is destined for so and so, the particular house is destined for so and so, and this particular field is destined for so and so.

This is not difficult; this concerning a first union and this concerning a second union."

After seeing the two passages quoted above several points can be noted as well as several questions asked.

---

1. Chapter 5 Mishna 19
2. Encyclopedia Britannica
3. Sota 2a (see Artscroll)

THE RABBI MICHAEL J ELJARRAT LEARNING PROGRAMME – CLASS EIGHTEEN

Point to note:

- Marriage sets rights and duties for the partners involved (paragraph1)
- Marriage serves a fundamental purpose (such as procreation, care of children and personal needs)
- Until recent times marriage was rarely motivated by romantic love.
- In more recent times same sex marriages became acceptable
- A person's spouse is determined in heaven (paragraph 2)
- There is a concept of a first and second union

Questions to ask:

- Why have the attitudes of people changed?
- Is a person's spouse one's own choice or something predetermined in heaven?
- What is considered a first union and a second union?

Why have the attitudes of people changed?

The key attitude to a successful relationship is: "What can I give?" the opposite attitude "What can I get?" results in failed relationships. It is most likely this attitude shift, that has lead to the new outlook with regards to marriage and it is most likely this attitude that has lead to the increase in divorce amongst all groups and cultures.

There are two ways in which we interact with people, either I-YOU or I-IT[4]. In an I-YOU relationship the person sees the other individual as a person just like him/her with wants, needs and desires. This is a healthy outlook, which promotes giving.

In the I-IT relationship the person sees the other individual as an object and not a person, this attitude promotes selfish behavior and the attitude "what can I get?" It may be that our attitudes are no longer focused on our obligations and responsibilities towards our partner, but rather focused on our own selfish gain that has led to the current situation.

Is a person's spouse one's own choice or something predetermined in heaven?

It would seem quite clear from the Talmud cited above, that every match is made in heaven. A person's first union is predestined even before he/she is born, and a person's second union is determined according to ones deeds but in any event all matched are determined in heaven. The Talmud teaches us that by nature it is impossible for a Man and Woman to live together in harmony as the differences are so great that they (the man & woman) are comparable to fire, which will consume one another. This is illustrated by the words in Hebrew for Man & Woman.

---

4. Daniel Coleman- Social intelligence

THE RABBI MICHAEL J ELJARRAT LEARNING PROGRAMME – CLASS EIGHTEEN

In Hebrew the word for Man is "ISH" and the word in Hebrew for Woman is "ISHA".

MAN = "ISH" spelt "ALEF" (א)
"YUD" (י)
"SHIN" (ש)

WOMAN = "ISHA" spelt "ALEF" (א)
"SHIN" (ש)
"HEY" (ה)

 Both man & woman contain the elements of fire "AISH" spelt "ALEF", "SHIN" (אש) and can therefore not co-exist. The only way a MAN & Woman can co-exist is if they have G-d between them. The Name of G-d being, "YUD", "HEY", the "YUD" taken from MAN = "ISH" and the "HEY" taken from Woman = "ISHA".

When one realizes that without G-d it is impossible to co-exist one can begin to appreciate the fact that it was G-d who made the match. When a Jewish couple gets married we bless them saying: "MAY YOU BUILD A FAITHFUL HOUSE IN ISRAEL." The word faithful/NE-MAN has its roots in the word trust, hence "May you build a home of trust". Trust is the foundation of any relationship, one of the blessings we give a newly married couple is:
"YOU SHOULD REJOICE (LIKE ADAM AND EVE) IN THE GARDEN OF EDEN".
The reason why ADAM & EVE were able to rejoice fully over their union was because they knew with absolute certainty that they had the best spouse in the world, since there was no other. If we appreciate that our "match" is made by G-d we can appreciate that there is no other and we can build a faithful home, a home of trust.

What is considered a first and a second union?

The Talmud cited above made a clear distinction between first and second union, a first union being predetermined from before birth, and a second union depending on one's deeds. The question is what is a first and second union? The commentaries explain[5] that if a man were to marry a woman not predestined for him[6], that union would soon disintegrate whether through divorce or premature death. Could the "wrong" person be a consideration with regards to a first/ second union?
The simple way to understand a first/second union is quite simple:
1st union = 1st marriage & 2nd union = 2nd marriage (if there is one).

However the commentaries offer various alternate understandings of the first/second union:

- first union = young people – second union = old people (Meiri)
- first union = ideal match – second union = second best (Chachmei Ha Emes)

The topic of marriage is vastly extensive and will be dealt with in greater detail in the advanced course.

---

5. RAN – Moed Koton – Kosvim BeMoed
6. He prayed for extended mercy

THE RABBI MICHAEL J ELJARRAT LEARNING PROGRAMME – CLASS NINETEEN

CLASS 19
LIFE CYCLE
DEATH AND BURIAL
PART ONE

The final two classes of this life cycle section we will deal with "Death and Burial." In part one we will try and understand how and why we die as well as some customs associated with death. In part two we will explore from Burial and beyond, and take a closer look at life after death and the various customs associated with burial, death and mourning.

The Mishna in Ovos[1] says "They each said three things. Rabbi Eliezer says (a) Let your fellow's honor be as dear to you as your own and do not anger easily; (b) Repent one day before your death; and (c) Warm yourself by the fire of the sages, but beware of their glowing coal lest you be burnt etc."

In statement (b) "Repent one day before your death", the students asked "Does a person know the day upon which he will die?" to which Rabbi Eliezer replied: "No; therefore, repent everyday, lest tomorrow be your last."[2]

The concept is apparent, we do not know when we will die, and therefore the way to live our lives is with the understanding, that every day may be our last. We see this concept in the Torah with regards to Avraham the Patriarch, the verse says "and Avraham came with his days", the commentaries explain that Avraham used each day to its maximum; hence he "came with his days". A successful life consists of successful days. Each day that we live is an opportunity to achieve, to grow and to change.

In a similar vain the Mishna in Ovos[3] says "Do not say when I have free time I will learn, for perhaps you will never have free time".

In our busy time consuming lives, we often procrastinate and push off important things because we simply do not have enough time. We may neglect friends and family, we may fail to pursue our hopes and dreams, we may even push off life itself. Then one day it's all over, our life has been spent, the only question which remains is; on what?

On closer inspection we can see that life is in actual fact very short, we spend the earlier and later years being depended on others and during the middle section which is more productive, we spend one third sleeping and perhaps another one third on other mundane activities.

---

1. Chapter 2 Mishna 15
2. Shabbos 153a
3. Chapter 2 Mishna 5

THE RABBI MICHAEL J ELJARRAT LEARNING PROGRAMME – CLASS NINETEEN

Understanding why we die:

As we saw above, on closer inspection life is very short, especially when compared to the history of the world. We all know this fact, and yet for some reason we almost never contemplate our own death. The question is why do we find it so difficult to conceptualize our own death?

To answer this question we need to understand the history of death. When G-d first created man, man was not intended to die, man was build to be immortal. It wasn't until Adam & Eve sinned by eating from the tree of knowledge, that the impurities of the world entered man's body, causing man's body to become impure and unworthy of its ultimate goal namely; being close to G-d and enjoying the radiance of G-d.

Therefore G-d introduced the concept of death into the world in order for man's body to decompose, and later be reconstructed in a pure form to bask in the radiance of G-d. This reconstruction of the body takes place during the period of "resurrection of the dead." [4]

Based on the above it is easy to understand why we find it difficult to conceptualize our own death. Since death is not really a part of the human "life cycle" we still have the mind set that we are immortal and will live forever, and for this reason we often procrastinate, thinking we have all the time in the world.

Since death is not a part of the "life cycle" rather just a means whereby the human body can decompose and be cleansed, death was originally introduced as a swift process. When the time came for a person to die, he/she would die with no warning, very suddenly and very unexpected. Up until the times of Jacob the patriarch, the way in which a person would die, would be by sneezing; i.e. when the time came for a person to die they would simply sneeze, and with that sneeze the soul would leave the body and the person would expire.

However Jacob the patriarch prayed that sickness should precede death in order to give mankind the opportunity to repent, and get his/her affairs in order before death. G-d except the prayers of Jacob and hence death is now a gradual process, and no longer occurs suddenly by sneezing. The custom of saying "bless you" or "you should be well" when hearing someone sneeze, is believed to originate from this time in history, when death no longer took place via sneezing, as if to say you should be well and not die.

---

4. See THIRTEEN PRINCIPLESS OF FAITH – PRINCIPLE 13

THE RABBI MICHAEL J ELJARRAT LEARNING PROGRAMME – CLASS NINETEEN

Understanding how we die:

The Talmud tells us[5] that there are 903 types of death in the world; the most difficult death is something called "ASKARA" which is as difficult as pulling thorns out a tuft of wool, the easiest death is "NESHIKA" (Lit. Kiss) (being kissed by G-d). Which is as easy as removing a hair from a glass of milk.

The Talmud[6] relates a story regarding Rav Nachman who after his death appeared to his student, giving an account of what he felt when he died. Rav Nachman said that the experience of death was not painful, but was as easy as taking a hair out of milk; however he said that he would not want to experience death a second time, due to the fact that it was a very frightening experience. The commentaries[7] ask an apparent contradiction between two pieces of Talmud, in one place it appears that death is easy "like taking a hair out of a glass of milk" and yet in another place it appears difficult "like taking thorns out of a tuft of wool". They answer, that for righteous people death is easy, but for ordinary people death is difficult.

It would seem clear why there is a distinction between the righteous people and ordinary people. When the angel of death appears to us; it is at that moment that we recognize our own potential and the value of life. If a person lived his/her life well then the transition between life and death is easy, since life was used, to its maximum potential.

However for ordinary people who may have wasted part or even all of their life's opportunities, the realization that life has now come to an end, leaves the person struggling with the angel of death, begging for just another moment. It is written that a person can obtain his entire merit of the world to come in just one hour; it is this realization which becomes so apparent at the time of death.

The way we want to be remembered, is the way in which we must live our lives. When we read an obituary or tombstone, it's always the little things which are remembered, the things which appear little now, but in the end mean so much.

In part two we will look at the laws and customs of burial & mourning, as well as the journey of the soul from death up until its final resting place.

---

5. Brochos 8a
6. Moed Koton 28a-28b
7. Marsha (ibid)

THE RABBI MICHAEL J ELJARRAT LEARNING PROGRAMME – CLASS TWENTY

CLASS 20

LIFE CYCLE
DEATH AND BURIAL
PART 2

LIFE AND BEYOND

With this lesson, we come to an end of the "life cycle" as well as the section "faith & doubt." However this is not the beginning of the end rather the end of the beginning. So too with life itself, death is not the end rather the start of a new beginning, hence this lesson is entitled "life and beyond". In this lesson we will explore some of the laws of death, burial and mourning and then take a deeper look at the journey of the soul and body from the time of death.

The Talmud[1] says that King David requested from G-d, to know exactly when he would die, to which G-d replied to David, "It is a decree before me that we do not reveal the time of man." David asked G-d: "On which day of the week will I die?" to which G-d replied, "You will die on Shabbos." Every Shabbos King David would study Torah the entire day[2]. However when the day came for King David to die, the angel of death distracted King David, and was therefore able to take his soul.

Although we would like to prepare for the traumas in life, and to perhaps prepare for our own death, or the death of our loved ones. Death, whether it be our own or that of others, always feels sudden. It almost seems impossible that a person once full of life and energy, a person full of character and personality is now reduced to an empty shell void of any character what so ever.

 This drastic change comes as a shock, both to the person whom has just died as well as to the family members of the deceased. This shock can last for several hours or even several days. A feeling of displacement is normal as the reality sets in, followed by feelings of grief and loss, which may or may not lead to depression, all these feelings are normal, and the Torah and Sages, have prepared a path for us to follow to not only cope and deal with the death, but to find comfort and peace, with the situation and within ourselves.

One who is deathly[3] ill is termed a "GOSES". A "GOSES" is considered a living person in all regards, and anyone who hastens the death of a GOSES is considered a murderer. If

---

1. Shabbos 30a
2. Since the angel of death cannot disturb one whois studying Torah
3. The commentaries explain that one who is expected to die within 3 days is considered deathly ill

PAGE 1

one is alone with one who is on the verge of death it is a Mitzvah to stay with that person so that he/she does not die alone.

 It is forbidden to touch a GOSES, and one may not close the eyelids of one who has died until several moments after death. The commentaries[4] explain that a person becomes anxious and confused when the soul leaves the body, and for this reason parents should not kiss their children after their death, nor should one hold the hand of the deceased and say "I will come with/after you" as this causes distress for the deceased.

If the deceased is a close relative namely; a parent, child, sibling or spouse, a period of "ANINOS" begins. The period of ANINOS lasts from the time of death until the time of burial. When one first hears the news of the passing there is a Mitzvah to do "KREE-AH" (tearing of ones clothes). The laws and customs of KREE-AH differ between men and woman, as well as with regards to the relation of the deceased (parent/child).[5]

One who is in the period of ANINOS is called an ONAIN. An ONAIN is exempt from all the Mitzvos; he/she does not make blessings, pray etc, but may not violate any prohibition even rabbinical. An ONAIN may wear leather shoes and leave his/her home, but may not sit upon a regular chair, bath/shower or do work. During the period of ANINOS both the deceased and the relatives are in shock, many explain that this is the reason for the exemption from Mitzvos due to the lack of concentration.

During the period between death and burial, the deceased is prepared for burial. The preparation is done as follows. First the body is washed thoroughly with warm water from head to toe, then the hair is brushed, then the nails of hands and feet are cut, after which the body is placed upright and water is pored over the head of the deceased in a way that it runs down the entire body. After that a mixture of egg (with the shell) and wine is pored onto the head of the deceased, and then the special shrouds are placed on the body of the deceased. In cases of unnatural death a special procedure is followed with regards to preparing the body for burial.

As soon as the body is ready for burial, burial takes place, however in many cases burial is postponed until the relatives of the deceased arrive, as this is deemed an honor for the deceased. It is also an honor for the deceased if words of praise are spoken prior to the burial.

The body once prepared is placed in a simple coffin[6] and escorted by groups of people up to the grave site. The body is then lowered into the ground, and then covered with sand. The custom is for the people attending the funeral to assist with the covering of the coffin. Once the grave is filled, several verses from psalms are recited followed by "KADISH". There are various customs regarding the verses said as well as the time and place where they are said.

After the burial those attending the funeral stand in a row and the relatives of the deceased pass by. Once the relatives have turned away from the grave, they begin a

---

4. Beis Lechem Yehudah (Yoreh Daieh 339-1)
5. In all practical cases a competent authority should be consulted.
6. This is the custom outside of Israel.

THE RABBI MICHAEL J ELJARRAT LEARNING PROGRAMME – CLASS TWENTY

period of mourning. Depending on the nature of the relation to the deceased mourning lasts for a year, and gradually eases over three distinctive phases. The first phase lasts for a period of seven days; this period is called "SHIVA". When one G-d forbid sits SHIVA the following restrictions apply:

- One may not leave ones home
- One may not bath/shower
- One may not wear leather shoes
- One may not have a haircut
- One may not sit on a regular chair

There are several other laws and customs such as not eating meat and drinking wine. Prayers are held at the house of the mourner, and KADISH is recited for eleven months.

The second phase is the period between the end of SHIVA up until thirty days after burial. During this second phase the majority of restrictions are lifted apart from hair cutting. This period is known as "SHELOSHIM". The third phase is from the end of SHELOSHIM until the end of the year. During this phase one is restricted from attending public parties and the like and this phase is known as "AVAYLOOS".

After AVAYLOOS has ended, all restrictions are dropped, and life returns to normal for the most part, there are some customs, such as changing places for davening in shul after AVAYLOOS, but other than that once AVAYLOOS has passed, then all forms of mourning and change end. Every year on the Hebrew date marking the anniversary a candle is lit in memory of the deceased, and KADISH is said on their behalf.

WHAT HAPPENS TO THE SOUL DURING THIS TIME?

Many of the laws and customs are clear indications as to the whereabouts of the soul during the time of death, burial and mourning. One such custom is that of lighting a candle during the days of SHIVA. The Shebolay Ha- Leket (Hilchos Semochos) writes that the soul returns and mourns for the deceased through out the seven days. There are those that say the reason for covering mirrors is also due to the returning soul.

From various discussions in the Talmud[7] it is clear that the dead are aware of the occurrences amongst the living as well as having some form of emotion. For more in depth detail of the passage between life and death see the – RAMBANS SHAR HAGEMUL.

The laws of death, burial and mourning are very detailed for further reading:
See – MOURNING IN HALCHAH - BY RABBI CHAIM BINYAMIN GOLDBERG ARTSCROLL PUBLISHERS

---

7. Brochos 18a and b

CLASS 21

FUNDAMENTALS OF OBSERVANCE

INTRODUCTION TO THE LAWS OF SHABBOS

The verse states[1] "Remember the Shabbos day to sanctify it. Six days shall you work and accomplish all your work; but the seventh day is Shabbos to Hashem, your G-d, you shall not do any work – you, your son, your daughter, your slave, your maidservant, your animal, and your convert within your gates. – For in six days Hashem made the heavens and the earth, the sea and all that is in them, and he rested on the seventh day. Therefore Hashem blessed the Shabbos day and sanctified it."

-THE TEN COMMANDMENTS (EXODUS)

The verse also states[2] "Safeguard the Shabbos day to sanctify it, as Hashem; your G-d has commanded you. Six days shall you work and accomplish all your work, but the seventh day is Shabbos to Hashem your G-d, you shall not do any work – you, your son, your daughter, your slave, your maidservant, your ox, your donkey, and your every animal, and your convert within your gates, in order that your slave and your maidservants may rest like you. And you shall remember that you were a slave in the land of Egypt, and Hashem your G-d has taken you out from there with a strong hand and an outstretched arm, therefore Hashem, your G-d, has commanded you to make the Shabbos day.

-THE TEN COMMANDMENTS (DEUTERONOMY)

For centuries Shabbos has been the corner-stone of Judaism, and for centuries Shabbos observation has been the key factor in the continuation of Judaism from one generation to the next.

If understood, appreciated and observed; Shabbos can be the most enriching experience for man on earth. However if not properly understood and appreciated, Shabbos observance is no more than a burden and an imposition on daily routine. For this reason the first place to start when learning the laws of Shabbos, is to understand the deeper meanings behind this special day, and to build an appreciation in order to have the motivation, not only to observe, but to enjoy this special day called Shabbos.

---

1. Exodus Chapter 20 Verses 8-12
2. Deuteronomy Chapter 5 Verses 12-15

THE RABBI MICHAEL J ELJARRAT LEARNING PROGRAMME – CLASS TWENTY ONE

The rewards for keeping Shabbos:[3]

- Hashem carries out the decree or will of one who keeps Shabbos
- Hashem gives financial success to one who keeps Shabbos
- Keeping Shabbos protects a person from heavenly decrees
- A person can be forgiven for all his/her sins if he/she keeps Shabbos
- A person who keeps Shabbos will merit to Yiras Shomayim
- Israel will be redeemed in the merit of keeping Shabbos
- One who keeps Shabbos, rests in Gehenom on the day of Shabbos

Hashem carries out the decree or will of one who keeps Shabbos:

The Mishna in Ovos says[4] "make His will your will in order that He should make your will His will."
"Nullify your will before His will, so that He will nullify the will of others before your will." Very often we can feel as if G-d forbid, G-d is not listening to our prayers' we pray for something and yet nothing seems to happen. However when one keeps Shabbos his/her prayers are put onto the "VIP" list as it were. When a righteous person makes a decree, Hashem fulfills his decree. If we realize what a powerful tool Shabbos is, in the fact that the creator Himself considers the will of one who keeps Shabbos, we will see why Shabbos is considered such a precious gift.

Hashem gives financial success to one who keeps Shabbos:

One of the difficulties facing, the observer is the challenge of not working on Shabbos and the resultant loss of income there-of. However when one realizes that income is not generated by work rather through the gift of G-d one can be rest assured that financial success will be given by G-d, through Shabbos observance.

Keeping Shabbos protects a person from heavenly decrees:

A heavenly decree is something very powerful which can almost never be broken. The law of gravity can be described as a heavenly decree. If G-d forbid one has a bad decree placed on him/her from heaven, it is almost certain that, that bad event will happen. However so great is the power of Shabbos that it can remove a heavenly decree.

A person can be forgiven for all his/ her sins if he/she keeps Shabbos:

As we saw in the previous section of faith and doubt in the class titled "Reward and Punishment," punishment is a direct result of sin. Therefore keeping Shabbos will reduce ones suffering in this world since Shabbos can atone for ones sins.

---

3. Source: THE 39 MELACHOS – RABBI DOVID RIBAT
4. Chapter 2 Mishna 4

THE RABBI MICHAEL J ELJARRAT LEARNING PROGRAMME – CLASS TWENTY ONE

A person who keeps Shabbos will merit to Yiras Shomayin:

Shabbos in its essence is the key to spirituality. This is indicated by the fact that the Torah states you shall work for six days and on the seventh you shall rest. If the intention of the Torah was for us merely to rest in order to be more productive at work, the Torah should have written, "Rest on the seventh day (in order that) you shall work for six days." Therefore Shabbos is clearly more than a day of rest. Furthermore the restrictions which apply on Shabbos is another clear indication that there is more to Shabbos that meets the eye. Thus Shabbos is a spiritual day and those who observe it will merit to be spiritually enlightened.

Israel will be redeemed in the merit of keeping Shabbos:

The Mishna tells us that if Israel were to keep two consecutive Shabbosim it would bring the redemption.
The merit of Shabbos has the power to end the exile.

One, who keeps Shabbos, rests in Gehenom on the day of Shabbos:

The Zohar states, that on the eve of every Shabbos a heavenly voice goes out in the realms of Gehenom and says "stop all punishment for the King is coming and it is a day of rest", immediately all punishment stops even for the wicked. However those who did not observe Shabbos in their life time, will not be afforded a day of rest in Gehenom. Therefore keeping Shabbos has the benifit of having a day of rest in Gehenom

THE RABBI MICHAEL J ELJARRAT LEARNING PROGRAMME – CLASS TWENTY TWO

CLASS 22

LAWS OF SHABBOS

KABOLLAS SHABBOS / PREPARING FOR SHABBOS

The Importance of Shabbos is so great that the Torah warns about its observance 12 times. The benefit of keeping Shabbos is so great that the sages say "Whoever keeps Shabbos it is as if he/she has fulfilled the entire Torah." Yet one who does not prepare for Shabbos can miss all the benefits of Shabbos week after week.

Kabollas Shabbos:

The word Kaballah means to receive, but receiving is more than just getting, receiving means allowing something to be contained within. When it comes to receiving Shabbos, we need to take a closer look at what this means. If Shabbos comes every week, then why do we need to receive it? Seemingly each and every week when the sun sets on Friday, Shabbos arrives whether we receive it or not. However the answer lies within the question itself, Shabbos may arrive week after week, but our job is to receive it, meaning to allow Shabbos to be contained within ourselves. At the end of each week a new Shabbos arrives, a Shabbos which is so unique, since each Shabbos only comes once. The impact Shabbos has on us, depends on how much we allow Shabbos in, and to what extent we allow Shabbos to be contained within ourselves.

There are two types of people who don't enjoy Shabbos, and therefore don't benefit from Shabbos and are unable to observe any of the laws.

- The first is, one who finds Shabbos as his/her "enemy". Usually out of ignorance one finds that there are too many restrictions and thus Shabbos becomes a burden. As we will see, the more one learns about the laws of Shabbos, the more one can act freely. It's not a matter of not being able to do certain things on Shabbos rather it's about learning how to do it in the correct way. A thorough knowledge of the laws of Shabbos removes any feelings of "burden". By way of parable imagine if one is placed in confinement with one's arch enemy; is there any way to enjoy that situation? Of course not! So too if one is placed within the confounds of Shabbos the "enemy" there will be no way to enjoy the situation, unless one makes peace and turns Shabbos from an "enemy" to a "friend". The only way to do that is by leaning the laws.

- The second is, one who sees Shabbos as his/her "friend". One who is willing to observe and to learn; however this person does not create a space within themselves for Shabbos to occupy. Hence there is no receiving of Shabbos. The person soon falls prey to frustration as the inspiration wears out so does the enthusiasm to observe and to learn. By way of parable imagine if one has a good friend, however they never get to see each other. The individual and his friend begin to grow distant and the relationship begins to fade. Thus if one wants to feel Shabbos one must allow Shabbos onto one's heart and this is done with the recovery Shabbos.

There was once a very poor man, who was very righteous and pious. Despite all his efforts and prayers all of his business ventures were unsuccessful. In his desperation he prayed to G-d, "G-d please let me win the lotto" week after week he waited in anticipation to win the jackpot millions, however as the weeks drew by his hopes began to diminish, as no winnings ever come his way. After several months he complained to G-d, "G-d, I depend on you, you have given me no success in my business, and moreover you have not made me win the lotto." Suddenly a once voice came out from heaven with a response, "I would have made you win the lotto, but you must buy a ticket!"

Preparing for Shabbos:

There is a famous expression "failing to plan, is planning to fail". The success of any endeavor is rooted in the planning stages of the project. The Talmud[1] says "One who makes an effort on Erev Shabbos will eat on Shabbos, but one who does not make an effort on Erev Shabbos from where will he eat on Shabbos?" The message is clear, one has to prepare for Shabbos. This fundamental concept applies not only to physical and practical endeavors, but also to spiritual and less tangible endeavors as the sages say "This world is comparable to a dry land and the world to come in comparable to the sea."

The Mishna in Ovos[2] says "Who is wise? One who learns from every person" On this Mishna Reb Zusha of Anipoli[3] makes the following comment, there are 7 things we can learn from a thief:

1. What he does he keeps to himself
2. He is ready to take risks in order to achieve his goal
3. The smallest detail is of great importance to him
4. He invests great effort and toil in what he does
5. He is swift
6. He is confident and optimistic
7. If at first he fails, he is back time and again for another try.

---

1. Avoda Zorah 3a
2. Chapter 4 Mishna 1
3. Meaningful life centre: Torah-Ethics

THE RABBI MICHAEL J ELJARRAT LEARNING PROGRAMME – CLASS TWENTY TWO

With these traits one can accomplish a great deal. The Chaiya Odom[4] says that it is a Mitzvah to wash your entire body on Erev Shabbos, and to wash your hair and cut your nails. It is also a Mitzvah to change into special Shabbos clothes and to clean your home in honor of Shabbos.

In the special prayer we say on the Eve of Shabbos called
"Rebon kol ho-Olamim"[5] "Please O king who reigns over kings, instruct your Angels, the ministering angles, servants of the exalted One, that they consider me with mercy and bless me when they enter my home on our holy day, for I have kindled my lights, spread my bed, and changed my clothes in honor of the Shabbos day"

In order to receive Shabbos in a state of joy, one must stop working early on Friday afternoon and prepare for Shabbos. It is ideal not to work from Mid-day Friday afternoon, on order to be fully prepared for Shabbos when it arrives.

The Friday service begins with Kabbolas Shabbos, with the prayers "Le-cho Neranana" – "come let us sing to G-d." This is a praise and acknowledgment to G-d being the creator and Master of the universe. These psalms are followed by the song "le-cha Dodi" – "come my beloved to greet the bride" – The Shabbos presence let us welcome. The last stanza " Boy ee Be Shalom" – "enter in peace" we turn around to face the entrance of the synagogue and bow. It is at this point that the holy "extra Soul" enters the body and the radiance of Shabbos fills the individual. It is at this point that the special holy day of Shabbos enters and the day of Shabbos has now begun.

In summary:
In order to feel the presence of Shabbos we should:

1. Learn the laws of Shabbos
2. Allow space within ourselves for Shabbos to occupy
3. Act like the thief who persists with diligence
4. Make physical preparations in honor of Shabbos
5. Pray to receive Shabbos with joy

---

4. Laws of Shabbos 1:10
5. Artscroll Siddur page 356-357

THE RABBI MICHAEL J ELJARRAT LEARNING PROGRAMME – CLASS TWENTY THREE

CLASS 23

LAWS OF SHABBOS

KIDDUSH AND CANDLE- LIGHTING

The Talmud[1] tells us that two angels escort a person, on Friday night when he leaves Shul and comes home- one good Angel and one bad Angel. If when the person enters his home he finds, the candles have been lit, the table set and the bed made, the good angel says "May it be the will of Hashem that it would be so next Shabbos" and the bad Angel also answers Amen. If however this is not so, the bad Angel says "May it be the will of Hashem that it should be so next Shabbos" and the good Angel answers Amen. For this reason the first thing we do upon arriving home from Shul is to sing "Shalom Aleichem" a song of welcome to the Angels. This is then followed by the song "Aishes Chayil" – "Woman of valour" and is praise both to the "bride" Shabbos and the Jewish woman. This is then followed by Kiddush.

What is Kiddush?

The word Kiddush comes from the adjective "le-kaddaish" (to sanctify or make holy) which has its roots in the word "Kodesh" (unique, special, holy). Therefore Kiddush can be described as the action which declares Shabbos as a special and holy day. This is accomplished by making a special blessing over wine. The wording for this blessing can be found in the siddur.[2]

Why do we use wine?

We find that wine is used for many ceremonies, such as weddings, circumcisions and for the sanctification of holidays. The reason why wine is used is owing to the fact that wine has a unique physical property. Unlike most physical items, wine improves with time. Wine although physical contains within it spiritual properties. Spiritual items improve with time. Therefore when creating a bridge between the physical and the spiritual, such as going from the mundane six days of the working week to the holy day of Shabbos, we therefore use wine as the conduit for spiritual transformation.

---

1. Shabbos 119b
2. Artscroll siddur page 360-361

THE RABBI MICHAEL J ELJARRAT LEARNING PROGRAMME – CLASS TWENTY THREE

Quick facts about the Mitzvah of Kiddush:

1. Making Kiddush on Friday night is a Torah commandment.
2. Both Men and Women are obligated to recite Kiddush or to listen to someone recite it.
3. Kiddush should be made as soon as possible after Maariv.
4. It is forbidden to eat or drink until Kiddush has been said.
5. One, who began to eat before Kiddush, must stop eating and recite Kiddush immediately.

Quick facts about Kiddush procedure:

1. There are different customs regarding standing for Kiddush:

    (a) Some stand only for the first 4 words
    (b) Some stand for the biblical passage and sit for the blessing
    (c) Some stand for the entire Kiddush

2. The Kiddush cup should be lifted with both hands and then placed in the palm of the right hand, 10cm above the table (one Tefach)

3. The Challas should be placed on the table and covered when reciting Kiddush

    (a) Since it is proper to make a blessing on bread before wine, we hide the bread.
    (b) To remind us of the dew which, covered the Mana in the dessert.

Quick facts about the wine and the cup:

1. The Kiddush cup must be whole and intact without any damage.
2. The Kiddush cup needs to be washed both on the inside and outside before being used
3. The Kiddush cup must be large enough to contain a "Re-veis" and the cup must be filled to the brim.
4. The remainder of wine from a cup or bottle which was drunk from is considered used wine and may not be used for Kiddush unless rectified.
5. One should use the highest quality wine for Kiddush.

Substitutes for wine:

1. For Friday night Kiddush, one may use bread instead of wine for Kiddish and follow the following procedure:

    (a) Wash for bread and recite the blessing on washing
    (b) Place both hands on the bread when covered and say the passage of "Va ye chulu"
    (c) Uncover the bread and say the blessing of Ha-Motzi
    (d) Cover the bread again, then continue with the remainder of the Kiddush blessing
    (e) After finishing the blessings cut and eat the bread.

2. For Kiddush on Shabbos morning, one may use "Chamar Medina" (Local beverage) as a substitute for wine this includes the following beverages
    - Beer
    - Liquor
    - Whiskey

Some also include the following:
   - Milk
   - Orange/apple juice
   - Tea/Coffee.

It is customary in many Shuls to have a communal Kiddush on Shabbos morning after davening, one should take care to eat a sufficient amount of "Mezonoz" (cakes, biscuits, pastries) to make an after blessing of "Al-hamichya." As ideally speaking Kiddush needs to be made in the place where one is having ones meal.

Making Kiddush for others:

It is preferable for one person to make Kiddush and exempt all those that are listening. The listener should pay attention and not talk while Kiddush is being said. Although there is no need for the listener to drink from the Kiddush wine, it is customary for the one making Kiddush to give some wine to all those listening. One may make Kiddush for another as many times as necessary, provided, that the listener has not yet heard Kiddush, however in such a case, the listener should drink some of the wine.

For further reading regarding the laws of "Lechem Mishna" (Two complete loafs) see:
THE RADIANCE OF SHABBOS
RABBI SIMCHA BUNIM COHEN
PUBLISHED BY: ARTSCROLL

THE RABBI MICHAEL J ELJARRAT LEARNING PROGRAMME – CLASS TWENTY THREE

CANDLE LIGHTING

Quick facts about the Mitzvah of candle lighting:

1. According to most opinions, candle lighting is a Rabbinical Mitzvah.

2. There are two primary reasons: (a) To honor Shabbos
　　　　　　　　　　　　　　　　(b) For the Joy of Shabbos

3. The obligation applies to all adult members of the household

4. If one member of the household lights, all the members are then exempt from lighting

5. It is customary for the women of the house to light on behalf of others:

   (a) Because woman are considered to be home makers
   (b) To atone for the sin of Adam in the garden of Eden

Quick facts about the candle lighting procedure:

1. The candles should be lit 18 minutes before sunset
2. The earliest time one can light is 1 and ¼ hours before sunset.
3. The candles should be of a high quality and produce clear burning flame. (oil may be used)
4. The candles should be placed where they can be seen during the meal
5. The candles should burn long enough to last up until the beginning of the meal
6. The obligation can be fulfilled with just a single candle
7. The custom is to light 2 candles, corresponding the two verses "Remember" and "Observe"
8. There is also a custom to light one candle for each member of the household
9. A woman lighting Shabbos candles must make the blessing after she has lit
10. One who is not excepting Shabbos at the time of lighting should make the blessing before lighting

THE RABBI MICHAEL J ELJARRAT LEARNING PROGRAMME – CLASS TWENTY FOUR

CLASS 24 — LAWS OF SHABBOS

APPLICATION OF LAWS

The laws of Shabbos are numerous, and without a basic framework one can drown in an infinite sea of details. For this reason this class will explore the basic concepts used when dealing with the laws of Shabbos and explaining some of the common terms used.

The Ramban in Mishna Torah explains the terms and concepts used by the sages, in regard to the laws of Shabbos. For the purposes of this lesson we will follow the order of the Rambam and elaborate the points where necessary. Before we begin, it is important to note the term "MELACHA" refers to one of the 39 categories of forbidden work on Shabbos, these categories and their reasons will be explained in the classes to follow.

- Resting on Shabbos from doing "MEACHA" is a positive commandment.
- Violating Shabbos and doing a "MELACHA" is a transgression of a negative commandment.

The punishment system[1]

INTENTION	WITNESSES	PUNISHMENT
WITH INTENTION	WITH OUT WITNESSES	KARES
WITH INTENTION	WITH WITNESSES	SKEILA
BY MISTAKE	-	SIN OFFERING

PUNISHMENT	MEANING
KARES	"TO BE CUT OFF" DYING YOUNG DEATH OF CHILDREN, POVERTY
SKEILA	DEATH BY STONING, ONLY DONE WHEN THE TEMPLE STANDS
SIN OFFERING	A SACRAFICE BROUGHT TO ATTONE FOR SIN ONLY DONE WHEN THE TEMPLE STANDS

---

1. Laws of Shabbos Chapter 1 Law 1

THE RABBI MICHAEL J ELJARRAT LEARNING PROGRAMME – CLASS TWENTY FOUR

Concepts:

CONCEPT NAME	MEANING
DAVAR SHE-AINO MISKAVEN	SOMETHING WITHOUT INTENTION

- SOURCE: RAMBAM LAW 5
- MALACHA: UPROOTING LIVING PLANTS IS FORBIDDEN
- ACTION: WALKING ON GRASS
- LAW: PERMITTED

CONCEPT NAME	MEANING
PSEIK REISHA	CUTTING OFF HEAD

- SOURCE : RAMBAM LAW 6
- MELACHA: IT IS FORBIDDEN TO KILL A LIVNING CREATURE ON SHABBOS
- ACTION: CUTTING THE HEAD OFF A CHICKEN
- LAW: FORBIDDEN

The difference between "DAVAR SHE-AINO MISKAVEN" and "PSEIK REISHA" is that with regards to a "DEVAR SHE AINO MISKAVEN" the action may or may not cause a violation of the Melacha, therefore so long as there is no deliberate intention to violate the Melacha, the action is allowed. However with regards to "PSEIK REISH" the action will defiantly cause a violation of the Melacha, therefore even if there is no intention to violate the Melacha the action is forbidden.

CONCEPT	MEANING
MELACHA SHE-AIN TZARICH LEGOOFA	A MELACHA WHICH IS NOT NEEDED FOR ITSELF

- SOURCE: RAMBAM LAW 7
- MELACHA: IT IS FORBIDDEN TO EXTINGUISH A FLAME ON SHABBOS
- ACTION: EXTINGUSING A FLAME TO USE OIL
- LAW: FORBIDDEN

THE RABBI MICHAEL J ELJARRAT LEARNING PROGRAMME – CLASS TWENTY FOUR

The difference between "PSEIK REISHA" and "MELACHA SHE-AIN TZARICH LEGOOFA" is that with regards to "PSEIK REISH" the person is doing an "ACTION" which causes a definite violation of the "MELACHA". However, with regards to Melacha She-ain Tzarich Legoofa the person is doing the Melacha itself but not for the result of the intended Melacha but rather for another reason. Another example would be digging a hole to use the sand, the "MELACHA" is digging a hole for the purpose of planting, thus one who digs a hole for the sand is violating the "MELACHA" but for a different intention.

CONCEPT NAME	MEANING
SHENYIM SHE-OSOO	TWO WHO DID

- SOURCE: RAMBAM LAW 15
- MELACHA: IT IS FORBIDDEN TO WRITE ON SHABBOS
- ACTION: TWO PEOPLE HELD THE PEN AND WROTE TOGETHOR
- LAW: EXEMPT (MEANING FORBIDDEN BUT EXEMPT FROM PUNISHMENT)

The law of "SHENYIM SHE-OSOO" applies only in a case where two people are not necessary to carry out the Melacha, for example writing with a pen. However if two people are needed to perform the Melacha then both parties are liable for the Melacha, for example if two people carry a plank of wood in the street on Shabbos, both people will be liable for the Melacha.

CONCEPT NAME	MEANING
ME KALKEL	DESTROYING

- SOURCE: RAMBAM LAW 17
- MELACHA: -
- ACTION: TEARING CLOTHES TO BE DESTRUCTIVE
- LAW: EXEMPT (MEANING FORBIDDEN BUT EXEMPT FROM PUNISHMENT)

The reason why "ME KALKEL" is exempt is owing to the fact that the Torah forbade "MELECHES MACHSHEVES" meaning thoughtful, constructive actions, not thoughtless, destructive actions. For this reason there are numerous laws regarding exemptions due to lack of thought such as "MISASAIK" – DOING WITHOUT THINKING, or having intention for one result and not another (See laws 8-15). It is interesting to note that the RAMBAM in law 17 gives the example of "digging a hole for the sand" as an example of "MEKALKEL", the commentaries explain that this is referring to digging a hole in a place that causes destruction for example in the living room.

ADVANCED CONCEPTS

CONCEPT NAME	MEANING	
PSEIK REISHA DE LO NICHA LAY	AN UNDESIRED PSEIK REISHA	New Concept

- SOURCE: TALMUD (KESUBOS 6a)
- MELACHA: SHEARING/CUTTING HAIR IS FORBIDDEN ON SHABBOS
- ACTION: BRUSHING HAIR
- LAW: VARIOUS OPINIONS

The concept is the same as "PSEIK REISHA" i.e. that the "action" will definitely cause a violation of a "Melacha" however the consequent "MELACHA" is either undesired or non consequential. There are various opinions regarding such a case. (See source for further details)

THE RABBI MICHAEL J ELJARRAT LEARNING PROGRAMME – CLASS TWENTY FIVE

CLASS 25
LAWS OF SHABBOS
39 MELACHOS

ORDER OF BREAD

As we have seen in previous classes the prohibition of "MELACHA" on Shabbos includes only those things that were considered "MELACHA" in the Mishkan. The Mishkan was the temporary temple in the desert, and there were 39 distinctive "MELACHOS" which needed to be done in both the establishing and the daily function of the Mishkan. Although these 39 "MELACHOS" are each unique, they can be logically grouped into 4 groups namely:

- The order of Bread (bread being a sacrifice offered in the Mishkan)
- The order of Garments/Fabrics (needed in making coverings for the Mishkan)
- The order of Hides (hides being used in the construction process and sacrifices)
- The order of Construction (the process of construction itself)

This class will look at the first order, namely "The order of bread". The order of bread includes all the necessary tasks involved in making bread, from plowing all the way to baking. Bread played an important role in the Mishkan, since bread was needed for the "Shulchan" (lit table). However the Shulchan was no ordinary table and the bread was no ordinary bread. The bread placed on the Shulchan had a special name; it was called "lechem ha-Ponim." (Lit. bread of faces), often referred to as "show breads". The table was no ordinary table; this table was covered in pure gold and was one of the primary ornaments placed within the "holy" of the Mishkan. There were many miraculous events surrounding these mysterious show breads, one of which was the bread's longevity. It would stay fresh for over a week, as the Talmud[1] says "Taking it out was as putting it in" meaning it remained perfectly fresh from the time it was placed in the Shulchan, until the time it was taken out.

The Order of Bread:
- Choraish (Plowing)
- Zoraya (Sewing)
- Kotzair (Reaping)
- M'amer (Gathering)
- Dosh (Threshing)
- Zoreh (Winnowing)
- Borer (Sorting)
- Tochain (Grinding)

---
[1] Yoma 21a

THE RABBI MICHAEL J ELJARRAT LEARNING PROGRAMME – CLASS TWENTY FIVE

- Merakaid (Sifting)
- Losh (kneading)
- Ofeh-Bishul (Baking – cooking)

Before we begin going into detail, there is one principle which needs to be explained, namely that of an "Av-Melacha" and a "Tolda." (literally "A father" and "child") they are both forbidden as a Torah law and the only difference is whether or not that action is specified by the Torah Melachos, for example digging for the purpose of planting is the "Av Melacha" of "Choraish/Plowing" where as loosening soil would be forbidden as a "Tolda."

CATEGORY: ORDER OF BREAD

MELACHA NUMBER 1

NAME: Choraish/Plowing

DEFINITION: Any activity that prepares soil for the purpose of planting

EXAMPLE: Plowing, digging, fertilizing

CATEGORY: ORDER OF BREAD

MELACHA NUMBER 2

NAME: Zoraya/Sowing

DEFINITION: Any activity which aids or promotes plant growth

EXAMPLE: Sewing, planting, watering

THE RABBI MICHAEL J ELJARRAT LEARNING PROGRAMME – CLASS TWENTY FIVE

CATEGORY: ORDER OF BREAD

MELACHA NUMBER 3

NAME: Kotzair/Reaping

DEFINITION: Any activity that uproots a living plant from its source of growth

EXAMPLE: Picking fruit off a tree, taking a leaf off a tree

CATEGORY: ORDER OF BREAD

MELACHA NUMBER 4

NAME: M'amer/Gathering

DEFINITION: Any activity whereby scattered produce is collected or combined

EXAMPLE: Gathering bundles, Raking leaves

CATEGORY: ORDER OF BREAD

MELACHA NUMBER 5

NAME: Dosh/Threshing

DEFINITION: Any activity that breaks apart a kernel from its stem

EXAMPLE: Threshing, pounding wheat stalks

THE RABBI MICHAEL J ELJARRAT LEARNING PROGRAMME – CLASS TWENTY FIVE

CATEGORY: ORDER OF BREAD

MELACHA NUMBER 6

NAME: Zoreh/Winnowing

DEFINITION: Any activity that uses wind to separate unwanted particles

EXAMPLE: Winnowing, blowing off dust

CATEGORY: ORDER OF BREAD

MELACHA NUMBER 7

NAME: Borer/Sorting

DEFINITION: Any activity of sorting or selecting

EXAMPLE: Removing unwanted raisins from peanuts

CATEGORY: ORDER OF BREAD

MELACHA NUMBER 8

NAME: Tochain/Grinding

DEFINITION: Any activity that breaks down a large item into smaller useable parts

EXAMPLE: Crushing, chopping, dicing

CATEGORY: ORDER OF BREAD

MELACHA NUMBER 9

NAME: Merakaid /Sifting

DEFINITION: Any activity that uses a sieve or similar device to separate

EXAMPLE: using a sieve or strainer

CATEGORY: ORDER OF BREAD

MELACHA NUMBER 10

NAME: Losh/ Kneading

DEFINITION: Any activity whereby a paste or dough is made by mixing particles with liquid

EXAMPLE: Mixing cement, making dough

CATEGORY: ORDER OF BREAD

MELACHA NUMBER 11

NAME: Ofeh-Bishul/ Baking - Cooking

DEFINITION: Any activity that improves a substance for consumption by means of heat

EXAMPLE: Cooking, baking, boiling

THE RABBI MICHAEL J ELJARRAT LEARNING PROGRAMME – CLASS TWENTY SIX

CLASS 26
LAWS OF SHABBOS
39 MELACHOS

ORDER OF FABRICS
PART 1

In this lesson we will take a look at the next set of forbidden Melachos, namely: The Order of fabrics. The order of fabrics consists of all the necessary steps involved in making garments from shearing all the way to tearing, a total of 13 processes.

In the Mishkan fabrics were needed for the special coverings, which would cover the top of the entire Mishkan and formed a blanket like roof. These coverings were made from wool and were dyed three different colors. The process of obtaining the wool started with shearing sheep, after which the wool was crushed. The next step was to comb the wool, followed by the dying of the wool into its 3 necessary colors, namely T'chayles – blue, Argomon – purple and Tola'as Shoney – red. Once dyed the threads were spun together and woven into a cloth. The weaving process was complex and for this reason we have broken up the order of fabrics into to parts.

The Order of Fabrics:

- Gozez (Shearing)
- Melaben (Bleaching)
- Minapaitz (Combing)
- Tzovaya (Dyeing)
- Toveh (Spinning)
- Oseh Shtay Botei Nirin (Making 2 Heddles)
- Maisach (Worping)
- Oraig (Weaving)
- Potzaya (Unraveling threads)
- Kosahair (Tying)
- Matir (Untying)
- Tofair (Sewing)
- Koraya (Tearing)

In this class we will take a closer look at the first seven Melachos, from Gozez (Shearing) to Oseh Shtay Botei Nirin (Making 2 Heddles). In part two we will take a closer look at the next six Melachos from: Oraig (Weaving) to Koraya (Tearing).

THE RABBI MICHAEL J ELJARRAT LEARNING PROGRAMME – CLASS TWENTY SIX

CATEGORY: ORDER OF FABRICS

MELACHA NUMBER: 1

NAME: Gozez/Shearing

DEFINITION: Any Activity that severs the growth of hair on humans and animals.

EXAMPLE: Shearing wool, cutting hair, cutting finger nails, shaving, plucking feathers

GEZEROS: Brushing hair with hard brush

CATEGORY: ORDER OF FABRICS

MELACHA NUMBER: 2

NAME: Melabain/Bleaching

DEFINITION: Any Activity that cleans a garment

EXAMPLE: Bleaching, soaking clothes, removing stains with water or other solutions

---

CATEGORY: ORDER OF FABRICS

MELACHA NUMBER: 3

NAME: Menapaitz/Combing

DEFINITION: Any Activity which separates raw materials into separate fibers

EXAMPLE: Combing raw wool, beating flax stalks into fibers

THE RABBI MICHAEL J ELJARRAT LEARNING PROGRAMME – CLASS TWENTY SIX

CATEGORY: ORDER OF FABRICS

MELACHA NUMBER: 4

NAME: Tzovaya/Dyeing

DEFINITION: Any Activity that changes an objects color

EXAMPLE: Painting, Make-ups such as eye liners etc, using nail polish

---

CATEGORY: ORDER OF FABRICS

MELACHA NUMBER: 5

NAME: Toveh/Spinning

DEFINITION: Any Activity by which thread is formed from fibers

EXAMPLE: Spinning thread, making rope, re-twining tzitzis

CATEGORY: ORDER OF FABRICS

MELACHA NUMBER: 6

NAME: Maisach/ Warping

DEFINITION: Any Activity by which lattice work is created in preparation for weaving

EXAMPLE: Aligning slots into the floor for lattice making, arranging and laying out reeds in basket making

CATEGORY: ORDER OF FABRICS

MELACHA NUMBER: 7

NAME: Oseh Shtay Botei Ninirin/Constructing two heddles

DEFINITION: Any Activity that allows for the passing of thread through the heddles

EXAMPLE: Threading reeds around warp reeds to allow other layers to be woven.

THE RABBI MICHAEL J ELJARRAT LEARNING PROGRAMME – CLASS TWENTY SEVEN

CLASS 27   LAWS OF SHABBOS 39 MELACHOS

ORDER OF FABRICS
PART 2

This lesson will explore the final six Melachos, pertaining to the order of fabrics, namely:

- Oraig/ Weaving
- Potzaya/ Unraveling
- Koshair/ Tying a knot
- Matir/ Untying a knot
- Tofair/ Sewing
- Koraya/ Tearing

CATEGORY: ORDER OF FABRICS

MELACHA NUMBER: 8

NAME: Oraig/ Weaving

DEFINITION: Any Activity whereby thread is passed under and over warp threads.

EXAMPLE: Basket weaving, making a straw hat.

CATEGORY: ORDER OF FABRICS

MELACHA NUMBER: 9

NAME: Potzaya/Unraveling

DEFINITION: Any Activity whereby a thread is unraveled under and over warp threads

EXAMPLE: Pulling loose threads out of a garment

PAGE 1

THE RABBI MICHAEL J ELJARRAT LEARNING PROGRAMME – CLASS TWENTY SEVEN

The next two Melachos involve tying and untying a knot, this was sometimes necessary for the weaving process itself, as well as for the nets which were made to trap the "Chelozon" fish, whose blood was used to make the blue – T'chayles dye. There are many types of knots that can be made those which are forbidden are permanent and professional knots. One who makes a knot which fulfills these two conditions has violated the Torah law.

CATEGORY: ORDER OF FABRICS

MELACHA NUMBER: 10

NAME: Koshair/Tying a knot

DEFINITION: Any activity by which a permanent type of professional knot is brought into being.

EXAMPLE: Making an overhand knot, or surgical knot.

CATEGORY: ORDER OF FABRICS

MELACHA NUMBER: 11

NAME: Matir/Untying a knot

DEFINITION: Ant activity by which a permanent type of professional knot is undone

EXAMPLE: Undoing a overhand knot, or surgical knot

CATEGORY: ORDER OF FABRICS

MELACHA NUMBER: 12

NAME: Tofair/Sewing

DEFINITION: Any Activity that permanently forms together two materials by means of a third substance.

EXAMPLE: Sewing, pasting

CATEGORY: ORDER OF FABRICS

MELACHA NUMBER: 13

NAME: Koraya/Tearing

DEFINITION: Any Activity that tears materials apart to facilitate re-joining

EXAMPLE: Removing stitches

CLASS 28

LAWS OF SHABBOS
39 MELACHOS

ORDER OF HIDES

The next category that we will explore is the "order of Hides". Hides were used in the Mishkan for a number of purposes. One of the main needs for hides in the Mishkan was for the coverings which formed the roof and ceiling of the Mishkan. In order to obtain these hides 7 processes had to take place, starting with the capturing of the animal all the way to cutting and fitting, the processed leather. These Melachos are listed below.

- Tzod/Trapping
- Shochait/Slaugtering
- Mafshit/Skinning
- M'abaid/Tanning
- Memachaik/Smoothing
- Mesartait/Scoring
- Mechataich/Measured cutting

CATEGORY: ORDER OF HIDES
MELACHA NUMBER: 1
NAME: Tzod/Trapping
DEFINITION: Any activity that restricts the movement of a non-domesticated creature, so that it comes under human control.
EXAMPLE: Fishing, catching a bird in a net

THE RABBI MICHAEL J ELJARRAT LEARNING PROGRAMME – CLASS TWENTY EIGHT

CATEGORY: ORDER OF HIDES

MELACHA NUMBER: 2

NAME: Shochait/Slaugtering

DEFINITION: Any activity that causes loss of life or blood to a living creature

EXAMPLE: Killing an animal, bird or insect

CATEGORY: ORDER OF HIDES

MELACHA NUMBER: 3

NAME: Mafshit/Skinning

DEFINITION: Any activity by which the skin of a dead animal is separated from its flesh

EXAMPLE: Skinning an animal

CATEGORY: ORDER OF HIDES

MELACHA NUMBER: 4

NAME: M'abaid/Tanning

DEFINITION: Any activity by which raw hide is made more useable or durable

EXAMPLE: All parts of the tanning process

CATEGORY: ORDER OF HIDES

MELACHA NUMBER: 5

NAME: Memachaik/Smoothing

DEFINITION: Any activity by which the surface of a material is smoothed out

EXAMPLE: Sanding, plastering, using solid soap

THE RABBI MICHAEL J ELJARRAT LEARNING PROGRAMME – CLASS TWENTY EIGHT

CATEGORY: ORDER OF HIDES

MELACHA NUMBER: 6

NAME: Mesartait/scoring

DEFINITION: Any activity that makes lines on a surface in preparation for cutting or writing

EXAMPLE: Making a margin to write a Mezuza

CATEGORY: ORDER OF HIDES

MELACHA NUMBER: 7

NAME: Mechataich/Measured cutting

DEFINITION: Any activity by which the size of an object is altered for more suitable use

EXAMPLE: Cutting out a newspaper article

Source references: Menucha ve' Simcha – JEP publications
The 39 Melachos – Rabbi Dovid Ribat

THE RABBI MICHAEL J ELJARRAT LEARNING PROGRAMME – CLASS TWENTY NINE

CLASS 29   LAWS OF SHABBOS
39 MELACHOS

 ## ORDER OF CONSTRUCTION

The final set of Melachos deals with the building and assembly of the Mishkan, and is named the order of construction. Unlike other buildings, the Mishkan was assembled and dismantled many times during its many journeys in and around the Sinai desert. The Mishkan was made from many planks and each coated in gold and slotted into special sockets made from silver. Each unit wad build to allow for easy dismantling and re- assembling, this required writing and erasing, lighting and extinguishing. Fire was needed to make charcoal and for smelting metals. During assembly and dismantling the planks had to be moved from a private domain to a public domain and vise versa. A total of eight Melachos were needed in the order of construction, these are listed below.

- Kosaiv/Writing
- Mochaik/Erasing
- Boneh/Building
- Sossair/Demolishing
- Makeh B'patish/Final hammer blow
- Mechabeh/ Extinguishing a flame
- Mavier/Kindling
- Hotzoa/Transferring

CATEGORY: ORDER OF CONSTRUCTION

MELACHA NUMBER: 1

NAME: Kosaiv/Writing

DEFINITION: Any activity that makes lasting and meaningful figures on a surface

EXAMPLE: Drawing, painting, typing

GEZEROS: Drawing on a moist windowpane

PAGE 1

CATEGORY: ORDER OF CONSTRUCTION

MELACHA NUMBER: 2

NAME: Mochaik/Erasing

DEFINITION: Any activity whose affect is the production of a clean surface for writing

EXAMPLE: Erasing writing to make space for new writing

CATEGORY: ORDER OF CONSTRUCTION

MELACHA NUMBER: 3

NAME: Boneh/Building

DEFINITION: Any activity connected with construction, repairing, or erecting a useable structure or shelter

EXAMPLE: Hanging a door, installing a window pane

GEZEROS: Opening an umbrella

CATEGORY: ORDER OF CONSTRUCTION

MELACHA NUMBER: 4

NAME: Sossair/Demolishing

DEFINITION: Any activity that prepares a surface for building, by demolishing an existing structure

EXAMPLE: Removing a broken window to put in a new one

THE RABBI MICHAEL J ELJARRAT LEARNING PROGRAMME – CLASS TWENTY NINE

CATEGORY: ORDER OF CONSTRUCTION

MELACHA NUMBER: 5

NAME: Makeh B'patish/Final hammer blow

DEFINITION: Any activity that puts the final touches upon, or improves or repairs an article

EXAMPLE: Removing hanging threads from a new suit

CATEGORY: ORDER OF CONSTRUCTION

MELACHA NUMBER: 6

NAME: Mechabeh/Extinguishing a flame

DEFINITION: Any activity which terminates, or diminishes a flame or hot glow, if for some productive purpose

EXAMPLE: Putting out a candle to improve the wick

CATEGORY: ORDER OF CONSTRUCTION

MELACHA NUMBER: 7

NAME: Mavier/ Kindling

DEFINITION: Any activity which initiates or prolongs a flame or hot glow

EXAMPLE: Lighting a fire, smoking, driving

THE RABBI MICHAEL J ELJARRAT LEARNING PROGRAMME – CLASS TWENTY NINE

CATEGORY: ORDER OF CONSTRUCTION

MELACHA NUMBER: 8

NAME: Hotzoa/Transferring

DEFINITION: Any activity by which an object is transferred from or within a forbidden domain*

EXAMPLE: Carrying objects in a public road

* terms and conditions apply

THE RABBI MICHAEL J ELJARRAT LEARNING PROGRAMME – CLASS THIRTY

CLASS 30   LAWS OF SHABBOS

MUKTZEH

Apart from the 39 Melachos seen previously, which are forbidden from Torah law and included various Gezeros which are Rabbinicaly forbidden, the sages also enacted laws of "Muktzeh". Muktzeh which literally means "set aside" is a system of laws which serves to protect the existing laws of Shabbos as well as preserve the sanctity of the day. This lesson will explore the laws of Muktzeh and some of its practical applications.

The implications of Muktzeh

If something is said to be Muktzeh, the following prohibition apply:

- It is forbidden to eat or use object
- It is forbidden to move the object (various types of Muktzeh contain this prohibition)

The main categories of Muktzeh:

- Kli she-melachto le–issur
- Muktzeh Machmas chesron kis
- Muktzeh Machmas gufo
- Bosis le-dovor ha-issur

General rule

(Each will be explained below in further detail)

Kli she-melachto le-issur- (A vessel that is used for forbidden)

A Kli she- Melachto le-issur is a abject or utensil who's primary use is for an activity which is forbidden on Shabbos, for example a pen which is used for writing an activity which is forbidden on Shabbos, or a fishing rod used for fishing, an activity that is forbidden on Shabbos. However an item whose primary use is for an activity which is allowed on Shabbos or even an item which is used with equal frequency for both forbidden and permitted activities is not treated as a kli she- melachto le-issur.

The laws pertaining to a Kli she-melachto le-issur: * **

A kli she-melachto le-issur may be moved only in the following two situations

- If one needs to use it for a permitted purpose
- If on Shabbos one needs to make use of the space it occupies

Examples of using a Kli she- melachto le-issur for a permitted purpose:

- Using a matchstick to pick ones teeth
- Using a hammer to crack nuts

* One may not adapt the kli she-melachto le-issur to make it more useable for its permitted purpose

** One should rather use a non restricted item if one has it available

Muktzeh machmas chesron kis - (Muktzeh as a result of loss of money)

Muktzeh machmas cheseron kis can be defined as any article or item that is:

- Valuable
- Used for an activity that is forbidden on Shabbos
- Safeguarded against misuse or damage

Examples include:

- Camera
- Cell phone
- Laptop
- Items with a fixed place (e.g. A valuable painting)
- Items intended for sale (Business stock)
- Valuable papers (e.g. Bank notes, stock certificates etc)

- Any item which is Muktzeh machmas chesron kis may not be moved even if one needs the space it occupies

- Any item which is Muktzeh machmas chesron kis may not be used even for a permitted purpose

Muktzeh machmas Gufo- (Muktzeh as a result of itself)

Muktzeh Machmas Gufo can be defined as any article or item that is:

- Not designed for any use (worthless)
- Not consisting of food for either human or animal consumption.

Examples include:

- Stones
- Peels
- Shells
- Forbidden foods (e.g. Chometz on Pasach)
- Animals
- Broken and discarded articles

Any item which would ordinarily be Muktzeh machmas Gufo, is not Muktzeh if one set it aside to be used before Shabbos, this can be achieved by merely thinking about using the item before Shabbos.

- Any item which is Muktzeh machams Gufo may not be moved even if one needs the space it occupies
- Any item which is Muktzeh machmas Gufo may not be used unless pre-designated before Shabbos.

Bosis le-dovor ha-issur - (A base for a forbidden article)

A Bosis le-dovor ha-issur can be defined as any article or item, on which there was placed or hung before Shabbos an item which is Muktzeh. This applies even if the article in question can in no way be deemed Muktzeh in its own right.

Any item, which has been classified as a Bosis le-dovor ha-issur:

- Acquires the same status as the Muktzeh item.
- May not be moved on the same fashion as the Muktzeh item.
- Even if the Muktzeh item has been removed or fell off on Shabbos

An item only becomes a Bosis le-dovor ha-issur if it fulfills the following conditions:

- The Muktzeh item is placed by the owner or with the owners consent.
- The Muktzeh item is placed with specific intent.
- The Muktzeh item is placed before Shabbos and is intended to remain there until Shabbos comes in.

THE RABBI MICHAEL J ELJARRAT LEARNING PROGRAMME – CLASS THIRTY

- The Muktzeh item can be seen as, being supported by the item beneath.
- The Muktzeh item is the only or most important item placed on the Bosis.
- The Muktzeh item is placed directly in the Bosis itself.

Any item which does NOT fulfill the conditions set above for Bosis ledovor ha-issur:

- May be moved once the Muktzeh item has been removed or fell off
- One may tilt the article to make the Muktzeh item fall off [1]

RECOMMENDED READING:
SHEMIRATH SHABBATH KE HILCHATHAH – RAV YEHOSHUA Y. NEUWIRTH

---

1. If one needs to use the article or if one needs the space that the article occupies

THE RABBI MICHAEL J ELJARRAT LEARNING PROGRAMME – CLASS THIRTY ONE

CLASS 31   LAWS OF SHABBOS

BORER/SELECTION

Previously we learnt about the 39 Melachos. The first order (the order of bread) contained within it, the Melacho of Borer (Selection). This lesson will take a closer look at some of the practical applications of this Melacho. It is worthy to note, that although some Melachos are more practical by nature than others, for example the Melacho of Bishul (Cooking) is more frequent than Oraig (Weaving), never the less all the 39 Melachos contain numerous laws. The next few lessons will explore some of the more practical Melachos, and some of their practical applications.

On Shabbos it is forbidden to separate any item which is mixed within others, whether it be food or even non edible items, as this would be a violation of Borer. For the purposes of clarity we will refer to a simple yet effective example of a bowl containing mixed nuts and raisins. Therefore to put it rather simply, on Shabbos it is forbidden to separate the nuts and raisins into two separate piles (one containing nuts the other raisins).

There are however several rules which apply to the law of Borer:

Borer is allowed when it is done in the "normal use of the item". Borer is considered "the normal use of the item" if all of the following three conditions are satisfied.

1. One separates the "good" from the "bad" (The item one wants is deemed "good").
2. Separation is done by hand and not using a utensil designed for separating.
3. Separation is done for immediate use and not for future use.

Therefore using our example above, concerning a bowl of mixed nuts and raisins:
If one wants the nuts and dislikes the raisins, hence;

        The nuts = "good" and the raisins = "bad"

then one may separate in the following way:

1. One may remove the nuts from the bowl.
2. Using one's hand
3. If one wants to eat the nuts immediately.

What is considered mixed?

Although it may be stating the obvious, the prohibition of separating only applies if the two (or more) articles are mixed together, and are in fact different in some way from one another. Therefore items which are:

- Lying next to one another with a clear line between them
- The same in terms of species, color and size

May be separated one from another, since they are not in fact considered mixed in any way.

A closer look at the three requirements:

One of the conditions mentioned above, was that the separation must be done for immediate use, this would include the following cases:

- immediate use for one's self or others
- immediate use for an animal
- immediately prior to a meal (this may be a long time if preparing for many)
- Food that is on one's plate is considered immediate use

As mentioned above the prohibition of separating dos not apply, when the act is done in the usual use of the item therefore the following actions are permitted:

- One may remove bones from one's mouth when eating
- One may spit out pips from fruit when eating.

Peels, shells and seeds:

Generally speaking one may remove peels, shells and seeds in the normal course of eating, however the following situations need particular attention:

1. One may remove dust off fruit under running water, for immediate use.
2. Edible peels such as those found on apples, pears etc may be peeled off

- Even with a utensil designed for peeling
- Even if not for immediate use

Inedible peels such as those found on bananas (or egg shells) may be removed
- Not using a utensil designed for separating (A knife is permitted)
- Only for immediate use.

THE RABBI MICHAEL J ELJARRAT LEARNING PROGRAMME – CLASS THIRTY ONE

Apart from the three requirements mentioned above which are considered the normal use of the item, another very practical rule is that separating only occurs when items are removed from one another and not together.

Thus the following situations are allowed:

1. One may remove a fly with a spoon from a bowl of soup, together with some soup.
2. One may remove a peach pip together with some peach.

In the above two cases the act is not considered separating since both the "good" and "bad" elements are being removed together. When in doubt this method can be used to "separate" without any violation.

Special cases:

1. Apricot pips separate entirely, and is therefore preferable not to separate but rather to spit or shake out the pip immediately before eating.

2. Mixed cutlery should not be separated and put away, but may be placed in order when laying the table (Since this is "good" from "bad" for immediate use)

3. Mixed clothing should not be separated and sorted unless it is for immediate use.

4. One may mot sort a pile of books; however one may return a book to its correct shelf to clear a table.

5. It may be preferable not to use a jug with a lid designed to separate ice, if not for immediate use.

THE RABBI MICHAEL J ELJARRAT LEARNING PROGRAMME – CLASS THIRTY TWO

CLASS 32 — LAWS OF SHABBOS

PERSONAL GROOMING

This lesson will look at the practical laws relating to personal hygiene and grooming on Shabbos. Although the topic of grooming and hygiene as well as the laws of Shabbos are extensive, we will try and cover as many applications as possible. However this class is by no means a complete list, and as always further study and analysis is needed.

The following areas will be covered in this lesson:

- Hair removal (Shaving/waxing)
- Oral hygiene (Brushing teeth/Dental floss)
- Cutting nails
- Bathing/Showering
- Make-up (Face, hand and feet)
- Hair care (Washing/ Styling)
- Fragrances (Deodorant, antiperspirant, aftershave and perfume)

Although this lesson will deal with personal grooming, needles to say personal grooming is in fact personal and vast differences occur between men and women, and between one person and the next. This lesson will therefore deal with the topics above in a general context.

HAIR REMOVAL

As we saw previously when learning the 39 Melachos, it is forbidden to remove the hair of any living animal, humans included as this would be a violation of the Melacho of Gozez/Shearing (order of fabrics). Therefore it is forbidden for Men and Women alike to remove any hair from any body part, by any means including but not limited to shaving waxing and plucking with a tweezers.

PAGE 1

THE RABBI MICHAEL J ELJARRAT LEARNING PROGRAMME – CLASS THIRTY TWO

ORAL HYGIENE

With regards to brushing one's teeth on Shabbos, there are various customs and practices ranging from brushing as per usual with toothpaste and toothbrush to the opposite, with those that forbid brushing with a toothbrush and toothpaste. For the correct practice further study is needed, however some of the concerns may include the violation of the Melocha of Shochait/ Slaughtering, causing bleeding when brushing, and the Melocha of Memachaick/Smoothing, causing the semi-solid toothpaste to be smoothed out. With regards to using dental floss on Shabbos, it would seem clear that it is forbidden, as cutting the dental floss would be in violation of the Melocha of Korayah/Tearing, in addition the likelihood of causing bleeding is greatly increased. If one needs to use dental floss on Shabbos a competent authority should be consulted.

With regards to using mouthwash on Shabbos, it would seem clear that it is permitted, as its use would not be in violation of any Melocha, however care should be taken not to use a measuring cup.

CUTTING NAILS:

With regards to cutting nails on Shabbos, whether it be the nails of the hands or of the feet, the cutting of nails is forbidden on Shabbos. The violation stems from the Melocha of Kotzair/Harvesting which was defined previously as severing a living, growing organism from its source of life. Cutting nails is forbidden by all means including but not limited to; cutting with a scissors, nail clipper and teeth.

BATHING/SHOWERING:

On Shabbos one is allowed to wash oneself in the ways and means which will be described below:

- One may wash one's hands, face and feet with water which was heated before Shabbos.
- One should not wash one's entire body with water that was heated before Shabbos.
- It is forbidden to wash even one finger in water that was heated in violation of Shabbos.
- Water which was heated by standing in the sun is treated like water heated before Shabbos
- The laws of washing oneself on Yomtov are different, since one may cook on Yomtov[1].

---

[1]. One may heat water on the 1st day of Yomtov to wash; hands, face and feet. There are those who permit washing ones' entire body in water which was heated on Yomtov on the 2nd day of Yomtov outside Israel.

PAGE 2

THE RABBI MICHAEL J ELJARRAT LEARNING PROGRAMME – CLASS THIRTY TWO

MAKE-UP:

With regards to applying make-up on Shabbos, the Melacha of Tzovayih/ Dying would Prohibit the vast majority of applications including, but not limited to:

- Foundation/Base
- Mascara and eye liner
- Lipstick and blush
- Nail polish and Nail varnish

HAIR CARE:

With regards to washing one's hair on Shabbos, the Melocho of Dosh/Threasing with the Tolda of Sochait/ Squeezing would prohibit the washing of hair on Shabbos since one may not squeeze the water out from one's hair. Similarly one may not use excess amounts of styling gels and mousse that would cause one to squeeze these products out of one's hair.

With regards to brushing one's hair on Shabbos one needs to be concerned about the Melacho of Gozez/ Shearing. Therefore one should not use a hard bristled brush, rather a soft brush which will not cause hair to be uprooted during brushing.

FRAGRANCES:

With regards to using aerosol (deodorant and antiperspirant) as well as natural spray aftershaves and perfumes, all are allowed on Shabbos provided that one sprays directly on to the skin and not onto clothing as this would be a violation of Molid. (A Rabbinical violation which, forbids the creating of a new smell on a fabric).

Recommended Reading:
Shemirath Shabbath ke-Hilchathah – Rav Yehoshua. Y. Neuwirth.

PAGE 3

THE RABBI MICHAEL J ELJARRAT LEARNING PROGRAMME – CLASS THIRTY THREE

CLASS 33   LAWS OF SHABBOS

SHABBOS BEHAVIOR-THE LAWS OF ISAIAH

Apart from the 39 Melachos which we have dealt with up until this point, there are further laws pertaining to one's behavior and general conduct on Shabbos. Unlike the 39 Melachos which are forbidden by Torah law, the laws pertaining to one's conduct are forbidden under Prophetic scripture [1] and can therefore be sourced in the scripture of the prophet (Isaiah 58:13-14).

The verse states as follows:

> If you restrain because of Shabbos, your feet refrain
> from accomplishing your own needs on my holy day,
> if you proclaim the Shabbos "a delight", the holy one
> of Hashem "Honored one", and you honor it by not
> doing your own ways, from seeking your needs or
> discussing the forbidden (58:13)
>
> Then you shall be granted pleasure with Hashem,
> And I shall mount you astride the heights of the world,
> And provide you the heritage of your forefather
> Jacob, for the mouth of Hashem has spoken. (58:14)

RUNNING:

From the verses quoted above, several laws are learnt both directly and indirectly. We will now examine "and you honor it by not doing your own ways" the way you walk on Shabbos, should not be the same as you would walk during the week, From this verse we learn that it is forbidden to run on Shabbos unless one is running to do a Mitzva, or to protect oneself from harm.

---

1. As was noted previously the words of the prophets are directly from G-d, and are thus treated as Torah Laws.

THE RABBI MICHAEL J ELJARRAT LEARNING PROGRAMME – CLASS THIRTY THREE

PREPARING FOR AFTER SHABBOS:

"And you honor it from seeking your needs" It is forbidden to go to a place on Shabbos, with the intention of doing a Melacho there directly after Shabbos, where one's intentions are clearly visible to others.

SEEKING YOUR NEEDS:

"Not doing your own ways, from seeking your needs" One may not pursue one's usual activity on Shabbos, this means to say that one may not pursue one's business on Shabbos. Therefore it is forbidden on Shabbos to make preparations such as stock checking, in order to re-stock after Shabbos, or to seek out a worker with the intentions of hiring him/her after Shabbos, as well as any case similar to the above.

TRADING:

Generally speaking all forms of trading are forbidden on Shabbos, and the prohibitions apply to both the buyer and the seller. However although rarely practiced there is scope within the halachic parameters, to take goods from a store and pay either before or after Shabbos, provided that no mention is made regarding, price, volume, weight and amount. This halacha has great practical benefit when it comes to staying in hotels over Shabbos[2] One can purchase a "meal voucher" before Shabbos, (which indicates what the recipient is entitled to) and redeem the voucher on Shabbos.

GIVING GIFTS:

It is forbidden on Shabbos to give or receive a gift, unless the recipient does not take ownership, until after Shabbos, by means of using a third party to receive the gift. However one may give/receive gifts on Shabbos if the gift is for the purpose of Shabbos. Therefore, one who wishes to present a gift to a host, should preferably give the gift before Shabbos, or choose a gift which may be deemed "for the purpose of Shabbos."

MEASURING AND WEIGHING:

It is forbidden to measure and weigh on Shabbos, unless the measurements/weights are not done precisely (for example when preparing food on Shabbos). However for the purposes of a Mitzva such as measuring a cup to ascertain if it is kosher as a kiddush cup or a piece of Matzah to see whether or not it contains a "ke-zyis" (an olives worth) is permissible on Shabbos. For the purpose of one who is ill, one may measure on Shabbos. However the laws relating to illness and emergencies will be dealt with in a separate class.

---

2. Kosher hotels that prepare Shabbos meals for guests.

THE RABBI MICHAEL J ELJARRAT LEARNING PROGRAMME – CLASS THIRTY THREE

READING:

On Shabbos one may not read papers which are connected to one's business such as accounts, invoices etc. However one may read about current events in a newspaper. One may also read professional literature which, are not of a business nature such as text books and the like. (If ones profession is an activity which is forbidden on Shabbos such as engineering etc it is forbidden to read literature pertaining to ones' profession on Shabbos).

SPEAKING:

It is forbidden on Shabbos to speak about doing something after Shabbos, which is forbidden on Shabbos itself. For example one may not say on Shabbos "Tomorrow I am going to write a letter" or "Tomorrow I am going to drive a car". Although speech is restricted on Shabbos, thought about forbidden activities is allowed, provided that the thoughts are not of a disturbing nature, as one is not allowed to grieve on Shabbos. If one needs to speak about an activity which will take place after Shabbos, one should do so without reference to the activity which is forbidden for example "Tomorrow I will give you a letter" without speaking about writing.

Recommended reading: Shemiras Shabbos Ke-Hilchasa.

THE RABBI MICHAEL J ELJARRAT LEARNING PROGRAMME – CLASS THIRTY FOUR

CLASS 34 — LAWS OF SHABBOS

ELECTRICITY ON SHABBOS

Although the potential for electricity has been around since the beginning of creation, it has only become commercially available since the early 19th century. The word electricity comes from the Greek word "elektron" meaning amber; it was the Greeks who discovered static charge, which was produced by the rubbing of amber with fur[1]. However, it wasn't' until 1881 that the first power station was built. Today electricity is part and parcel of every day life, and the question therefore stands; May one use electricity on Shabbos and why?

Bearing in mind that only those activities that violate the 39 Melachos or the prohibitions of Isaiah, or Rabbinical decrees are forbidden on Shabbos, which, if any prohibition does the use of electricity violate?

In this lesson we will examine some of the possible reasons, why the use of electricity should be forbidden on Shabbos.

MOLID/CREATING SOMETHING NEW:

The first possible basis for forbidding the use of electricity on Shabbos is based on the Rabbinical prohibition of "Molid" (creating something new). According to Rabbinical law it is forbidden to apply fragrances to ones clothes on Shabbos, as one is creating a "new scent" on one's clothes. In a similar vein when one switches on an electrical appliance, one is creating a "new function" within the appliance. By applying electricity, one renders a previously "dead" appliance into a "live" functioning item. Therefore switching on an electrical appliance may be in violation of the law of "Molid".

BUILDING:

The next possible basis is offered by the Chazon Ish[2], who maintains that the use of electricity on Shabbos is comparable to Building. Both the turning on and the turning off of an electrical appliance, constitutes "building" and "destroying" a circuit. Therefore the use of electricity, or more specifically the opening and closing of a circuit is in violation of a Torah law namely the Melocho of building.

---

1. Encyclopedia Britannica
2. Rabbi Avraham Yishaiah Karelitz

THE RABBI MICHAEL J ELJARRAT LEARNING PROGRAMME – CLASS THIRTY FOUR

FINAL HAMMER BLOW:

A third possible reason to forbid the use of electricity on Shabbos stems from the Melocho of "Makesh be Patish" the final hammer blow. The Melocho forbids activity which is the final step in the production of an item. Based on this reasoning, turning on an electrical appliance[3], may be considered to be the final step in the production of the appliance, since the appliance was made with the intention of being used. Therefore one could say that the act of turning on an appliance is the "final hammer blow".

SPARKS:

A forth reason is based on the Rabbinical prohibition of creating sparks on Shabbos. Based on the Melocho of, creating fire on Shabbos. Chazal added a decree against creating sparks from wood or stones. In a similar vein the switching on and off of electrical appliances causes sparks to be generated[4], and would thus be prohibited under the Rabbinical decree.

ADDITIONAL FEEL CONSUMPTION:

An additional reason based on the causative affect that is produced by using electricity on Shabbos, namely causing more coal to be burnt as a result of the greater demand. Thus using electricity on Shabbos is causing a violation of the Melocho of creating fire. It is important to note that this reason is only problematic when the causative affect is definite and the violation is done by Jews.

COOKING:

A final reason to prohibit the use of electricity on Shabbos is based on the Torah Melocho of cooking. This reason is particularly true when it comes to turning on an incandescent light bulb, whereby the wire filament within is raised to a considerably high temperature. This action may be considered as "cooking" the wire filament within. Thus the prohibition is based on a Torah violation.

For more details see presentation: "electricity on Shabbos"

Sources: The use of electricity on Shabbos and Yomtov.
Rabbi Michael Broyde/Rabbi Howard Jachter.

---

3. For the first time and possibly each switching on is considered the "first time".
4. This version would not be applicable to solid state electricity.

THE RABBI MICHAEL J ELJARRAT LEARNING PROGRAMME – CLASS THIRTY FIVE

CLASS 35 — LAWS OF SHABBOS

COOKING AND REHEATING

PART ONE

From all the Melachos which were covered in previous lessons, the melacha of Bishul/ Cooking may be the most extensive in terms of its numerous laws and practical applications. For this reason the laws relating to cooking and reheating food on Shabbos will be broken into five parts, each part dealing with a specific aspect namely:

- Part one: Defining the term "cooking"
- Part two: Grades of vessels
- Part three: Laws relating to reheating
- Part four: Maintaining and returning to a heat source
- Part five: Insulating

Defining the term "cooking"

The final step of the Order of bread was baking, and as was defined previously this melacha incorporates any activity that uses heat to improve the quality of an item. Therefore the term cooking is used in a broad sense and incorporates: Boiling, Baking, Frying, Roasting etc.

The next question which needs to be addressed is: At what point is the quality of an item considered to be "Improved"? For example if an item can be used in its current state without the application of any heat, such as fruits or cold drinks, is there any prohibition to heat such items? Since the application of heat does not in fact improve the item?

Tosfos in the Gemorrah in Shabbos[1] makes a distinction between items such as apples which can be eaten entirely raw with full benefit, to items such as onions were even though they can be eaten in their raw state, cooking improves the onion to remove its sharp taste. This matter is a large discussion, however for the purposes of this lesson we will assume that all raw items are subject to the prohibition of cooking, regardless of quantifiable improvement.

---

1. Shabbos 48a

THE RABBI MICHAEL J ELJARRAT LEARNING PROGRAMME – CLASS THIRTY FIVE

The next concept which needs to be addressed is spectrum of cooking itself. This means to say that food can be cooked to various degrees, all the way from very rare to overdone and burnt. The question pertaining to this lesson is, at what degree of cooking does one violate the Torah prohibition of Bishul/ Cooking?

Another important question which needs to be addressed is, is there any difference between the laws relating to solids and liquids? And if so what in fact is the difference? All the above questions will now be addressed.

Returning to the definition of cooking, namely using heat to improve the quality of an item, or in other words transforming an inedible item into an edible food product[2], the question now becomes one of defining the terms "edible" and "inedible".

Solids:

The Talmud in various places states that food is considered edible when it reaches the point of "Mychel Ben Droosai" literally the "food of Ben Droosai". Ben Droosai was a thief in the times of the Talmud who was always on the run from the authorities. Since Ben Droosai was always on the move he never had sufficient time to fully cook his food, and would therefore cook his food to the point were it was barely edible[3]. Hence one who cooks food on Shabbos to the point where it is barely edible, like the food of Ben Droosai has violated the Torah prohibition of cooking.

Rabbinical decree prohibits cooking even to a point which is less than the food of Ben Droosai for fear that one will continue past the initial point and come to violate the Torah prohibition. Therefore one may not place a raw item in a place where it will eventually become cooked.

Liquids:

The minimal degree of cooking liquids on Shabbos is reached when liquids are raised to a temperature of "Yad Soledes Bo" literally "the hand is scalded by it" this temperature is deemed to be 43℃ (The concept of Yad Soledes Bo will be discussed in greater detail in the following classes). Rabbinicaly it is forbidden to place cold liquids in a place where the liquids will eventually be raised to a temperature of Yad Soledes Bo.

---

2. Transforming an item into an edible food product may be considered the greatest form of improvement.
3. This is either half cooked or one third cooked

THE RABBI MICHAEL J ELJARRAT LEARNING PROGRAMME – CLASS THIRTY FIVE

The table below summarizes the laws pertaining to both solids and liquids

MBD = Mychel Ben Droosai
YSB = Yad Soledes Bo

General rule

Substance	Degree of cooking	Law
Solid	Less than MBD	Rabbinical Forbidden
Solid	MBD	Torah Forbidden
Solid	MBD - Fully cooked	Torah Forbidden
Liquid	Less than YSB	Rabbinical Forbidden
Liquid	YSB	Torah Forbidden
Liquid	YSB – Boiling point	Torah Forbidden

Cooking can be accomplished in numerous ways, all of which are forbidden on Shabbos. In addition one may not accelerate the cooking process by means of:

- Changing the position of the pot on the stove
- Reducing the amount of food in the pot
- Stirring the pot
- Covering the pot with a lid
- Closing the oven door

All the laws in this lesson have dealt with food that is <u>not fully cooked</u> and therefore can still be improved. Once a food has been fully cooked, the improvements which can be made are limited. Fully cooked food is considered to be "reheating" as apposed to "cooking" when heated. The laws of reheating will be dealt with in class 37.

Sources and Recommended reading:
The Shabbos Kitchen- Rabbi Simcha Bunim Cohen
Published by Artscroll

THE RABBI MICHAEL J ELJARRAT LEARNING PROGRAMME – CLASS THIRTY SIX

CLASS 36

LAWS OF SHABBOS

COOKING AND REHEATING

PART TWO

As we saw in the previous class cooking can be accomplished in a number of different ways, such as roasting, frying etc. This lesson will deal with one particular way of cooking, namely cooking with hot liquids.

We are all familiar with the concept of cooking with hot liquids we often refer to this method of cooking as boiling. However when we think of boiling we generally tend to think of placing a food item into boiling water. There are however several types of boiling, or more correctly ways to cook with hot liquids. We will now explore these various ways and define them in terms of the laws of Shabbos.

Any liquid which has been heated to the point of Yad Soledes Bo[1] is capable of cooking even after it has been removed from its heat source. The question we have to ask is whether or not transferring the hot contents will reduce this ability to cook? There are in fact five different levels when it comes to cooking with hot liquids.

The diagram below illustrates:

1st Vessel was in contact with the heat source
2nd Vessel and 3rd vessel had no contact with the heat source

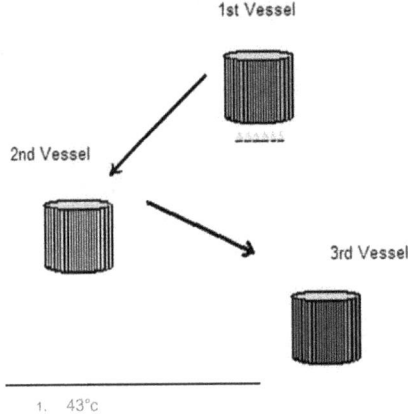

1. 1st Vessel
2. Pouring from a 1st vessel
3. 2nd Vessel
4. Pouring from a 2nd Vessel
5. 3rd Vessel

1. 43°c

PAGE 1

THE RABBI MICHAEL J ELJARRAT LEARNING PROGRAMME – CLASS THIRTY SIX

Each stage listed above has less cooking potential, as we move down the scale. Hence a first vessel has the greatest ability to cook, and the third vessel has the least ability to cook. The laws pertaining to each of the five stages will now be discussed in detail.

Before we move on to discuss the laws of relating to each of the five stages, we will need to look at two general rules that pertain to cooking on Shabbos.

1. **Ein Bishul Achar Bishul** (There is no cooking after cooking): This law states that once a **solid** food has been fully cooked, one cannot subsequently cook it further. Meaning there is no prohibition to reheat food, in the manner in which it was cooked. However there is a prohibition to reheat food, in a different manner in which it was cooked. For example if food was fully cooked by means of roasting, one may reheat the food using a method of roasting, but one may not reheat the food using a method of boiling, frying, baking etc.

2. **Yaish Bishul Achar Bishul** (There is cooking after cooking): This law states that once a **liquid** has cooled down past the point of Yad Soledes Bo, it becomes subject to all the laws of cooking raw liquids on Shabbos.

These two laws will be discussed in further detail in the next class dealing with reheating food on Shabbos.

The First Vessel (Was in contact with the heat source):

A first vessel is like the heat source in almost every regard, even once removed from the heat source. Consequently one may not place any raw item into a first vessel. Similarly one may not put liquids which have been cooked and have cooled down below the point of Yad Soledes Bo into a first vessel.

However one may place fully cooked solid foods into a first vessel (As indicated in the two laws mentioned above) In this regard soluble food stuffs should be treated as a liquid, and therefore may not be placed in a first vessel.

Pouring from a First Vessel:

Pouring from a first vessel is equivalent in almost all regards to the first vessel itself. Subsequently one may not pour hot liquids from a first vessel directly onto raw food, or cold liquids. However the cooking ability is slightly diminished when pouring, and can only cook the surface of a raw item, and not beyond. Therefore one may place raw food within a container, and pour hot liquids from the first vessel onto the container. Since the liquids being poured will not be able to penetrate the raw food within the container.

THE RABBI MICHAEL J ELJARRAT LEARNING PROGRAMME – CLASS THIRTY SIX

The Second Vessel (Was not in contact with the heat source):

As a general rule a second vessel cannot cook. This means to say that a second vessel does not have the ability to cook a raw item, since the second vessel did not come into contact with the heat source.[2] Therefore one may place raw items (Baring several exceptions mentioned below) in a second vessel. One may also place liquids which have cooled down into a second vessel, and one may also place soluble foods into a second vessel. However one may not place raw foods which cook easily into a second vessel. Since we do not have an exact qualification for "raw foods which cook easily", practically speaking we only place foods which will definitely not cook easily into a second vessel, such as water, oil, ginger and cinnamon sticks.

Pouring from a Second Vessel:

Pouring from a second vessel has the same law as the third vessel. This will now be dealt with below.

The Third Vessel (Was not in contact with the heat source):

Once a liquid has been transferred to a third vessel it no longer has the ability to cook raw items. Except for several items which cook almost instantaneously such as eggs, very salty fish and tea leaves[3].

Grades of Vessels with regards to solids:

The five grades of vessels dealt with above all refer to liquids which cool down somewhat during a transfer. However solid foods retain more heat during a transfer. Some therefore maintain that the laws of the five grades of vessels do not apply, and solids have the law of a first vessel regardless of how many transfers are done. Others maintain that the laws of the five grades of vessels do apply to solids as well. Therefore in practice with raw foods we maintain the stricter view and with precooked condiments we follow the lenient view[4].

The status of the ladle:

With regards to the ladle some maintain that the ladle is a first vessel, while others maintain that the ladle is a second vessel thus making the soup bowl the third vessel. In practice we follow the stricter view with regards to raw food, and the lenient view with regards to precooked condiments and baked foods. However if the ladle is left in the pot for a considerable period of time, all agree that the ladle is considered a first vessel.

Sources and Recommended reading:
The Shabbos Kitchen- Rabbi Simcha Bunim Cohen
Published by Artscroll

---

2. See Tosfos Shabbos 40b "Ve Shema"
3. There are those that permit tea leaves in a third vessel.
4. Precooked condiments are only a question of reheating, and may therefore be placed in a second vessel containing solids.

THE RABBI MICHAEL J ELJARRAT LEARNING PROGRAMME – CLASS THIRTY SEVEN

CLASS 37

LAWS OF SHABBOS

COOKING AND REHEATING
PART THREE

"לֹא־תְבַעֲרוּ אֵשׁ בְּכֹל מֹשְׁבֹתֵיכֶם בְּיוֹם הַשַּׁבָּת"

"You shall not kindle fire in any of your dwellings on the Sabbath day."[1]

Cooking on the Sabbath is forbidden as it transgresses one of the 39 *Melachot* and yet enjoying warm food on the Sabbath is a common *minhag* world-wide – why? Firstly, an explanation brought down concerns the Cuthites[2], known for their very literal observance of Torah. Their interpretation of the verse quoted above resulted in their not lighting fires even prior to the Sabbath as the fires would burn into Saturday, a violation of what they believed to be an admonition against any fires on the Sabbath at all. The Sages[3] have taught us through the Oral Law that the Torah is not meant for literal analysis in every instance and often requires a deeper study. Preparing warm meals on the Sabbath today is a reminder of that lesson.

Secondly, and as discussed previously, an important aspect of Sabbath observance is the enjoyment of the day (*oneg Shabbos*). For many people, this includes eating warm, hearty meals. This class deals with the following issues:

- How does one enjoy warm food on Shabbos, without violating *melacha*?
- How do these methods apply to different foods?
- How does the method in which food was prepared influence the way in which it can be reheated?

We know that there is an Issur d'Oraisso against cooking on the Sabbath – it is one of the 39 *melachot*. There is also an Issur d'Rabbonon against heating all <u>partially cooked</u> foods, or placing them near a heat source, on the Sabbath, as this can lead to cooking.

 When discussing reheating foods on the Sabbath, we are referring <u>only</u> to foods that are fully cooked prior to the Sabbath.

---

1 The Artscroll Chumash. Exodus 35:3
2 The Cuthites were a people living in Samaria around 500 BCE - Wikipaedia
3 Mechilta

Ein bishul achar bishul - cooking after cooking

This principle is vital when it comes to understanding the *halacha* surrounding reheating food on the Sabbath. *Ein bishul achar bishul* says that food cannot be re-cooked after being cooked initially. In other words, certain fully cooked foods may be reheated in a permissible manner as doing so is not considered cooking. However, the Sages[4] decided that this rule needed limitations and therefore, it applies only to food "cooked in a pot", but not necessarily to food baked, fried or roasted. For example, it is not advisable to place challah into soup in a *kli rishon* or *kli shaini* as it is considered cooking after baking.

Ein afiyah achar afiya – baking after baking – is a related principle. Challah that is already baked, but which has been frozen may be placed on a blech to defrost as halachically, it cannot bake any further.

 When it comes to reheating food on the Sabbath, it is important to remember that it is forbidden to re-heat food by a method not previously employed in its preparation.

Re-heating solids

Although we are permitted to re-heat certain foods on the Sabbath, rabbinical law forbids us from placing food directly on to a blech or other heat source for two reasons:

- It looks like cooking (*maris ayin*)
- It could lead to cooking

Therefore, food must be re-heated in an unusual manner that is clearly not cooking and which cannot lead to cooking. There are four such methods:

- Food may be placed into a pot or other vessel and then placed on top of a second pot which has been on the blech since before the Sabbath. There must be food of some kind in the pot directly on the blech; otherwise it is considered the same as placing the food directly on to the blech.
- Food may be placed <u>near</u> a flame, for example, in the middle of a blech
- Food may be placed in a *kli rishon* off the fire
- Food may be placed on to a hot plate or in a warmer that has only on/off settings (the hot plate or warmer must have been on prior to the Sabbath)

Re-heating liquids

As liquids (e.g. soup) are usually re-heated to improve their temperature and not to improve their flavour, the principle of *ein bishul achar bishul* does not apply. Many *poskim* therefore hold that it is forbidden to re-heat liquids on the Sabbath. While other *poskim* disagree, the stringent view is held by all communities.

---

[4] Chazal

There is a further stringency that applies to liquids which solidify when they are cold, like gravy or fat which may accompany a solid food like chicken. Some *poskim* hold that if the cold gravy or congealed fat is absorbed into the chicken when the dish is re-heated, then re-heating is permissible. However, if the gravy or fat liquefies, then re-heating is not permissible[5] as a new substance has been created, which violates the *melacha* of *molid*.

Should this situation occur, the chicken must be removed from the gravy (be careful of violating separation laws) and reheated on its own in a permissible manner.

 If food has been heated in a forbidden manner on the Sabbath, whether purposefully (*b'mazid*) or accidentally (*b'shogaig*), consult a local rabbi as it may not be permissible to eat the food.

The use of a *blech* when heating food
As discussed previously, a *blech* may be used in certain ways for the re-heating of food on the Sabbath. Halachically, a *blech* is divided into three "heat zones" as described below:

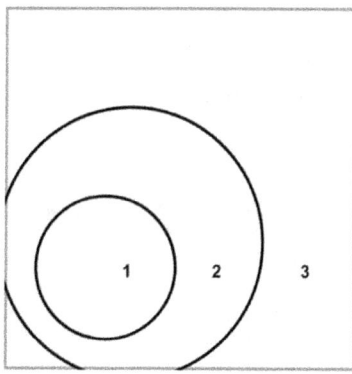

1. Directly above the hot plate

2. Near enough to the source of heat to warm food to approximately 45°C (the minimum requirement for *yad soledes bo*)

3. Perimeter of the blech – food placed here will get warm but will never cook

These "heat zones" impact upon the way we heat food on the Sabbath in the following ways:

- Food directly out of the fridge may only be placed in zone 3
- Food placed in zone 3 prior to the Sabbath may not be moved into zones 1 or 2
- Food in zone 2 prior to the Sabbath may be moved to zone 1
- Food in zones 1 and 2 that were moved to zone 3 during the Sabbath may be moved back to zones 1 or 2 if they are still warm

---

[5] Shabbos KeHalacha pg. 205

Learning outcomes - by the end of the lesson, students should:
1. Be able to discuss the rule *Ein bishul achar bishul* and give practical applications.
2. Be able to differentiate between reheating solids and liquids on Shabbos, with practical applications.
3. Be able to discuss the "heat zones" on a blech with practical applications.

Review questions
1. Does the rule *Ein bishul achar bishul* permit cooking food that was previously baked?
2. If food is edible, but not fully cooked, may it be reheated? If yes, describe the method.
3. If a cup of tea is completely cold, may it be reheated? If yes, describe the method.
4. Is it permissible to reheat fully cooked, dry potato kugel? If yes, describe the method.
5. Is it permissible to reheat a piece of chicken in gravy? If yes, describe the method.
6. Draw a diagram of a blech, detailing the "heat zones" discussed in class.

Additional reading
1. The Shabbos Kitchen - Rabbi Simcha Bunim Cohen (Artscroll Publishers)
2. Shemirath Shabbath - Rabbi Yehoshua Neuwirth (Feldheim Publishers)

Online sources
1. The Shabbos Kitchen – an online course by Shema Yisroel Torah Network (http://www.shemayisrael.co.il/)

THE RABBI MICHAEL J ELJARRAT LEARNING PROGRAMME – CLASS THIRTY EIGHT

CLASS 38
LAWS OF SHABBOS

COOKING AND REHEATING

PART FOUR

Maintaining and Returning to a heat source

Maintaining:

The previous three lessons have dealt with the prohibition of cooking on Shabbos, as well as the laws which allow one to reheat pre-cooked food on Shabbos. We will now turn our attention to a question, namely; may one leave **uncooked** food on a heat source **before** Shabbos with the intention of allowing that food to cook **on** Shabbos?

It is important to note the difference between placing raw food on a heat source on Shabbos, and leaving raw food on a heat source before Shabbos. In the latter case one has not been actively involved in the cooking process which occurs on Shabbos. One could also say that in the latter case all the activities relating to the cooking of the food have been done in a time which is permitted (Before Shabbos starts). Hence placing raw food on a heat source before Shabbos is merely a causative, passive act, where as placing raw food on a heat source on Shabbos is an active violation.

Based on the paragraph mentioned above it should be clear that one may in fact leave raw food on a heat source before Shabbos and allow the food to cook on Shabbos. However just as the sages were concerned with regards to re-heating pre-cooked foods so too the sages were concerned that leaving raw food on a heat source before Shabbos, may temp one to adjust the heat and promote cooking on Shabbos. Thus the sages allowed one to leave raw food on a heat source before Shabbos only when certain conditions are met.

In the days of the sages cooking was usually done in a coal oven, and thus the sages maintained that if one were to remove the coal and/or cover the coal with ashes before Shabbos the "temptation" to cook on Shabbos will be eliminated.

- **Removing the coals** indicates ones intention not to cook further
- **Covering the coals with ashes** indicates hampering the speed of cooking and subsequently ones intention not to cook further.

PAGE 1

THE RABBI MICHAEL J ELJARRAT LEARNING PROGRAMME – CLASS THIRTY EIGHT

Today however we predominantly use gas and electric stoves and ovens. We therefore need an equivalent to "removing the coals" and "covering the coals with ashes". The wide spread custom is to cover the surface of the stove tops with a sheet of metal which is wide enough to cover the knobs which control the temperature setting. This metal sheet covering is known as a "BLECH".

The blech is equivalent to covering the coals with ashes as it shows ones intention not to cook further[1].

Although the use of a blech may not slow down the cooking process, it acts as a recognizable feature which indicates ones intention not to cook on Shabbos.

Therefore when using a blech on Shabbos, one must insure to cover all the heat sources, as well as the temperature controls.

- Stove tops can be covered with a sheet of metal (as explained above).
- Ovens would require coverings on all sides, such as a metal box.
- Crock pots can be covered with aluminium foil in the inside as well as over the knobs.
- Urns are difficult to cover therefore one should insure that the water is boiling before Shabbos.
- Warming trays and hot plates which have no temperature control do not require a blech[2].

With regards to all raw foods[3], a blech is required if one wishes to maintain food on Shabbos.

However one exception is made with regards to raw meat, since raw meat takes a very long time to cook, the sages were not concerned that one would be tempted to speed up the cooking (Since in any event it would not be ready for the Friday night meal).

Subsequently one may place a piece of raw meat in a pot before Shabbos with the intention of allowing it to cook on Shabbos, and no blech is required. However it is preferable to use a blech in all circumstances.

---

1. See Tzitz Eliezer 7:15 (The custom of the Gaonim was to be lenient and not require covering of the ashes, just a recognizable feature.)
2. Since it is clear that this item is not a cooking utensil.
3. Solids which are not Mychel Ben Droosai and liquids which are not Yad Soledes Bo.

THE RABBI MICHAEL J ELJARRAT LEARNING PROGRAMME – CLASS THIRTY EIGHT

Returning to a heat source:

The next concept that we will discuss is that that of **"Chazorah"** (Returning). On Shabbos the need sometimes arises to transfer food from one blech to another. Provided that the food is fully cooked there should be no problem with doing a transfer.

Once again the sages were concerned that this may cause others to stumble in the laws of cooking on Shabbos. Therefore the sages required five conditions which will now be discussed:

Before we begin to discuss the five conditions needed in order to permit Chazorah, we must emphasise that the term Chazorah (Returning) only refers to an item which was already on the blech before Shabbos, hence the action of removing the item from the blech, and then back to the blech a second time can be considered as returning as apposed to initially placing.

The five conditions for Chazorah:

- The heat source must be covered with a blech
- The food must be completely cooked
- The food must still be warm when returned
- One must not let go of the pot
- Ones intention must be to return the pot at the time when the pot was removed

Further laws of Chazorah will be discussed in the advanced courses

Sources and Recommended reading:
The Shabbos Kitchen- Rabbi Simcha Bunim Cohen
Published by Artscroll

THE RABBI MICHAEL J ELJARRAT LEARNING PROGRAMME – CLASS THIRTY NINE

CLASS 39   LAWS OF SHABBOS

COOKING AND REHEATING

PART FIVE

The laws of Insulating

In this lesson, the last in the series of cooking and reheating on Shabbos, we will discuss the laws relating to "**Hatmona**" (Insulating food in order to maintain the heat within).

In general it is forbidden to insulate on Shabbos. The prohibition stems from a Rabbinical decree, which was put in place in order to prevent one from cooking on Shabbos. The sages were concerned that if one would insulate a pot which is on the stove, one would first try to raise the temperature of the pot prior to insulation, in order to retain the maximum amount of heat. The actions taken to raise the temperature of the pot may involve making a fire or directly cooking, both of which are forbidden from Torah law. Thus in order to protect against the possible violation of a Torah law, the sages made a decree that it is forbidden to insulate on Shabbos.

Although the general rule is that it is forbidden to insulate on Shabbos, there are several laws ands exceptions as well as several definitions as to what is considered insulating. All of these will now be discussed below.

What is considered insulated?

The term insulated is used only under the following conditions:

- The covering is **not** the primary container in which the food is placed.
- The covering is wrapped in such a way that it covers the pot from all sides.

Therefore any container which is either the primary container of the food (such as the pot itself), or which does not cover the pot entirely from all sides is not deemed as insulating. These cases will be dealt with towards the end of this lesson.

THE RABBI MICHAEL J ELJARRAT LEARNING PROGRAMME – CLASS THIRTY NINE

Categories of substances:

1. **Type A: Heat retaining substances** (Including but not limited to)

   - Cloth
   - Paper
   - Aluminium foil

2. **Type B: Heat intensifying substances** (Including but not limited to)

   - Salt
   - Sand
   - Grass

Laws of insulation relating to Type A substances:

- A pot may be wrapped before Shabbos with a Type A substance.
- If a pot was wrapped with a Type A substance before Shabbos, and it then became unwrapped, one may rewrap the pot on Shabbos.
- A Type A substance may be used to wrap a **Kli Sheini (Second Vessel)** on Shabbos itself.
- In cases of great need a Type A substance may be used to wrap a Kli Rishon (First Vessel) which has cooled down to below Yad Soledes Bo.

Laws of insulation relating to Type B substances:

- Type B substances may not be used even before Shabbos.
- Although cloth is considered a Type A substance, if cloth is used to wrap a pot which is **on the blech**, the cloth is transformed into a Type B substance, since the heat of the blech and the cloth combine.
- One may not submerge a small pot of food into a big pot of food, to raise the temperature of the small pot, as this is considered insulating with a Type B substance.
- One may submerge food[1] into a pot if ones intention is to add flavour to the submerged food.

Non Technical Insulation:

If a pot is wrapped in such a way that either the majority is exposed, or the covering does not touch the majority of the pot, then it is permitted as technically no insulation has taken place.

Sources and Recommended reading:
The Shabbos Kitchen- Rabbi Simcha Bunim Cohen
Published by Artscroll

---

1. Even in a container

THE RABBI MICHAEL J ELJARRAT LEARNING PROGRAMME - CLASS FORTY

CLASS 40   LAWS OF SHABBOS

THE LAWS OF ERUV

In this lesson we will examine the laws relating to "ERUV". The first point which must be stressed is that, the laws of ERUV are very extensive; in fact an entire tractate in the Talmud is dedicated to the laws of ERUV[1].

Therefore in this lesson we will only touch upon some of the fundamental concepts related to the laws of ERUV, and expand a little upon the Melocha which we learned about previously[2], to the point where we can draw some practical implications.

This lesson will cover the following points:

- The meaning of the word ERUV
- The definitions of the various domains
- How to carry in a permissible way when there is no ERUV

What is an ERUV?

Before we can look at the laws of an ERUV, we need to establish what exactly is an ERUV? The word ERUV has its roots in the letters ערב which means to mix a substance with no change in character[3]. An ERUV therefore is a device which enables the "mixing" of domains in such a way, that what would normally be considered as two separate domains, can now be considered as one domain, due to the ERUV which is in place.

What is a domain?
The next question which we have to ask is what is a domain?
The simple answer to this question is, a domain is any area which fulfills certain basic criteria. These domains have names and requirements which will now be dealt with below.

---

1. Tractate Eruvin
2. Class 22 Hotzoa/ Transferring
3. Etymological dictionary – Rabbi M. Clark based on Rabbi S. R Hirsh

THE RABBI MICHAEL J ELJARRAT LEARNING PROGRAMME - CLASS FORTY

In halacha there are four main categories of defined areas. In certain instances it is forbidden to transfer from one domain to another, and in other instances it is forbidden even to carry within the domain itself. The four main domains are:

- Re Shoos-ha Yachid - (a private domain)
- Re Shoos-ha Rabim - (a public domain)
- Carmelis - (an open space)
- Mokom – Petoor - (an undefined space)

Re Shoos-ha Yachid

For an area to be considered a re Shoos-ha Yachid it must fulfill the following requirements:

- The area must measure 4 x 4 Tefachim (1 Tefach = 10cm)
- The area must be surrounded with a wall or fence which is at least 10 Tefachim high.

The general rule is that it is permissible to move and carry items within the re Shoos-ha Yachid itself. The laws relating to transferring items to and from a re Shoos-ha Yachid will be dealt with shortly.

Re Shoos-ha Rabim

The requirements for an area to be considered a re Shoos-ha Rabim are more complex and subject to various opinions. The general outline is that a re Shoos-ha Rabim is qualified if it has the following properties:

- The area must not be roofed
- The area must not be surrounded with a wall or fence
- The area must be at least 16 Amos wide (approximately 7.5m)
- The area must have a large number of people passing through every day

A highway or large busy street would be the classic example of a re Shoos-ha Rabim.

Carmelis

For an area to be considered a Carmelis it must fulfill the following requirements:

- The area must measure 4 x 4 Tefachim (1 Tefach = 10cm)
- The area must not be a re Shoos-ha Yachid or a re Shoos-ha Rabim

Examples of Carmelis include: The Sea, a desert, or a small road where the area is large enough to be considered a domain, but cannot fulfill the requirements of either a re Shoos-ha Yachid or a re Shoos-ha Rabim.

THE RABBI MICHAEL J ELJARRAT LEARNING PROGRAMME - CLASS FORTY

Mokom – Petoor

For an area to be considered a Mokom – Petoor it must meet the following requirements:

- The area must be less than 4 x 4 Tefachim[4] (1 Tefach = 10cm)
- The area must be more than 3 Tefachim high
- The area must be located within a re Shoos-ha Rabim

An example of a Mokom – Petoor would be the top of a pole standing in a re Shoos-ha Rabim.

Carrying and Transferring:

The Torah prohibition forbids the transfer of items from a re Shoos-ha Rabim to a re Shoos-ha Yachid and visa versa. As well as carrying items a distance of 4 Amos (approximately 2m) within a re Shoos-ha Rabim. However the Rabbinical prohibition extends to forbid transferring from a re Shoos-ha Rabim/ Yachid to a Carmelis and visa versa, as well as carrying items a distance of 4 Amos (approximately 2m) within a Carmelis.

The table below summarizes:

Transfer from	Transfer to Reshoos- Ha Rabim	Transfer to Reshoos- Ha Yachid	Transfer to Carmelis	Transfer to Mokom Petoor	Carrying within
Reshoos- Ha Rabim	✗ (Torah)	✗ (Torah)	✗ (Rabbinical)	✓ *	✗
Reshoos- Ha Yachid	✗ (Torah)	✓ **	✗ (Rabbinical)	✓	✓
Carmelis	✗ (Rabbinical)	✗ (Rabbinical)	✓ ***	✓	✓ ***
Mokom Petoor	✓	✓	✓	✓	N/A

* One may not however transfer from a Reshoos Ha Yachid/Rabim through a Mokom Petoor into another reshoos.
** When using an Eruv Chazayros
*** Within 4 Amos (Approximately 2m)

Definition of Transfer:

When we speak of transferring an item, the following 3 events must take place to violate the Torah prohibition. If these 3 events do not take place the transfer will only be subject to a rabbinical violation. The 3 events are:

- Akirah – Lifting the object
- Havarah – Moving the object
- HaNochah – Setting the object down

---

4. Any area which is less than 4 x 4 Tefachim wide and less than 3 Tefachim high is negated to the surrounding area, and is not considered an area in its own right.

THE RABBI MICHAEL J ELJARRAT LEARNING PROGRAMME - CLASS FORTY

What to do when there is no ERUV?

We said above that the word ERUV has its roots in the word "mix". Today around the world there are many large cities which have an ERUV surrounding them, thus enabling those who dwell within the ability to "carry" on Shabbos.

There are many types of ERUV, each with their own principles and mechanics. The ERUV which is employed to surround a large town or city is a form of ERUV chatzayros. This type of ERUV uses the principle of "AMOOD VE LECHI" (literally a pole and a string).

Poles and strings are erected at various strategic points around the town or city, which serve to enclose the given area. Thus making the area enclosed within, a single domain, enabling permissible carrying within the town or city. .

There are however, many large towns and cities which do not have an ERUV erected, and carrying within those cities on Shabbos may violate the full Torah prohibition. Thus if one finds oneself in an area which does not have an ERUV, the following principles should be kept in mind:

- An item which is a "TACHSHIT" (an ornament of attire other than clothing) is not subject to the laws of carrying.

There are two types of TACHSHIT

1. Items worn as jewelry
2. Items which serve the need of a person (such as glasses)

Therefore if an item needs to be carried on Shabbos, one would need to transform that particular item into an acceptable TACHSHIT before Shabbos, to enable its permissible carriage. However the laws relating to this subject are extensive and a competent rabbinical authority should be consulted for all practical applications.

Sources and recommended reading:

Shemirath Shabbath KeHilchatha – Rav Yehoshua Y Neuwirth

THE RABBI MICHAEL J ELJARRAT LEARNING PROGRAMME - CLASS FORTY ONE

CLASS 41   LAWS OF SHABBOS

EMERGENCIES ON SHABBOS

In this lesson we will address some of the issues that may arise in an emergency situation, and how to deal with such situations on Shabbos. By their very nature emergency situations are unpredictable, and can span anywhere from a minor inconvenience to a major life threatening disaster. By the same token the laws of Shabbos are also vast and expansive. Therefore to deal with every emergency situation and every related Shabbos law, would be practically impossible, and beyond the scope of this particular course. Thus this lesson will only cover a few basic concepts with regards to emergency situations, which can then be applied to various situations.

Emergency situations can be divided into two categories

- Those affecting the body
- Those affecting property

We will deal with each category separately. Emergency situations can be further divided into three levels of urgency:

- Major situations
- Intermediate situations
- Minor situations

Of course these distinctions are not set within the laws themselves; however making these distinctions will enable us to compartmentalize the various laws into practical guidelines.

Emergency situations affecting the body:

As a general rule, in the same way as one is obligated to observe Shabbos under normal circumstances, so too one is obligated to violate the laws of Shabbos in order to save a human life. This law is known as "Pikuach Nefesh Docheh es Ha-Shabbos " (Life threatening situations override the laws of Shabbos.

THE RABBI MICHAEL J ELJARRAT LEARNING PROGRAMME - CLASS FORTY ONE

Major situations

The following cases are deemed to be potentially life threatening, and thus Shabbos must be violated.

If a person/patient has:
- A medical doctor claiming that the person in question is in life threatening danger
- Expressed him/her self that they feel that they are in life threatening danger
- Developed a high temperature
- An internal wound
- Developed a strong internal pain
- Uncontrollable bleeding
- Or may have a broken or fractured bone
- A deep cut
- An infected wound
- Been bitten by or stung by an insect which one is severely allergic to
- Been bitten by an animal
- Swallowed poison
- Lost consciousness
- Given birth within the last three days

Intermediate situations

Intermediate emergency situations are those in which a person's life is not in danger. The general rule in such cases is; one should either attend to the person/patient without violating the laws of Shabbos, or one may ask a non Jew to treat the patient even if the non Jew would violate what would normally be a Torah violation if performed by a Jew.

The following situations are deemed as being intermediate

If a person/patient has:

- An illness which makes him/her confined to bed rest
- Pains throughout his/her body

Examples include:

- Migraines
- Acute diarrhea/ indigestion
- Nausea and vomiting

Sufferers of chronic illnesses may take their prescribed medications in order to prevent themselves from becoming ill. One who is experiencing an intermediate emergency situation on Shabbos may take the necessary medications[1].

---

[1]. Taking medications on Shabbos is normally forbidden under the rabbinical decree stemming from the melocha of grinding. (The laws relating to medication on Shabbos will be dealt with separately).

Minor situations

Minor emergency situations, are those in which a person is only suffering a minor inconvenience. The general rule is that one suffering from such a condition may not take medications unless the situation worsens, or one fears that the situation will worsen if left untreated. In the latter cases medication may be taken as the situation is deemed to be that of an intermediate situation as indicated in the laws stated above.

The following situations are deemed as being minor

If a person/patient has:

- A toothache
- A sore throat
- A headache
- A common cold
- A cough

Emergency situations affecting property:

As a general rule one may not violate Shabbos in order to save ones property. When we speak of emergency situations affecting property, we mean specifically just that. Meaning that there is no doubt whatsoever that a person or peoples life/lives will be in danger, rather it's just a matter of loss of property alone.

In emergency situations such as fires, one may rescue only a minimal amount of property such as food and clothing needed for immediate use. However one may ask a non-Jew to extinguish the fire in order to save sacred writings, in addition one may use methods of indirectly causing the fire to become extinguished.

What ever the emergency situation may be, whether it is fire, flood, earthquake or hurricane, the question which must be asked is whether there is any danger to human life, or if it is a danger to property and personal possessions alone.

Sources and recommended reading:

Shemirath Shabbath KeHilchatha – Rav Yehoshua Y Neuwirth

THE RABBI MICHAEL J ELJARRAT LEARNING PROGRAMME – CLASS FORTY TWO

CLASS 42 — LAWS OF SHABBOS

THE LAWS OF HAVDALA

This class brings us to the end of the laws of Shabbos, and as such we will conclude with the laws of Havdala; the laws of terminating Shabbos.

In the same way as we welcome and invite Shabbos upon its arrival, so too we announce and escort Shabbos upon its departure. Shabbos is the "special guest" Who we welcome into our homes, when it arrives, and who we escort out when it leaves. Just as there is a special procedure upon the arrival of Shabbos; called Kiddush, so too there is a special procedure upon the departing of Shabbos called Havdala.

What is Havdala?

The word Havdala comes from the active word "le – havdil", which means to separate. Hence the act of Havdala separates the holy day of Shabbos from the other less holy days of the week. (The question of which act in particular acts as the separating act, will be dealt with below)

How does one separate?

 According to many opinions the Torah obligation is fulfilled by saying "Ato Chonuntanu" in Shemoneh Esrei, or by saying "Boruch Hamavdil Bein Kodesh Le-Chol".

However M'Drabanan one is obligated to recite Havdala over a cup of wine. When the Jews moved back from Bavel to Eretz Yisroel, (After the destruction of the first temple) not everyone could afford wine for Havdala, and so the sages enacted that Havdala be said in the Shemoneh Esrei on Motzei Shabbos. (Saturday evening).

When the Jews prospered once again, the sages re-instituted the law of making Havdala over a cup of wine.

Subsequently the Jews once again faced difficult times; and so the sages declared that Havdala should be said in the Shemoneh Esrei, as well as over a cup of wine by those who could afford it.

THE RABBI MICHAEL J ELJARRAT LEARNING PROGRAMME – CLASS FORTY TWO

The order of Havdala:

There are various customs with regards to the verses which are said before the blessings which are made before the blessing of Havdala itself. However all customs include the following blessings:

- The first blessing is on the wine[1]
- The second blessing is on the spices.
- The third blessing is on the fire.
- The forth blessing is the blessing of Havdala itself.

The blessing on the wine:

As is the case whenever drinking wine; the blessing "Borei Pre HaGoffen" (Who created the fruit of the vineyard) is recited. The reason why wine is used is similar to the reason why wine is used for Kiddush on Friday night; namely for its unique physical properties: That even though wine is a physical substance, it displays spiritual properties as it improves with age. Therefore wine is used as the bridge when crossing over from mundane to holy as well as when crossing over from holy to mundane as we saw in class 23.

The blessing on the spices:

The blessing which is made on the spices is "Borei Minei Besomim". The reason we smell spices on motzei Shabbos, is because during Shabbos we have an extra soul, however when Shabbos ends this soul departs. Therefore in order to consol the remaining soul we smell spices[2].

The blessing on the fire:

The blessing which is made on the fire is "Borei MeOrei Ha-Aish". The flame which is used for havdala must be a multi wicked flame, since the blessing is in plural tense "MeOrei" (Lights). The reason why we make a blessing on fire on Motzei Shabbos is because the first fire which was light by Adam, was light on a Motzei Shabbos[3]. There is also a custom to look at ones finger nails after reciting this blessing, as Adam did when he first made a fire[4].

The Havdala blessing:

The Havdala blessing is the blessing of "HaMavdil Bein Kodesh LeChol". This blessing concludes the Havdala process. After which all activities which were forbidden on Shabbos, now become fully permissible.

---

1. When using wine, however when using "Chamar Midinah" (Local Beverage) the blessing of Shehakol is made.
2. This idea will be explained in detail in an advanced class.
3. Ta-amei Haminhagim 411
4. Ta-amei Haminhagim 414

Prohibitions before Havdala is made:

- It is forbidden to eat before hearing Havdala, however one may drink water.
- One who started a meal with bread at least half an hour before sunset does not need to stop eating when the time for havdala arrives.
- However in the above case, once birchas ha-mozon has been said it is forbidden to eat or drink until after Havdala.
- One may not do Melocho until Havdala has been said (Either Havdala in the Shemoneh Esrei, or Havdala over wine is sufficient to permit one to do Melocho)

Sources and recommended reading:
The radiance of Shabbos – By Rabbi Simcha Bunim Cohen
Published by Artscroll

THE RABBI MICHAEL J ELJARRAT LEARNING PROGRAMME – CLASS FORTY THREE

CLASS 43 — LAWS OF KASHRUS

INTRODUCTION TO KASHRUS

This lesson is the first in a series of lessons which will deal with the laws of Kashrus (The laws of Kosher). The word "Kosher" may be familiar to many, but its meaning remains a hidden mystery. The observance of kosher has been essential for observant Jews for hundreds of years, and its laws have been preserved since the giving of the Torah on Mount Sinai.

This lesson will address the following questions:

- What exactly is kosher?
- What does the word kosher mean?
- Why do we keep kosher?

What is Kosher?

The Torah in Parshas Shemini[1] (Leviticus 11) describes to us which animals, birds, fish and insects are considered "kosher" The states that for each category of creature certain requirements must be met, these are as follows:

An animal:
- Must have completely split hooves
- Must chew the cud

A bird:
- May not be a bird of prey

A fish:
- Must have fins
- Must have scales

An insect:
- Is not kosher[2]

---

1. Starting from 11:1
2. Barring a few exceptions, however today all insects are considered forbidden as we no longer can differentiate between kosher and non-kosher insects.

THE RABBI MICHAEL J ELJARRAT LEARNING PROGRAMME – CLASS FORTY THREE

What does the word "kosher" mean?

As we saw above the Torah states the requirements needed for an animal, bird etc to be kosher. For example a cow fulfils the criteria of having fully split hooves and chewing the cud.

But does this mean that:
- All cows are kosher?
- All limbs, fats and sinews of a cow are kosher?

The answers to the above questions will become clear once we have explained the word "Kosher".

- **Kosher:** Prepare; connect properly[3]
- **Trief:** Snatch; secure food

In colloquial terms the word kosher is used, to refer to permissible foods, while the word trief is used to refer to forbidden foods.

Although regarding the laws of slaughtering the word "trief" refers to an animal which is terminally ill, due to a triefa (a tear) in a vital organ, in the broader sense the word trief refers to all that is forbidden, in the sense that one has grabbed or snatched that food from nature without authority and without forethought.

By contrast the word "kosher" comes from the word; "prepare". Hence kosher food is not merely snatched from nature, it is prepared for consumption. This means to say, that in order for food to be considered "kosher" it must be prepared in such a way that all the laws regarding that particular food have been taken into consideration.

Apart from the requirements needed with regards to the various species of animals, birds and fish, other Torah requirements are needed with regards to the preparation and the handling of the foods in order for them to be fit for kosher consumption.

Some of the additional requirements are[4]:

- Slaughtering: Kosher animals and birds must be ritually slaughtered.
- Removal of blood: Kosher animals and birds require a process of removing the blood.
- Removal of the "CHELEV": Kosher animals require the forbidden fats to be removed.
- "Nikkur": Kosher animals require the forbidden nerves and sinews to be removed.
- "Bedikka": Kosher animals and birds require expert inspection to ascertain that there was no terminal illness present in the animal/bird at the time of slaughtering.

Any animal or bird which was not slaughtered according to the prescribed method is deemed to be a "Nevayla", and may not be consumed. Likewise any animal or bird presenting a terminal illness at the time of slaughter is deemed to be a "Treifa" and may not be consumed.

---

3. Etymological dictionary – Rabbi S R Hirsh (M. Clark)
4. These laws will be dealt with in a later class.

THE RABBI MICHAEL J ELJARRAT LEARNING PROGRAMME – CLASS FORTY THREE

The five examples given above are just some of the requirements needed in order to produce a kosher product.

Any animal, bird, fish or insect which is deemed to be non-kosher:
Not only is it forbidden itself, but even any by-product such as eggs or milk etc is forbidden too.

Why do we keep kosher?

Although there may be some health benefits or social advantages of keeping kosher, these benefits are by no means the "reason" as to why we keep kosher. The real reason why we keep kosher is simply because we are commanded to do so by G-d. However, having said that we can assume that the commandments of G-d contain within them many inherent benefits, seeing as G-d is both the designer and creator of the Human being.

In the same way as the food which we eat impinges on our mind and behaviour, so too the food which we eat impacts our soul and our closeness to G-d. Keeping kosher maintains our soul's sensitivity to spirituality, where as eating non kosher causes a "clouding" of the soul.

Recommended reading: Kashruth by Rabbi Yacov Lipschutz

THE RABBI MICHAEL J ELJARRAT LEARNING PROGRAMME – CLASS FORTY FOUR

CLASS 44
LAWS OF KASHRUS

THE SHECHITA AND MELICHA PROCESS

As we saw previously[1], in order for kosher meat to be rendered kosher for consumption, a number of processes are required, above and beyond the mere selection of a "kosher species" of bird or animal. The first in a series of processes is that of "Shechita" (Ritual slaughtering).

What is Shechita?

The Torah states:[2]

"…You may slaughter from your cattle and your flock….As I have commanded you…"

Rashi on the above verse explains, that from here we see that we are commanded how to slaughter, and that these are the laws of Shechita that were given to Moses on Mount Sinai.

The laws of Shechita are numerous, in fact many chapters of the Shulchan Aruch are dedicated entirely to discussing such laws as; who may perform the ritual slaughter, what instruments may be used, the procedure to follow when performing a ritual slaughter etc.

For the purposes of this lesson we will only briefly outline some of the fundamental concepts regarding the ritual slaughter.

The person performing the Shechita is called a "Shochait". The Shochait must be a trained professional who is an expert in the laws of Shechita. The instrument which is used to perform the Shechita is called a "Chalef". The Chalef is an exceptionally sharp knife-like instrument, which has a completely smooth blade. In fact a single nick on the surface of the blade renders the Chalef invalid, and any subsequent slaughtering void.

Before carrying out a ritual slaughter, the Shochait tests the Chalef to insure that there are no "Pegimas" (Nicks) on the blade. The way in which the Shochait tests the blade, is by running the back of his finger nail up and down the length of the blade. If a nick is detected, the blade is sharpened and re-tested.

---

1. Class 43
2. Devarim / Deuteronomy 12:21

THE RABBI MICHAEL J ELJARRAT LEARNING PROGRAMME – CLASS FORTY FOUR

How is Shechita done?

Before the Shochait slaughters the animal, he makes the following blessing[3]:

"Blessed are you Hashem, our God, King of the universe, who has sanctified us with his commandments, and has commanded us regarding slaughtering."

Before the animal is slaughtered, the animal is restrained (usually in an upright position). The head of the animal is placed between a bracket and a chin lift, in order to expose as much of the neck surface as possible.[4]

After the animal is positioned correctly, the neck of the animal is washed down, in order to remove any dirt which would possibly obstruct the blade during slaughtering.

The Shochait then makes the above blessing and proceeds to slaughter the animal. The incision is made towards the middle of the animal's neck.

The Shochait insures that the following is done:

- The cut severs both the trachea and the oesophagus.
- The cut is made with a single continuous stoke motion without any hesitation.
- The cut is made without any external pressure.[5]
- The cut is made in the correct location upon the animal's neck.
- The blade is exposed during slaughter.

A short while after the animal has been slaughtered, the chest cavity is opened and the lungs are checked by an expert to insure that the lungs are healthy and contain no adhesions.

This first checking is called "Bedikas Pe'nim" (Internal Checking) and it is done whilst the lungs are still within the animal. After the animal has been flayed and the internal organs removed, the lungs are checked once again. The second checking is a thorough investigation, whereby the lungs are inflated and examined for any adhesions. If adhesions are found they are removed and the lungs are further tested to insure that no holes are present in the lobes of the lung. This second checking is called "Bedikas Chootz" (External Checking) and is done once the lungs have been removed. If holes are found after the removal of any adhesions, the animal is deemed a Triefa and is not fit for Kosher consumption.

---

3. This blessing is made before the first animal is slaughtered, and the blessing covers all subsequent slaughtering done in that period.
4. There are various restraining methods, however whichever method is used, the primary goal is to expose the surface area of the neck.
5. The cut must be made using the sharpness of the blade alone.

THE RABBI MICHAEL J ELJARRAT LEARNING PROGRAMME – CLASS FORTY FOUR

What is Melicha?

The Torah states:[6]

"…and all blood, you should not eat…"

From this verse we learn that; it is forbidden to consume any blood from both animals and fowl alike, however it is permissible to consume the blood of fish and Kosher locusts.

In order for meat to be deemed "kosher and ready to eat", the blood found within the meat must be removed. The process of removing the blood is called "Kashering"

Kashering can be done in one of two ways:

1. Kashering using a process of Melicha and Hadacha.
2. Kashering using a process of roasting.

The process of Melicha and Hadacha:

The most common way of koshering meat is by using the Melicha (meaning salting) and Hadacha (meaning washing) method. After the animal has been checked and deemed to be kosher, it is cut both length ways and horizontally. Most commonly only the forequarter is taken for kosher consumption. The forequarter is then processed through the following steps:

1. The meat is washed in order to remove any surface blood.
2. The meat is salted with a course salt on all sides.
3. The meat is rinsed off/ washed three times to remove the salt.

The process of roasting:

Some meats and organs contain large amounts of blood, one such organ is the liver. The liver is kashered using a process of roasting. The liver is first cut in a criss-cross fashion, and then lightly salted, after which it is placed on a grill within a roasting oven, thus allowing the blood to be drained as a result of the heat. This process insures that the blood is fully removed from the liver, thus allowing the liver to be kosher for consumption.

Recommended reading: Kashruth by Rabbi Yacov Lipschutz
Published by: Artscroll.

---

6. Vayikra / Leviticus 7:26

THE RABBI MICHAEL J ELJARRAT LEARNING PROGRAMME – CLASS FORTY FIVE

CLASS 45   LAWS OF KASHRUS

MEAT AND MILK FORBIDDEN MIXTURES

We have seen previously, that although a particular species of animal may be in the "Kosher" category, it is not deemed Kosher to eat until all the processes of slaughtering, examining and Kashering have been completed to a satisfactory level.

However the laws of Kosher do not stop there; even after meat has been rendered kosher to eat, it can loose its "Kosher" status if it has been cooked incorrectly.

This lesson will deal with some of the laws relating to the preparation of food, as well as mixtures which are forbidden to eat.

The Torah states the following phrase on three separate occasions:

"You shall not cook a kid in the milk of its mother.[1]"

From the fact that the Torah stated this verse three times, we learn three separate laws, namely:

1. One may not cook a mixture of meat and milk
2. One may not eat a mixture of meat and milk
3. One may not have benefit from a mixture of meat and milk

Thus the following actions are forbidden by Torah law regarding a mixture of meat and milk. (We will soon see the Rabbinical restrictions which were included in this law)

1. Cooking (even if you don't eat it) is forbidden
2. Eating (even if someone else cooked it) is forbidden
3. Having benefit (even if someone else cooked it and you don't eat it) is forbidden

---

[1]. Exodus/ Shemos 23:9, 34:26 and Deuteronomy/ Devarim 14:21

THE RABBI MICHAEL J ELJARRAT LEARNING PROGRAMME – CLASS FORTY FIVE

The following Rabbinical restrictions also apply:

1. Mixing meat and milk together (without cooking[2])
2. Eating a mixture which has been mixed (but not cooked[3])
3. Eating a mixture containing poultry and milk

The laws are derived from the verse as follows:

"You shall not cook"

From this section we learn that the Torah only forbade the cooking of meat and milk together. If one would simply mix cold meat and milk together, one would not have violated this Torah law, and subsequently the cold mixture would not be subject to the Torah laws (eating, and having benefit). However Rabbinical law forbids even mixing without cooking, as well as the eating of such a mixture.

"A Kid"

From this section we learn that the Torah only forbade the meat of a domesticated animal, similar to a "Kid" which is a domesticated animal. However if one would cook the meat of a wild animal or the meat of a fowl together with milk, one would not have violated the Torah laws (cooking, eating and having benefit). However Rabbinical law forbids the eating of a dish consisting of the meat of a wild animal or the meat of a fowl cooked together with milk.

Another law which is learned from this section of the verse is: The Torah only forbade the cooking of kosher meat together with milk; however the cooking of a non-kosher species of animal together with milk is not subject to the laws of "Meat and Milk". We learn this law from the fact that the Torah wrote "A Kid", just as a kid is a kosher animal, so too all the laws of meat and milk only applies to kosher animals.

"In the milk of its mother"

From this section of the verse we learn that the Torah only forbade the "milk of its mother". Meaning the milk which is forbidden to cook is similar to the meat which is forbidden to cook, hence the term "its mother". Just as the meat which is forbidden to cook comes from a kosher domesticated animal, so too the milk which is forbidden to cook is the milk of a kosher domesticated animal.

---

2. For example mixing cheese sauce into a meaty lasagne.
3. For example eating a meaty lasagne which has cheese sauce mixed in.

THE RABBI MICHAEL J ELJARRAT LEARNING PROGRAMME – CLASS FORTY FIVE

Forbidden mixtures:

Cooking utensils:

Any utensil which was used to cook either meat or milk becomes "meaty" (Fleishick) or "milky" (Milchick) respectively.

The reason why the utensil gains the status of that, which was cooked within, is due to the fact that the walls of the utensil are porous, giving the utensil the ability to absorb the flavours from that which was cooked within.

Furthermore, the flavours which have been contained and absorbed within the walls of the utensil are further released back into the utensil once the utensil is again used for cooking. (As demonstrated in the example below)

Stage 1:
If one were to cook meat in a pot, the pot being used will absorb meat flavours during the cooking process, and the pot will be deemed a "meaty pot" (or a "milky pot" should milk have been cooked within)

Stage 2:
If one would then cook milk in that "meaty pot" (or meat in that "milky pot"); the flavours which had previously been absorbed into the walls of the pot will be released into the meat (or milk) cooking within the pot at present, thus creating a forbidden mixture of meat and milk.

Moreover the forbidden mixture within the pot will create its own forbidden flavours which will then be absorbed into the walls of the pot, thus rendering the pot itself not kosher.

Should the above occur the following laws apply:
- The contents of the pot are forbidden to eat
- The pot itself may not be used until it has been Kashered.

The 24 hour rule:
An exception is made when a utensil has not been used within 24 hours. After 24 hours have elapsed since cooking, the flavours absorbed within the walls of the utensil become "stale". Such a utensil releases "bad" flavours when cooking, and thus does not render the food being cooked within non-kosher. However the utensil itself may not be used until it has been kashered.

The Botel Be Shishim rule:
Another important law is that of "Botel Be Shishim" (Meaning nullified in sixty). This law states that if meat/milk fell into a utensil containing its counterpart, and the meat/milk is sixty times smaller than the contents of the utensil, then the flavours which are released from the fallen meat/milk are nullified against the flavours of the contents of the utensil, and the contents of the utensil remain kosher to eat. These and other laws will be addressed in further detail in the lessons to follow.

Sources and recommended reading:
Meat and Dairy by Rabbi Ehud Rosenburg.
Published by: Artscroll

THE RABBI MICHAEL J ELJARRAT LEARNING PROGRAMME – CLASS FORTY SIX

CLASS 46   LAWS OF KASHRUS

CHECKING VEGETABLES

As we learnt previously, not all species of animal, fowl and fish are Kosher. Even those species that are Kosher are not permissible to eat, until further requirements have been met.

However when it comes to fruits, vegetables, legumes and seeds the Torah did not limit those species which are Kosher and subsequently all species of fruits, vegetables, legumes and seeds are intrinsically kosher.

However just as "Kosher" species of animals are not permissible to eat until certain requirements have been met, so too when it comes to fruits, vegetables, legumes and seeds certain requirements must be met, before they become permissible to eat.

The fundamental difference:

There is a fundamental difference between animal, fowl and fish compared to fruits, vegetables, legumes and seeds. When it comes to foods coming from a living source of a category B nature (see below), the "food" in question is intrinsically forbidden[1] until it has been slaughtered. However foods comings from a category C nature (see below) are intrinsically permitted and only external prohibitions[2] can forbid food in this category.

There are four categories of living creatures:

- Category A – Human Beings
- Category B – Animals, fowl, fish and insects
- Category C – Plant life and vegetation
- Category D – The inanimate

Hence the laws of Kosher were only given in the context of category B creatures, and not for category C and below. Thus it would seem fairly simple that all fruits, vegetables, legumes and seeds are kosher. However the habitat of one of the smallest forbidden category B creatures namely insects, is vegetation itself. Some of the world's smallest insects are found in common fruits and vegetables, and these insects must obviously be removed before one eats the said fruit or vegetable.

---

1. Talmud Beitza 25a
2. Such as insect infestation, or laws of Terumos and Mai's ros

THE RABBI MICHAEL J ELJARRAT LEARNING PROGRAMME – CLASS FORTY SIX

How does one remove insects from fruits and vegetables?

It would seem fairly simple, that insects which are visible to the naked eye can be removed by hand. However the situation becomes more complex, since some insects are too small to grasp (although visible to the naked eye). Further complicating the matter; some small insects attach themselves to the fruits or vegetables in such a way that they are almost impossible to remove.

Thanks to the research of individuals who have dedicated their lives entirely to the study of insects and their behaviour, we now know a great deal about insects and their natural habitats.

Using this important information we now know which fruits and vegetables are prone to insect infestation. We also know how these insects behave in terms of their eating, nesting and mating habits.

After gathering all this information, these experts compiled a list of the various fruits and vegetables, the insects commonly affecting them and the procedure to remove them.

There are three distinctive methods; each method is applicable according to the nature of the fruit or vegetable in question.

Method 1 Cleaning:

In certain instances, where infestation is very rare and where insects are only loosely attached to the fruit or vegetable, a simple washing is enough to remove any insects. In other instances the insects grab hold of the vegetable, such as is the case with Thrips on cabbage. In such cases soaking in soapy water helps to remove all insects. However certain insects such as Aphids, do not come off when soaking in soapy water, insects such as these can however be removed by wiping a soapy sponge over both sides of the vegetable, as is the case when cleaning lettuce.

Method 2 Checking:

Some vegetables such as lettuce, spinach and butter beans, require checking to insure that the method used for cleaning was in fact effective. (see below for a list of vegetables which require checking)

Method 3 testing:

Certain vegetables cannot be cleaned and checked due to the nature of the vegetable and the relevant type of insect infestation. In these cases it is impossible to visually detect the presence of insect infestation. Therefore a third method is used called "testing". Testing is a process whereby we either shake off the vegetable onto a surface such as a cloth, or we wash or cook the vegetable, after which we examine the cloth or the water in which the vegetable was cooked or washed in. If we find insect infestation on the cloth or in the water which the vegetable was cooked in, we disregard the vegetable.

THE RABBI MICHAEL J ELJARRAT LEARNING PROGRAMME – CLASS FORTY SIX

Some examples include the following:

Fruit/Vegetable	Cleaning	Checking	Testing
Artichoke	x		
Asparagus			x
Basil			x
Butter beans		x	
Chick peas			x
Cabbage	x		
Cauliflower	x		
Celery	x		
Coriander			x
Dates		x	

For a complete list consult the Beth Din kosher guide published annually

Food for thought:

A lesson to be learnt from this lesson is that small things are important, and that we need to be aware of our situations in which we find ourselves. We need to pay attention to small details and be aware of subtle changes in our environment.

In closing let us say:

"We need to spend more time searching for God and less time searching for insects".

THE RABBI MICHAEL J ELJARRAT LEARNING PROGRAMME – CLASS FORTY SEVEN

CLASS 47   LAWS OF KASHRUS

SIFTING FLOUR AND CHECKING EGGS

In this lesson we will look at two practical skills needed, in order to maintain a kosher kitchen. In the lessons to follow we will look at the laws of kosher relating to manufactured products, and some specific laws relating to bread.

When it comes to baking and cooking, the two most common ingredients are flour and eggs; however as common are the ingredients, so too are there common problems which may arise, the first of which we will look at are the issues related to flour.

Sifting flour:

As we saw previously, it is forbidden for one to eat insects, and we therefore check our fruits and vegetables before we eat them. Another common source of insect infestation is in flour, especially when left open and in a semi damp environment. For this reason before we begin cooking and baking using flour, we first sift the flour in order to remove any possible insect infestation. It is common practise both for Halachic and hygienic reasons to discard flour, if any insect infestation is present. Another law which is specific to flour and baking is that of "Challah". We will learn about the laws of "Challah" in a separate class.

Checking eggs:

As we saw previously, not all animal, fowl and fish are kosher, and amongst the kosher species not all parts of the animal itself are kosher. We also saw that the by-product of any species carries the same law as the species itself. That means to say that a by-product such as milk or eggs etc can only be considered kosher if they come from a kosher species of animal or fowl. Therefore only the milk or eggs etc of a kosher species can be considered kosher.

Are all Chicken eggs kosher?

It would seem from what we said in the above paragraph that all chicken eggs are by default kosher. The question we need to ask therefore, is this true? Are all chicken eggs Kosher?

THE RABBI MICHAEL J ELJARRAT LEARNING PROGRAMME – CLASS FORTY SEVEN

To answer this question, we will examine a piece of Talmud. The Talmud[1] says "An animal has a status of being non-kosher, until we know how it was slaughtered. Once it has been slaughtered it has the status of being kosher, until we can identify a reason why it should be non-kosher". Rashi on that piece of Talmud explains: that an animal has a status of "non-kosher" when it is alive since one is forbidden to eat a limb from a living animal. However once the animal is slaughtered its status changes to "kosher" even though we may find fatal organ damage; (Thus rendering the animal "Trief") however until we actually find fatal organ damage we can assume the animal to be kosher, since most animals do not have fatal organ damage.

Thus even though a chicken which has fatal organ damage will be rendered as "Trief" and subsequently the eggs from a Trief chicken are also Trief. However we can assume that an ordinary chicken is healthy and therefore its eggs can be assumed to be kosher.

When eggs are no longer eggs:

It is important to note, that eggs can only be considered a by-product of a chicken so long as the egg has not been fertilized. However once an egg has been fertilized, it is no longer considered an "egg" rather a "chicken embryo". Since a chicken needs to be slaughtered and the "chicken" has not yet been formed; by default a fertilized egg/embryo is forbidden to eat.[2]

Egg fertilization:

Since a fertilized egg is forbidden to eat, the question then arises; how does one tell the difference between a fertilized and non-fertilized egg?

We learnt previously that one is forbidden to eat the blood of an animal or fowl. The commentaries ask, what is the law regarding blood found within eggs? There are several opinions as to the status of this blood. Some maintain that even if the blood is indicative of fertilization, the blood is forbidden only Rabbinicaly, while others maintain that if the blood is indicative of fertilization then the blood is forbidden by Torah law, since it is considered a "fowl", due to the fact that a fowl would eventually have been formed.

Thus in practice if one cracked open an egg and found a blood spot within, the halacha is that we throw away the egg. Since both the blood and the egg would be forbidden to eat according to what we said above.

However there are several opinions as to where exactly on the egg, is a blood spot indicative of fertilization. Therefore the law would be as follows:

- When a blood spot is found within one egg, we throw away the egg.

- When a blood spotted egg has been mixed with two or more eggs:
    1. If the blood spot is on the yolk we throw away the mixture.
    2. If the blood spot is on the albumen, the blood spot together with as much of the "infected" egg is thrown away, and the rest of the mixture is permitted.

---
1. Beitza 25a
2. This may be the reason according to the second opinion below.

THE RABBI MICHAEL J ELJARRAT LEARNING PROGRAMME – CLASS FORTY SEVEN

Battery hens:

Today many eggs come from battery hens. Battery hens are kept in cages and do not roam around freely. Therefore eggs with blood spots coming from battery hens could not possibly be fertilized.

When it comes to eggs from battery hens the following laws apply:

- When a blood spot is found within one egg, we throw away the egg, (To maintain the tradition).

- When the blood spotted egg has been mixed with two or more eggs, then only the blood spot need be removed, and the rest is permitted.

Sources and further reading:

Kashruth by Rabbi Yacov Lipschutz
Published by Artscroll.

Also see presentation: "Checking eggs".

THE RABBI MICHAEL J ELJARRAT LEARNING PROGRAMME – CLASS FORTY EIGHT

CLASS 48   LAWS OF KASHRUS

KASHERING UTENSILS AND IMMERSING NEW VESSELS

In this lesson we will look at two concepts which are common place in the kosher kitchen. The first concept is that of "Kashering" utensils. "Kashering" is a slang word for "Making Kosher", the root of the word being "Kasher" or Kosher. The second concept is that of immersing new vessels commonly known as "Tevilas kaylim" (Tevila – Immersing and Kaylim – Vessels).

Kashering utensils:

So what is Kashering all about?

To answer this question we need to understand, that the vast majority of utensils are porous, thus giving them the ability to absorb some of the food that was cooked within. Hence a pot which was used to cook milk is "Milchick" (Milky) and a pot which was used for cooking meat is "Fleishick" (Meaty), and a pot which was used to cook non-kosher food is non-kosher. Sometimes mistakes are made in the kitchen and a Milchick pot is used to cook meat and visa versa. (In a later class we will look more into the laws which are relevant to mistakes in the kitchen.)

Therefore to answer our question, Kashering is the process whereby we eliminate any previous status of a utensil and return the status of the utensil back to neutral. Perhaps one could think of Kashering as pressing the "Reset" button.

The general rule regarding Kashering is: "Ke Derech she-bolo, Kach palto" (In the way it absorbs, so too it excretes). This means to say, that the method which was used to absorb, the same method can be used to excrete that which was absorbed. Hence if a pot became "Milchick" through boiling, the pot can be Kashered through boiling.

As you may recall from the laws of cooking on Shabbos, there are various degrees of heat intensity when it comes to cooking. The hottest form of cooking is "Tzli" (Roasting on an open flame), the mildest form of cooking is cooking from a third vessel. We will now look at each form of cooking and the appropriate method of Kashering.

THE RABBI MICHAEL J ELJARRAT LEARNING PROGRAMME – CLASS FORTY EIGHT

It is important to note that "taste flavours" are only absorbed into a utensil through the application of heat. If a utensil was used for cold non-kosher substances, then the utensil will not absorb non-kosher tastes, and Kashering would not be required. All that is required in cases pertaining to cold substances is thorough cleaning using cold water.

The exception to this rule is knives which were used to cut "Sharp" cold non-kosher foods, May in fact absorb the taste from the non-kosher food[1].

Earlier we mentioned that the vast majority of utensils are porous and can therefore absorb tastes, however utensils which are non-porous would not need to be kashered. Glass is deemed by some to be non-porous and does not need kasheing. Another important point to note is that not all materials can be koshered. In general only metal utensils may be kashered, earthenware utensils may not be kashered, and must therefore be discarded should they absorb non-kosher tastes.[2]

Grades of heat intensity:

The following table illustrates the various degrees of heat intensity and the method required for kashering. We will explain briefly what is required by each method.

Method of cooking	Method of Kashering
Tzli – Roasting on an open flame	Libun Gamur
First vessel	Hagala / Libun Kal
Pouring from a "First vessel"	Hagala
"Second vessel" / "Third vessel"	Pouring from "First vessel"

- Libun Gamur: Placing the utensil into a direct flame (such as under a blow torch) thus destroying any tastes absorbed by the utensil.

- Libun Kal: Heating the utensil until it becomes hot enough to create a fire.

- Hagala: Placing the utensil into boiling hot water and then rinsing the utensil with cold water.

- Pouring from a "First vessel": Pouring boiling water over utensils.

---

1. The commentaries discuss whether or not liquid or grease plays a role in taste transference.
2. See source and reference for a comprehensive list of materials.

THE RABBI MICHAEL J ELJARRAT LEARNING PROGRAMME – CLASS FORTY EIGHT

Immersing new vessels:

The verse states[3]:

"Only the gold and the silver, the copper and the iron…..you shall pass through the water…"

From this verse we learn that vessels require immersing in water, when transfer of ownership is passed from a non-Jew to a Jew.

Which utensils require immersion?

Since the Torah states gold, silver and other metals; only metallic utensils require immersion. Therefore the following utensils would not require immersion.

Items made of:
- Wood
- Stone
- Plastic (And other synthetic materials)
- Disposable items
- Electrical appliances[4]

Glass is an exception and does require immersion.

The obligation of immersing utensils is limited to utensils which come into direct contact with food. Utensils such as hot trays etc, which do not come into direct contact with food, do not have to be immersed. Utensils which are coated with a substance which does not require immersion should be immersed without a blessing.

How immersion is done:

The procedure for immersing utensils is done as follows:

- First all labels and tags are removed from the utensil.
- Then one makes the blessing "Al Tevilas Kli" for one utensil or "Al Tevilas Kaylim" for many utensils.
- Next the utensils are fully immersed into a Kosher Mikveh, until water surrounds and covers every part of the utensil.

Sources and recommended reading:

The Kosher Kitchen – A Practical Guide.
By: Rabbi Binyomin Forst.
Published By: Artscroll – Halachah Series.

---

3. Bamidbar/Numbers 31:22-23
4. Since they can only be used when plugged in, it is considered as part of the building and not a utensil.

THE RABBI MICHAEL J ELJARRAT LEARNING PROGRAMME – CLASS FORTY NINE

CLASS 49   LAWS OF KASHRUS

MISTAKES IN THE KITCHEN

In this lesson we will look at some of the mistakes that can occur in a kosher kitchen, and the ways in which these mistakes can be rectified. Certainly it goes without say that we could not possibly cover every potential mistake that could occur. Rather we will look at some basic principles which will determine the nature of the problem which has occurred, and the way in which to phrase a question to your local Rabbi should the need arise.

As we have learnt previously, a kosher kitchen requires strict separation between meat and milk, as well as cautious observance to insure that only kosher ingredients are found in the home. However even when the above is adhered to; still, mistakes can occur.

Let us look at some common issues.

- What do I do if; I placed a Milchick lid on a Fleishick pot, while cooking?
- What do I do if; Milk has dropped onto some meat while it was in the fridge?
- What do I do if: I find Milchick cutlery in the Fleishick draw?

In order to gain clarity on the above cases we will look at some basic principles regarding the laws of meat and milk. Once we have seen the concepts it will be easier to navigate our way through the laws and know how to ask a question.

Bottle Be Shishim:

The Talmud[1] explains that tastes are nullified in a ratio of 1 to 60. That means to say, if a piece of meat were to fall into a pot of boiling milk, and the volume of milk were 60 times greater than that of the meat; then the milk would be permitted to drink. (The meat however would be forbidden as it has absorbed and has been saturated with milk.) Subsequently since the milk is kosher it will not contaminate the pot, and the pot can be used again without koshering.

---

1. Chulin 97a

Ben Yomo:

In halacha we refer to a vessel as either being "Ben Yomo" (Lit son of its day) or not "Ben Yomo". A vessel which is Ben Yomo, has been used to cook either meat or milk within the last 24 hours. As a rule a vessel only has the ability to absorb and retain milk/meat tastes for up to 24 hours. After 24 hours have elapsed, the tastes which have been absorbed into the pot go stale, and are no longer considered tastes of milk/ meat.

Temperature:

As a general rule, the transfer of taste only occurs when heat is applied, as we saw in the previous lesson. Therefore dry and cold foods which touched each other will not absorb tastes from one another. However if one or both of the foods are wet/damp or fatty, even though the foods will not transmit tastes, still they should be rinsed prior to eating in order to remove any surface contamination.

Davar Charif:

As a general rule, the laws regarding tastes can be applied as we have seen above. However an exception is made when it comes to food which is regarded as "Davar Charif" (A sharp tasting food). Foods such as onions, garlic and chillies are considered to be sharp foods, and subsequently their tastes are more potent, and can spread tastes in a ratio greater than 1:60, and perhaps can last longer than 24 hours.

Kavoosh:

In halachah we find another type of "cooking" with regards to taste transferral. Kavoosh (Soaking) allows tastes to be transferred. As a general rule something which was soaked in a liquid for a period of 24 hours, is considered to be "cooked" by that liquid. Subsequently if meat were soaked in milk for a period of 24 hours, the meat will absorb the tastes of the milk. Depending on the type of liquid, some liquids such as salty brine can achieve the status of Kavoosh after just several minutes.

Zayah:

Another method by which tastes can be transferred is through Zayah – Steam. The general principle is that steam coming from a liquid is the same as the liquid itself, however steam coming from a solid only has the same law as the solid if the steam is visible.

THE RABBI MICHAEL J ELJARRAT LEARNING PROGRAMME – CLASS FORTY NINE

To phrase the questions above:

What do I do if; I placed a Milchick lid on a Fleishick pot, while cooking?

To answer this question we would need to know the following:

- When were the pot and lid last used?
- What was cooking in the pot?

What do I do if; Milk has dropped onto some meat while it was in the fridge?

To answer this question we would need to know the following:

- Was the meat smooth on the outside?
- How long was the milk dripping for?
- How saturated was the meat?

What do I do if: I find Milchick cutlery in the Fleishick draw?

To answer this question we would need to know the following:

- Did you see the wrong utensil being used?

In this case unless we saw a meat/milk mistake taking place while cooking, we can safely assume that the only "mistake" which has occurred is that of misplacing the cutlery.

Further reading and sources:
The Kosher Kitchen – Rabbi Binyomin Forst

THE RABBI MICHAEL J ELJARRAT LEARNING PROGRAMME – CLASS FIFTY

CLASS 50 — LAWS OF KASHRUS

MANUFACTURED PRODUCTS AND TRAVELLING

In this lesson we will take a closer look at what goes into manufactured products, with regards to the halachic implications and issues which need to be taken into account. We will examine some of the common additives, preservatives, colourings and flavourings, to see which may be problematic with regards to the laws of kosher. We will also look at the issues that may arise when travelling to foreign places, where ones usual products cannot easily be obtained.

In the late 18th century, the world under went some drastic changes. The industrial revolution had a major impact on almost every industry, especially on agriculture and manufacturing. With the great advances being made, food could be mass produced and sold in great quantities. This sparked a new era in commercialism and the birth of many manufacturing companies. Gradually the foods that people ate were no longer home made but rather the product of a manufacturing company. Manufactured foods had to maintain certain standards, for instance; the product shelf life had to be extended, due to the fact that goods had to be kept in storage or exported to foreign countries a great distance away, which required weeks of travel.

For this reason preservatives were added to food to insure that the food would remain "fresh" weeks after their non-manufactured counterparts would have long gone stale.

Due to the pressing needs of the companies to beat competitors and insure profit margins which were sustainable, synthetic additives were added to food to improve tastes or to cut costs.

Despite all this change, the laws of kosher remained constant and strict supervision of factories became essential in order to keep track of the changes being made.

Today in almost every city with a large Jewish community, establishments have been set up to monitor and control the Kashrus quality of manufactured products. Inspectors are sent out to factories to check the ingredients, and to insure that only kosher ingredients are being added to manufactured products. This checking often requires a great amount of research, and food technologists are required to gain an understanding of some of the complex additives. Once a product has been checked and passed as kosher, the product is then listed, and in many cases the mark of approval is added to the packaging of the manufactured product.

THE RABBI MICHAEL J ELJARRAT LEARNING PROGRAMME – CLASS FIFTY

We will now take a look at some of the common additives, their purpose and their halachic status. It is important to note that even though these additives may only be used in small quantities, never the less they are not negated, due to the fact that they are added for a purpose.

Acetic acid: Often used as a preservative which inhibits the growth of mould and bacteria (may be produced from wine)

Ascorbic acid: (Vitamin C) used as a preservative for its anti oxidant properties. (Often used in processed meats and fish)

Aspartic acid: Found in plants and animals and can be produced synthetically. Used as a synthetic sweetener (Aspartame)

Beta Carotene: Found in plants and used as a colouring (Orange/Yellow) (Often used in cheese and butter).

Calcium stearate: Produced from stearic acid (from plant or animal origins) and calcium chloride. Used as a free flowing agent.

Citric acid: Produced by means of enzymatic conversion and used as a natural preservative in canned fruit and juices.

Cystein: Produced from keratin (the protein found in hair and in feathers) used to improve dough and the speed of baking.

Food Flavourings: There are more than 1500 flavour ingredients both of natural extracts and synthetic chemicals.[1]

- **Ambergris** – Taken from the intestines of sperm whales and has blending qualities.
- **Castoreum** – Extracted from the glands of beavers and used to enhance berry type flavours.
- **Civet** – Produced from the secretions of the civet cat, and used to blend flavours.
- **Lipase** – is an enzyme derived from calf glands and used in dairy products.

Food Colourings: In the USA the FDA (Food and Drug Administration) is responsible for governing additives such as colourings. There are at present 9 colouring substances which are certified by the FDA[2]. Depending on the source of the colouring, kashrus supervision is required.

Gelatine: Produced from collagen extracted from animals and used to produce gel like substances.

Glycerides: Produced either synthetically or from plant or animal origin and used as an emulsifier (see below)

Hydrogenated vegetable shortening: Produced by converting liquid oils; into solid fat by introducing hydrogen under pressure.

---

[1]. Kashruth – Rabbi Yacob Lipschutz.
[2]. www.fda.gov

THE RABBI MICHAEL J ELJARRAT LEARNING PROGRAMME – CLASS FIFTY

Monosodium glutamate: Produced either synthetically or from plant extract and used as a flavour enhancer.

Pepsin: Produced from animal gastric juices and used in the production of some cheese.

Potassium sorbate: Made from potassium and sorbic acid and used as a preservative.

Riboflavin: Found naturally and produced synthetically and used as a nutritional supplement.

Sulphur dioxide: Produced from sulphur and used as a preservative. (In the USA there various prohibitions regarding this substance)

Xylitol: Produced from wood pulp and used as an artificial sweetener.

What are E numbers?

E numbers are additives which have been approved by the European union standards, and are coded as follows:

- 100 - 199 – Colours
- 200 – 299 – Preservatives
- 300 – 399 – Antioxidants and acidity regulators.
- 400 – 499 – Thickeners, stabilizers and emulsifiers[3]
- 500 – 599 – Ph regulators and anti caking agent.
- 600 – 699 – Flavour enhances
- 700 – 799 – Antibiotics

(Additional E numbers are used for other miscellaneous additives and range up to 1599+)

Below is a complete list of the various E- numbers:

---

[3]. Emulsifiers help to combine substances which would not naturally combine

E number range	Subranges	Description
100–199 (full list) Colours	100–109	yellows
	110–119	oranges
	120–129	reds
	130–139	blues & violets
	140–149	greens
	150–159	browns & blacks
	160–199	gold and others
200–299 (full list) Preservatives	200–209	sorbates
	210–219	benzoates
	220–229	sulphites
	230–239	phenols & formates (methanoates)
	240–259	nitrates
	260–269	acetates (ethanoates)
	270–279	lactates
	280–289	propionates (propanoates)
	290–299	others
300–399 (full list) Antioxidants & acidity regulators	300–305	ascorbates (vitamin C)
	306–309	Tocopherol (vitamin E)
	310–319	gallates & erythorbates
	320–329	lactates
	330–339	citrates & tartrates
	340–349	phosphates
	350–359	malates & adipates
	360–369	succinates & fumarates
	370–399	others

A full list can be found at: http://en.wikipedia.org/wiki/E_number

Guidelines for travelling:

When it comes to travelling, good preparation always pays dividends.

When travelling to civilized countries and towns with moderately large Jewish communities, one needs to familiarize oneself with the symbols and markings of the local Kashrus authorities.
It is important to note:

- Not all familiar branded products are kosher abroad as ingredients may differ from one country to the next.

When travelling to smaller towns and cities without a Jewish population, one should investigate the large cities nearby and enquire about local kashrus authorities, and important food.

When travelling to rural/uncivilized countries and towns one would need to bring ones own food from home. In certain instances it is forbidden to take food across boarders, and in such cases one would need to insure that one stays in a self catering type of accommodation. In such cases one would need to keep a very limited diet consisting of fresh fruits and vegetables, legumes and the like. One may also eat fish presenting fins and scales (of familiar species of fish).

If one plans on visiting uninhabited areas, it is highly recommended that a thorough investigation is done beforehand, to insure not only adequate food supply, but other areas of health and safety.

THE RABBI MICHAEL J ELJARRAT LEARNING PROGRAMME – CLASS FIFTY ONE

CLASS 51   LAWS OF KASHRUS

CHALLAH

In this lesson we will look at some of the laws and customs relating to "Challah". The word Challah has its roots in the word Challah which means to weaken, and in our context we are referring to a particular portion of dough. Perhaps there is a connection between the two meanings?

What is Challah?

When we hear the word Challah, we often think of the bread which we eat on Shabbos, which has been nick-named "Challah". It is not by coincidence that the bread we eat on Shabbos has been nick-named "Challah", as we will now explore the idea of Challah and its meanings are deeply rooted in the very heart of Judaism, and its significance spills over into many aspects.

The verse states[1]

    "As the first of your kneading you shall set aside a loaf as a portion...."

From this verse we learn the Mitzvah of Challah, that is, the Mitzvah to separate a portion of dough when baking, in order to give to the Kohen. The Chinuch[2] explains that the root of this Mitzvah is based on the fact that human life is dependent on sustenance, and one of the primary sources of sustenance is bread. Therefore Hashem wanted to give us a Mitzvah which would be applicable on a continuous basis, while simultaneously helping and enabling those who serve Hashem, by providing them with sustenance.

The laws of Challah:

Since the verse states "When you come to the land" we learn that the laws of Challah are only applicable in Israel, and when most of the Jews are living in Israel. However the sages enacted the laws of Challah to be practised outside the land of Israel, in order that the laws of Challah should not be forgotten by the Jews. Since the Torah did not state any particular amount to be given as Challah; By Torah law even if one separates the smallest amount, one has fulfilled ones obligation of separating Challah. However the Sages created standard measurements, namely one twenty-forth for home use, and one forty-eighth for bakers/commercial use.

---

1. Bamidbar / Numbers 15:20
2. Minchas Chinuch Mitzvah 385

THE RABBI MICHAEL J ELJARRAT LEARNING PROGRAMME – CLASS FIFTY ONE

Challah in practice:

The law of Challah only applies when one is baking bread from flour coming from one of the five species of grain, namely: wheat, barley, spelt, oats and rye. The obligation begins from the time the flour is mixed with the water and dough is formed. Only when one makes enough dough (Measuring an "Omer") is one obligated to separate Challah.

There are several customs regarding the amount of dough needed to encounter an obligation. According to the Noda Bi-Yehudah (Rabbi Ezekiel Landau 1713 – 1793) the amount of flour must be measured by volume, this is also the opinion of the Rambam, however it is customary to rely on weight as well.

The local custom is as follows: (See the Beth-Din Kosher guide)

- If the dough contains less than 2.5 litres, Challah is not seperated.
- If the dough contains between 2.5 – 4.3 litres, Challah is separated but without a Brocha.
- If the dough contains more than 4.3 litres, Challah is separated with a Brocha.

The weight equivalents for the above measurements are as follows:

Cake flour 1.30kg (without a Brocha)	Cake flour 2.35kg (with a Brocha)
White bread flour 1.32kg (without a Brocha)	White bread flour 2.28kg (with a Brocha)
Home ground flour 1.245kg (without a Brocha)	Home ground flour 2.15kg (with a Brocha)
Bought brown flour 1.390kg (without a Brocha)	Bought brown flour 2.4kg (with a Brocha)

Other customs include[3]:

- Russian Jews of pre-war generation[4]: 3 pounds with blessing.
- German Jews of pre war generation: 2.5 pounds without a blessing, 4 pounds with a blessing.
- Jews in England in recent years: 3.5 pounds with a blessing.

The conversion between pounds and kilograms:
Pound divided by 2.2046 = Kg.
Kilogram multiplied by 0.4536 = Pounds.

---

[3]. The Jewish dietary laws – Dyan Dr. I Grunfeld.
[4]. Pre 1939

THE RABBI MICHAEL J ELJARRAT LEARNING PROGRAMME – CLASS FIFTY ONE

The procedure of taking Challah:

Once the dough has been kneaded, and a sufficient amount of dough has been produced to require a blessing;

The following blessing is recited[5]:

"Blessed are you, Hashem, our God king of the universe, who has sanctified us with his commandments, and has commanded us to separate Challah from the dough."

After the blessing is recited the Challah is separated, and then the separated piece of Challah is burnt, since it can no longer be given to a Kohen, due to the fact that Kohanim are in a state of ritual impurity.

The message of Challah:

The Mishna in Bameh Madlikin states:[6]

"For three transgressions women die during childbirth; for being careless regarding the laws of Niddah, Challah and Kindling the Shabbos light"

The commentaries explain that due to the fact that Eve ate from the tree of Knowledge, several curses came to the world, and it is through her special Mitzvos that good can be restored to the world.

One of the curses which befell Mankind was: "By the sweat of your brow, shall you eat your bread". Because of this curse, some are afflicted with the suffering of not having bread to eat. These people are "Weakened".

As the Chinuch explained, bread is the staple diet of Man, and Challah is for those who dedicate themselves to the service of God. Hence the Mitzvah of Challah is there to remind us, that every time we put a piece of bread in our mouths, we must stop and think for a moment:

"Do the people who dedicate themselves to God have what to eat?"

Perhaps the most important time to stop and ask ourselves this question is on Shabbos. While you may be enjoying many delicacies, those who are immersed in the service of God may have nothing to eat. Perhaps it is for this reason that, the loaves of bread which we eat on Shabbos have been nicked-named "Challah".

---

5. See artscroll siddur page 226 – 227
6. Shabbos Chapter 2 Mishna 6

THE RABBI MICHAEL J ELJARRAT LEARNING PROGRAMME – CLASS FIFTY TWO

CLASS 52 — LAWS OF KASHRUS

PAS YISROEL AND CHALAV YISROEL

As we have seen in previous lessons, the nature and quality of food has drastically changed over the last several decades. One of the most noticeable changes can be seen with the staple food, bread. Where as in the past bread was made from simple ingredients, namely flour, water, yeast and salt. Today bread contains dough conditioners, shortenings as well as other additives and preservatives. In the past where simple baking trays were used, today specialized baking trays are used and a variety of releasing agents are also used.

What is Pas Yisroel?

Pas Yisroel (lit. Jewish bread), is bread baked by a Jew. According to Jewish law one is not allowed to eat bread which has been baked by a non-Jew. This law was enacted by the sages to prevent inter-marriage.

The sages prohibited three things in order to prevent assimilation, by limiting the amount of social interaction between Jews and non-Jews. These three things are related to food and eating. The sages felt that by restricting certain foods, Jews and non-Jews would find it difficult to dine together, and thus have limited contact.

The three things will now be briefly explained:

- Pas Akum – Bread baked by a non-Jew
- Bishul Akum – Food cooked by a non-Jew
- Yayin Nesech – The wine of non-Jews (Lit. Shaken wine)

Pas Akum:

The Shulchan Oruch[1] states that bread made from the five grains, which has been baked by a non-Jew, is forbidden to eat. However there are those that are lenient and allow bread baked by a non-Jewish baker, when there is no Jewish baker in the nearby vicinity. (Since the reason for the prohibition was to prevent inter-marriage, and one would not have a social interaction with the baker[2]).

---

1. Y"D 112
2. Bread baked by a commercial non-Jewish baker is not Pas Akum, but Pas Palter- Bread of a baker. No social relationship occurs in the commercial setting.

THE RABBI MICHAEL J ELJARRAT LEARNING PROGRAMME – CLASS FIFTY TWO

The Shulchan Oruch states two main customs:

- Those that forbid Pas Akum – The bread baked in the home of a non-Jew for personal consumption. But allow Pas Palter – The bread baked by a non-Jewish bakery for commercial use, in cases where there is no Pas Yisroel available or when the quality of the Pas Yisroel is inferior to that of the Pas Palter.
- Those that forbid Pas Akum - The bread baked in the home of a non-Jew for personal consumption, and also forbid Pas Palter – The bread baked by a non-Jewish bakery for commercial use.

It is important to note that, even those who are lenient and allow Pas Palter, only do so when the ingredients have been checked to insure that they are kosher, and that all additives which have been added to assist in the baking process are kosher compliant. Needless to say bread which is made from non-kosher ingredients is non-kosher regardless of who bakes it.

Bishul Akum:

There are various laws and customs relating to Bishul Akum - The prohibition of eating food cooked by a non-Jew. The Basic framework of this law revolves around three main principles. The basis of these laws can be found in the Talmud[3].

Any food which fulfils all three criteria may not be eaten by a Jew on account of it being Bishul Akum.

1. Food which has been cooked entirely (from start to finish) by a non-Jew.
2. Food that cannot be eaten raw, and thus requires cooking.
3. Food which is of high enough stature to be presented on the "King's Table".

Any food which does not fulfil all three criteria would in most cases not be subject to the prohibition of Bishul Akum.

For example if a non-Jew were to cook an apple, even though the apple has been fully cooked (fulfilment of criteria 1) and an apple has enough status to be presented on a Kings table (fulfilment of criteria 3), however since an apple can be eaten raw (Hence criteria 2 has not been fulfilled); the apple in question is permissible to eat.

Yayin Nesech:

The laws of Yayin nesech are numerous, and for the purpose of this lesson we will just outline two basic principles.

1. All wine (and grape products) made by non-Jews is forbidden.
2. Wine which has been touched by a non-Jew becomes Yayin Nesech unless the wine is Mevushal[4].

---

3. Avoda Zarah 37b- 38a
4. Yayin Mevushal is wine which has been cooked- Cooking depletes the quality of the wine.

THE RABBI MICHAEL J ELJARRAT LEARNING PROGRAMME – CLASS FIFTY TWO

What is Chalav Yisroel?

Chalav Yisroel (Lit. Jewish milk), is milk which has been milked by or supervised by a Jew. Unlike the three food prohibitions mentioned above (Pas Akum, Bishul Akum and Yayin Nesech) which were made forbidden to prevent inter-marriage, Chalav Akum (The milk of a non-Jew) is forbidden due to the concern that the ingredients placed within the milk may not be Kosher. The sages therefore decreed that milk must be supervised by a Jew to insure that no milk from a non-Kosher animal has been added to the kosher milk.

Supervision versus Knowledge:

Rabbi Moshe Feinstein writes[5] that we find a concept in the Talmud known as "Anan Sehadi" (We are witness) which in the context of our discussion means, that having absolutely clear knowledge about a matter is equivalent to having seen that particular event. This means to say that if we have absolutely clear knowledge that no non-Kosher milk has been added to the kosher milk that is equivalent to having "seen" (or supervised) the milking process and we can therefore say that no non-Kosher milk has been added to the kosher milk in question.

Thus he writes, in places such as the USA where strict control is taken at the dairy, to insure that the milk has not been contaminated with non-Kosher milk, as well as there being forceful penalties for dairies which do not adhere to the local laws and regulations; We can know with absolute certainty that no non-Kosher milk has been added, and it is therefore as if we have "seen" (or supervised) the milking process. Thus the milk of such companies fulfils the requirements of the Sages to supervise the milking.

In short we can say that the milk produced by such dairies, has been "supervised through knowledge".

Geveenas Akum:

Geveenas Akum is the cheese made by a non-Jew. There is a concern that when it comes to cheese made by a non-Jew, especially hard cheese (Since hard cheese requires additives to enable hardening) that the ingredients may not be kosher. The additive which is used in the production of hard cheese is called rennet. Rennet can be found in nature within the stomach lining of young calves. Our main concern is that a non-Jew may have acquired the rennet from a non-Kosher animal thus rendering any cheese produced non-kosher. Thus in order for cheese to be guaranteed as being kosher it must be made by or supervised by a Jew. Today rennet can be produced synthetically therefore the concern is slightly diminished.

5.Igros Moshe Y'D Siman 47

THE RABBI MICHAEL J ELJARRAT LEARNING PROGRAMME – CLASS FIFTY THREE

CLASS 53   PRAYER

MODEH ANI
AND
MORNING BLESSINGS

This lesson starts a new section dealing with prayer and Torah. In the first several lessons we will examine the daily prayers, and explore some of the deeper meanings found in these every day prayers. The lessons dealing with prayer are there to serve a dual purpose:

1. To improve reading and translation skills (used in combination with basic Hebrew skills).
2. To understand what (and why) we are saying when praying.

Reading and translation:

Reading and translating are two skills which are needed in prayer. As we will soon see, the words found in the daily prayers are not random babblings as some think, rather they are powerful tools with powerful abilities.

Reading:

For the best results, I recommend that those who are participating in this course acquire a siddur which has only Hebrew print, and no translations. The print should be large enough, that the nekudos are clearly visible. The best way to improve reading skills is to practise. By revising the Aleph – Beis, the shape of the letters and their sounds as well as the nekudos, their forms and sounds, one should find reading less challenging.

Unfortunately today we have lost the tradition of pronouncing the letters and the nekudos. Subsequently today we find many different pronunciations, all of which are most likely not the way the sages spoke. For more information about the various styles of reading refer to the course on Basic Hebrew Skills.

Translation:

Translation of prayer is not an added bonus, or something which is secondary to prayers. Translation is at the very core of the prayers themselves, since it is impossible to have any intentions, when saying words without knowing their meanings. Translation is the very first step in understanding the meaning of prayer. Once again one could not possibly examine the deeper meanings behind the words, without knowing what the words even mean in the first place. Having a good

THE RABBI MICHAEL J ELJARRAT LEARNING PROGRAMME – CLASS FIFTY THREE

knowledge of the translations, enable one to punctuate the sentences properly and place the emphasis on the correct word. An example of this can be found in the Mariv service, in the sentence found in the first blessing after the Shema.

"With great joy – and they all said"

בשמחה רבה ואמרו כלם

Without translation, one would run these two sentences together, and place the emphasis on the incorrect word. As in any language, reading can either be done in a mono-tone voice with no expression, or with enthusiasm and expression. The reading of prayers is no different one can either read the words in a mono-tone voice without expression, or one can read with enthusiasm and expression. Without translation one may read completely inappropriately; for example by saying happy/joyful prayers in a sad tune/voice and unhappy/solemn prayers in a happy/exciting tune or voice. Not only does this sound foolish, but it also makes a mockery of the prayers.

Understanding the prayers:

When we speak of understanding the prayers, we are referring to; knowing the context of the prayer, why certain words were used and the reason why we say these prayers.

One could view the depth of ones prayers as having three distinct levels:

- Level one: Knowing the translations, and punctuating correctly.
- Level two: Understanding the context of the prayers.
- Level three: Understanding the deep mystical aspects of the prayer.

In the lessons to follow, we will focus mainly on level one and two aspects of prayer and occasionally touch upon the level three aspects of a particular prayer.

We find a verse in the Torah[1] which says "With my sword and with my bow and arrow" The Talmud[2] explains that the sword refers to "Teffila" and the bow and arrow refers to "Bakasha" (Requests). The commentaries explain that there are two kinds of prayer:

1. The fixed prayers – called Teffila which is comparable to a sword.
2. An individual's private talk to God – called Bakasha, which is comparable to a bow and arrow.

The fixed prayers are powerful in their own right, just as a sword is dangerous in its own right. The sharpness of the blade makes the sword a great weapon regardless of ones skills. No matter who picks up the fixed prayer/sword, great results can be accomplished. Ones personal talk to God is like a bow and arrow, just like a bow and arrow are only effective when used with strength and accuracy, so too ones personal talk to God can be powerful when used with deep emotion and sincerity. When fighting the battles of life it's not a question which single weapon is most effective, but rather which weapons are needed in the cavalry. Similarly one should develop the skills in all the weapons, both the sword and the bow and arrow, to successfully win the battles of life.

---

[1]. Bereishis / Genesis 48:22
[2]. Bava Basra 123a

THE RABBI MICHAEL J ELJARRAT LEARNING PROGRAMME – CLASS FIFTY THREE

In the next several lessons I will translate the words of the prayers in the most simplistic way possible. This is done deliberately for the simple reason, that prayers are primarily emotional tools, the more formal the language the less accurate the translation. Many who have translated the siddur have criticised the use of simplistic language used in the translation of prayer, on the grounds that the prayers have deep significance and therefore require formal language. However what they have failed to realize is that the deeper meaning can only be accessed via emotional awareness which can only occur when one can attribute meaning to the very words themselves.

Ones translation of the prayers should be on par with ones general speech, in order to connect emotionally with the words.

> For example: "With abundant gladness – and said unanimously"
> Becomes: "With great joy – and they all said"

Modeh Ani:

"I give thanks, in front of you, King who lives and exists, that you have returned my soul to me with compassion, great is your faith."

The morning blessings:

1. It should be blessed[3] Hashem our God king of the universe, who gave the chicken[4] understanding, to distinguish between day and night.
2. It should be blessed Hashem our God king of the universe, that you didn't make me a Goy.
3. It should be blessed Hashem our God king of the universe, that you didn't make me a slave.
4. It should be blessed Hashem our God king of the universe, that you didn't make me a woman.
5. It should be blessed Hashem our God king of the universe, who gives sight to the blind.
6. It should be blessed Hashem our God king of the universe, who clothes the naked.
7. It should be blessed Hashem our God king of the universe, who unties those that have been bound.
8. It should be blessed Hashem our God king of the universe, who straightens the bent.
9. It should be blessed Hashem our God king of the universe, who spreads out the land on the water.
10. It should be blessed Hashem our God king of the universe, who has made for me everything that I need.
11. It should be blessed Hashem our God king of the universe, who prepares man's footsteps.
12. It should be blessed Hashem our God king of the universe, who girds the Jews with strength.
13. It should be blessed Hashem our God king of the universe, who crowns the Jews with splendour.
14. It should be blessed Hashem our God king of the universe, who gives strength to the weak.
15. It should be blessed Hashem our God king of the universe, who removes sleep from my eyes, and deep sleep from my eye lids.

---

3. See Chayay Odom 6:1
4. Brachos 60b (Rashi)

THE RABBI MICHAEL J ELJARRAT LEARNING PROGRAMME – CLASS FIFTY FOUR

CLASS 54   PRAYER

PESUKEI D'ZIMRAH

In this lesson we will look at the next section of the morning prayers, called Pesukei D'Zimrah (Verses of song). Pesukei D'Zimrah starts with "Baruch She-amar" and ends with "Yishtabach", the verses between "Baruch She-amar" and "Yishtabach", come from Psalms with the exception of "The song of the sea" and "David blessed" which comes from the Torah and Prophets respectively[1]. Since Pesukei D'Zimrah contains many verses we will focus only on the beginning, middle and end. Namely:

- Baruch She-amar
- Ashrei
- Yishtabach

Baruch She-amar:

May he be blessed;
The one who said, and then there was a world, blessed is he.
Blessed (is the one) who makes creation,
Blessed (is the one) who says and does,
Blessed (is the one) to decrees and fulfils,
Blessed (is the one) who has mercy on the land,
Blessed (is the one) who has mercy on the creatures.
Blessed (is the one) who pays rewards to those that fear him.
Blessed (is the one) who lives forever and exists for always.
Blessed (is the one) who redeems and saves.
Blessed is his name.
Blessed are you Hashem, our God, King of the universe;
The God,
The father,
The merciful,
The one who is praised by the mouth of his nation.
Praised and glorified in the speech of his pious and his servants;
And with songs of David your servant, we will praise you Hashem our God, with praises and with songs. We will make you great, and we will praise you, and we will glorify you, and we will mention your name, and we will make you our King.
Our King our God:
You are unique, life of the worlds, King who is praised and glorified, forever his name is great.
Blessed are you Hashem, King who is praised with praises.

---

[1]. There are other sections which do not come from Psalms such as "Hodu" and "Nishmas" on Shabbos and Yomtov.

THE RABBI MICHAEL J ELJARRAT LEARNING PROGRAMME – CLASS FIFTY FOUR

Ashrei:

Praiseworthy are those who live in your house, may they always praise you. Praiseworthy is the nation who is like this to him. Praiseworthy is the nation that Hashem is their God.

Praise by David:

1. I will always lift you up my God the King, and I will bless your name forever.
2. Every day I will bless you, and I will praise your name forever.
3. Great is Hashem, and very praise worthy, and his greatness is beyond comprehension.
4. Each generation will praise your work, and they will speak about your greatness.
5. Beautiful is your majestic honour, and words of your wonder I will speak.
6. And your awesome power, they will speak, and I will tell your greatness.
7. A recollection of your many (kindnesses) good, they will speak, and about your righteousness they will sing.
8. Gracious and merciful is Hashem, slow to anger and great in kindness.
9. Hashem is good to all, and his mercy is on all his creations
10. All your creations will thank you Hashem, and your pious ones will bless you.
11. The honour of your Kingship they will speak about, and of your strength they will tell.
12. To inform people of his strength, and the honour of his majestic Kingship.
13. His Kingship, is a Kingship of all worlds, and his rule is in every generation.
14. Hashem supports all those that have fallen, and straightens all those that are bend.
15. The eyes of everyone, look to you with hope, and you give them their food on time.
16. Open your hand, and satisfy every living desire.
17. Hashem is righteous in all his ways, and pious to all his creatures
18. Hashem is close to all those that call to him, to all those that call him sincerely.
19. The will of those that fear him, he does. And he will listen to their cries and save them.
20. Hashem protects all those who love him, and he will destroy all the wicked people.
21. May my mouth speak Hashem's praises, and may everyone bless his holy name forever.
22. And we will all bless Hashem, from now until forever, praised be Hashem.[2]

---

[2]. The word Halleluya is made up of two words: Hallelu meaning let us praise and Ya meaning Hashem.

THE RABBI MICHAEL J ELJARRAT LEARNING PROGRAMME – CLASS FIFTY FOUR

Yishtabach:

May your name be blessed forever;
Our King,
The God,
The King,
The great
And the holy one, in heaven and in earth.
Because to you its pleasant, Hashem our God,
And the God of our fathers.
Songs and praise,
Praise and song.
Power and domination
Eternity, greatness and strength.
Praise and splendour
Holiness and Kingship.
Blessings and thanks
From now until forever
May you be blessed Hashem,
God,
King,
Great in praises,
God of thanks giving,
Master of wonders
Who chooses musical songs
King,
God,
Life giver of the world.

THE RABBI MICHAEL J ELJARRAT LEARNING PROGRAMME – CLASS FIFTY FIVE

CLASS 55 — PRAYER

SHEMAH AND IT'S BROCHOS

The next section of the morning prayers is the reading of the Shemah and its brochos.[1] This section begins with "Borchu".

Borchu:
Let us bless; Hashem the blessed one. (Chazzan)
Blessed is Hashem, the blessed one, always and forever (Response)

The First Blessing of the Shemah:

"Yotzer Ohr"

Blessed are you Hashem, our God, King of the universe, who forms light and creates darkness, who makes peace, and creates everything.

The one who lights up the land and those that live on it, with mercy. And in his kindness, renews creation, each and every day continuously.

How great are your works Hashem,
You have made all of them with wisdom, the world is filled with your creations,
The King who lives above alone, from before creation.
Who is praiseworthy, and who is splendid, and who is raised since the beginning of time.

God of the world; In your great mercy have mercy on us.
Master of our power, the rock of our strength, shield of our salvation.
Be a stronghold for us.

Blessed God, who is great in wisdom.
Who prepares and works the rays of the sun,
He has formed good for the honour of his name.
He puts lights around his power.

The leaders of his army,
Holy ones, who exalt Hashem, who always tell the holiness and honour of God.

May you Hashem, bless your praiseworthy handiwork.
And the lights that you have made, may they always glorify you (etc)

---

[1]. We will only translate the first paragraph of each section.

THE RABBI MICHAEL J ELJARRAT LEARNING PROGRAMME – CLASS FIFTY FIVE

The Second Blessing of the Shemah:

"Ahavah Rabah"

A great love: You have loved us Hashem our God.
Great and extended compassion; You have been compassionate on us.
Our father, our King.
For the sake of our forefathers, who trusted in you,
And who taught us the laws of life.
So too give to us, and teach us.

Our father, the merciful father, the merciful one,
Have mercy on us, and put into our hearts,
So we can understand and know,
To listen, to learn and to teach.
To protect, to do, and to fulfil,
All the words of your Torah with love.

And stick our hearts onto your Mitzvos,
And focus our hearts, to love and fear your name,
And we should never feel shame. (etc)

The First Paragraph of the Shemah:

"Shemah Yisroel"

Listen all Jews; Hashem is our God, Hashem is one[2].

Blessed is the name of his honoured Kingship for always (In an undertone)

And you should love Hashem your God, with all your heart and with all your soul, and with all your possessions.
And it should be these words that I have commanded you Today;
On your heart.
And you should teach it to your sons, and you should speak about it when you are sitting in your home, and when you are travelling, and when you go to sleep, and wake up.
And you should tie it as a sign on your hand, and as a "Four" between your eyes, and you should write it on the door posts of your house and gates.

---

[2]. All Jews listen to this; YHVH "Hashem" is the God of the Jewish people, not Buddha, not Jesus, not Money, but YHVY- "Hashem" and there is only one Hashem, and don't forget it.

PAGE 2

THE RABBI MICHAEL J ELJARRAT LEARNING PROGRAMME – CLASS FIFTY FIVE

The Blessing after the Shemah: **"Ve-Yatziv"**	And stable, And correct, And existing, And straight, And trustworthy, And loved, And liked, And cherished, And pleasant, And awesome, And powerful, And fixed, And excepted, And good, And beautiful, is this thing forever.

True, God of the universe, our King, the rock of Yakov, the shield of our salvation, for generation after generation.

He exists and his name exists, and his throne is correct, and his Kingship, and his faithfulness exists forever.

And his words are living and existing, trusting and cherished for always and forever.

On our forefathers and on us, and on our children, and on our generation, and on all the generations of your servant "Yisroel" (etc)

THE RABBI MICHAEL J ELJARRAT LEARNING PROGRAMME – CLASS FIFTY SIX

CLASS 56   PRAYER

THE AMIDA/SHEMONEH ESREI

The "Amida" or "Shemoneh Esrei", has these two names based on the nature of the prayer. This prayer is said whilst standing hence the term "Amida" which means standing. This prayer is also called "Shemoneh Esrei" which means eighteen; this is because there are eighteen blessings within this prayer.

The Shemoneh Esrei which consists of eighteen blessings is made of two types of blessings:

1. Praises to God
2. Requests from God

The structure is set out as follows:

- The first three blessings are praises to God
- The next thirteen blessings are requests from God
- The last three blessings are praises to God

Although this brings the total count to nineteen and not eighteen, the original Shemoneh Esrei had just twelve blessings of request. However in the era shortly after the second temple was destroyed, Anti-Semitism rose and observant Jews were under threat from slanderers. It was then that a nineteenth blessing was added; the blessing of "Against Heretics". Although the Amida no longer consists of eighteen blessings, never the less the name "Shemoneh Esrei" remained.

The Shemoneh Esrei is the climax of the prayers; it is a personal conversation with God. The Shemoneh Esrei is said quietly, at a volume which is audible only to one's self. It is absolutely forbidden to make any interruptions while one is praying Shemoneh Esrei, and one who does interrupt has to start again from the beginning.

Our Sages tell us that it is essential for one to have absolute concentration while praying the Shemoneh Esrei, and one who does not have concentration has to repeat the Shemoneh Esrei. However owing to the fact that our concentration abilities have diminished over the years, the minimum requirement is to have concentration on the first three blessings. In this lesson we will look only at the first three blessings.

THE RABBI MICHAEL J ELJARRAT LEARNING PROGRAMME – CLASS FIFTY SIX

Hashem open my lips, and my mouth will tell your praises.

The First Blessing: Blessed are you, Hashem our God, and the God of our Fathers,
Ovos/Fathers: The God of Avraham, the God of Yitzchak and the God of Yakov.

The God, who is great, who is powerful and who is awesome.
God above,
Who bestows good kindness,
And creates everything,
And remembers the kindness of our Forefathers,
And brings redemption to their children's children,

For the sake of his name,
With love.
King (who)
Helps and saves,
And protects like a shield.

Blessed are you Hashem, who protects Avraham.

The Second Blessing: You are strong forever my master,
Gevooros/Strengths: You resurrect the dead,
Abundant ability to save,
You sustain life with kindness,
You resurrect the dead with great mercy,
You support those who have fallen,
You heal the sick,
You untie the bound,
And you keep your faith, with those sleeping in the dust.
Who is like you, owner of strengths
And who can compare to you,
King who gives death and life, and sprouts salvation,
And you are trusted to resurrect the dead,

Blessed are you Hashem, who resurrects the dead.

The Third Blessing: You are unique, and your name is unique,
Kedusha/ Uniqueness And your unique people praise you every day,
Of Gods name:
Blessed are you Hashem, the God who is unique.

THE RABBI MICHAEL J ELJARRAT LEARNING PROGRAMME – CLASS FIFTY SIX

During the repetition of the Amida, a special prayer is inserted in place of the third blessing. This prayer is called "Kedusha" and is said in a dialog format with the Chazzan and congregation responding to one another.

Congregation followed by Chazzan: Your name should be sanctified in the world, just as it is sanctified in heaven.
As it is written by the prophets, and they will call out to one another and say:

All: "Kodosh, Kodosh, Kodosh" Hashem "Tzvaos" the whole world is filled with his honour.

Chazzan: Those (angels) facing then say:

All: Blessed is the honour of Hashem, from his place.

Chazzan: And in the holy writings it is written:

All: "Hashem will rule forever, the God of Tzion, for every generation praised be Hashem"

THE RABBI MICHAEL J ELJARRAT LEARNING PROGRAMME – CLASS FIFTY SEVEN

CLASS 57   PRAYER

TACHANUN

After the Chazzan has completed the repetition of the Amida, we say the prayer called "Tachanun". Tachanun is a prayer where we humble ourselves before God and plead for God's mercy. The Talmud refers to this prayer as "Nefilas Apyim" (Falling on our faces). This prayer is recited with a "Fallen face" meaning we cover our face whilst reciting this prayer.

Tachanun is recited on every week day both at Shacharis and at Mincha. For Kabalistic reasons we cover our faces with our left arm, meaning we place our heads upon our left arm[1] when saying Tachanun. However when saying Tachanun whilst wearing Tefillin, we place our heads upon our right arm instead.

Since Tachanun is a prayer asking for mercy, Tachanun is omitted on days where it is not befitting to ask for mercy; such as on Shabbos and Yomtov. We also omit Tachanun on other days of happiness such as Rosh Chodesh, Purim and Chanukah, as well as several other minor festivals.

Once again since Tachanun is a prayer asking for mercy, the prayer of Tachanun is lengthened on days which are considered merciful; namely Monday and Thursday. At Shacharis on Monday and Thursday the prayer of Tachanun begins at "Ve Hu Rachum" (And he the merciful one). On all other days the prayer of Tachanun begins at "Va Yomer Dovid" (And David said).

Since the prayer of Tachanun starting from "Ve Hu Rachum" (And he the merciful one) is lengthy, we will only translate the Tachanun prayer from "Va Yomer Dovid" (And David said), until the end of the prayer.

The context of this prayer is set; Where King David is informed by the prophet that he has sinned. King David accepts responsibility for his actions, and begins to plead with God for mercy.

We too have sinned and it is befitting for us to plead with God to have mercy on us too. Just as God accepted King David's whole hearted repentance, so too may God forgive us, when we have whole hearted repentance.

---

1. Since the face must be covered, the skin of the arm should not be exposed, as skin covering skin is not considered covered.

THE RABBI MICHAEL J ELJARRAT LEARNING PROGRAMME – CLASS FIFTY SEVEN

Va-Yomer Dovid: **And David Said:**	And David said to Gadd; I am very troubled, May I fall into the hands of God, for he is very merciful, And may I not fall into the hands of Man. Merciful and compassionate one, I have sinned in front of you, Hashem full of mercy, Have mercy on me, and accept my submissive prayer.
Hashem Al Be-Apecha: **Hashem don't rebuke me in your anger**:	Hashem don't rebuke me in your anger, And in your rage, don't make me suffer. Favour me Hashem, because I am weak, Heal me Hashem, because my bones shake, And my soul is very distressed. And you Hashem, until when?! Return Hashem, free my soul, save me, for the sake of your kindness. Because on death, there is no mention of you, In the grave, who will thank you?! I am exhausted from groaning. Every night I wet my bed, With tears I soak my couch, I am wasted, from the anger of my eyes, I've been uprooted, from all my troubles. Leave me alone all evil doers. Because Hashem has heard me crying, Hashem has listened to my plea. Hashem take my prayer, Let all my enemies be embarrassed and weakened, They will regret, and be instantly shamed.

THE RABBI MICHAEL J ELJARRAT LEARNING PROGRAMME – CLASS FIFTY SEVEN

Shomer Yisroel: Protector of the Jews:

Protector of the Jews,
Protect the remainder of the Jews,
And don't let the Jews be destroyed,
Who say:
"Shemah Yisroel"

Protector of the Nation,
Protect the remainder of the nation,
And don't let the one nation be destroyed,
Who unite your name,
(And say)
"Hashem our God, Hashem is one"

Protector of the unique Nation,
Protect the remainder of the unique nation,
And don't let the unique nation be destroyed,
Who triplicate with the three "Kedushos"
(And say)
"Kodosh" (Kodosh, Kodosh, Kodosh)

CLASS 58

PRAYER

MINCHA AND MARIV

In this lesson we will look at the prayers of Mincha (The afternoon prayer) and Mariv (The evening prayer).

The Mincha prayer consists of the following sections:

- Ashrei (The translation of Ashrei was dealt with previously)
- Shemoneh Esrei / Chazzans repetition of Shemoneh Esrei (Dealt with previously)
- Tachanun – On most weekdays (Dealt with previously)

One can daven Mincha from half an hour after midday, all the way until dusk. There are several opinions regarding when the most befitting time to daven is.

The Mariv prayer consists of the following sections:

- Two pre-Shema blessings
- The Shema (Dealt with previously)
- Two post-Shema blessings
- Shemoneh Esrei / There is no Chazzans repetition at Mariv (Dealt with previously)

In this lesson we will look at the two pre and post Shema blessings.

THE RABBI MICHAEL J ELJARRAT LEARNING PROGRAMME – CLASS FIFTY EIGHT

The First Pre-Shema Blessing: **Ha Mariv Arovim: Who Brings Evenings:**	Blessed are you Hashem, our God, King of the universe, Who with his word, brings evenings With wisdom, opens gates, With understanding, changes seasons, and switches the times, And arranges the stars in their constellations in the sky, As he want, He created day and night, he rolls out light before dark, and dark before light, And he passes day, and brings night, And he separates between day and night, "Hashem Tzevaos" is his name, Living and existing God, Always reign over us, forever, Blessed are you Hashem, who brings evenings.
The Second Pre-Shema Blessing: **Ahavas Olam: A Love Forever:**	A love forever, the house of the Jewish nation, you have loved, You have taught us: Torah and Mitzvos, laws and statutes, Therefore, Hashem our God, When we go to sleep and when we wake up, we will talk about your statutes, And we will be happy in the words of your Torah, and your Mitzvos forever, Because they are our life, and the length of our days, And in them we will vocalize day and night, And your love; never take it away from us, Blessed are you Hashem, who loves his Jewish nation.
The First Post-Shema Blessing: **Ve Emunah Kol Zos: And Faithful is all of this:**	And faithful is all of this, and existing for us, For he Hashem is our God, and none other, and we are his Jewish nation, Who redeemed us from the hands of Kings, our King who redeemed us, From the grip of all terrorists, The God who loosens us from our oppressors, and who pays due debt to the haters of our soul, Who does countless wonders, Who placed our soul in life, and did not allow our foot to slip, Who lead us high above our enemies, and lifted our pride over all that hated us, Who did miracles for us, and took revenge on Paroh, Miracles and wonders in the land of Cham, Who; with anger struck all the first born in Egypt, and took out his Jewish nation from them, for a freedom forever, Who; brought his children through the split parts of the Yam Soof, and those who chased them, and hated them, he sunk to the deapths. And his children saw his greatness, and they praised and thanked his name, and they willingly accepted his Kingship, Moshe and the Jewish people, To you they answered in song, with great happiness.

THE RABBI MICHAEL J ELJARRAT LEARNING PROGRAMME – CLASS FIFTY EIGHT

Me Kamo-Cha:
Who is like you:

And they all said:
Who is like you amongst the deities Hashem!
Who is like you, so powerfully unique,
Too awesome to praise,
Who does wonders,

Your children saw your Kingship, as you split the sea in front of Moshe,
This is my God they answered,

And said:
Hashem shall rule forever,

And it says "Because Hashem has redeemed Yakov and delivered him from a hand which is stronger than ours"

Blessed are you Hashem, who redeemed the Jewish people.

The Second Post-Shema Blessing:

Hash-Key-Vaynu:
Lay us down:

Lay us down Hashem our God in peace,
And stand us up our King in life,
And spread the canopy of peace over us,

Set us up with good advise in front of you,
And save us for your names sake,
And build a shield for us,
And take away from us:
Enemies,
Plague,
Sword,
Hunger,
And sadness,
And remove Satan from in front of us and from behind us,
And in the shade of your wings, hide us,
Because you, God, are our protector and saviour,
Because you, God, are merciful and compassionate,

Protect our comings and goings, for life and peace, from now until forever,

Blessed are you Hashem, who protects his Jewish nation forever.

THE RABBI MICHAEL J ELJARRAT LEARNING PROGRAMME – CLASS FIFTY NINE

CLASS 59　　PRAYER

FRIDAY NIGHT SERVICE

As we learnt previously in the laws of Shabbos, the Friday night service begins with "Kabolas Shabbos" (The receiving of Shabbos).

Kabolas Shabbos begins with "Le chu Nerana" (Come let us sing) – Psalm 95 – which praises God for the creation of the world. This is followed by Psalms 96 – 99 and then Psalm 29 followed by the Kabalistic Prayer: "Ono-Bekoach".

This is then followed by the song of "Lecho Dodi".

In this lesson we will look at the song of "Lecho Dodi".

> The song of Lecho Dodi was written by: Shlomo Ha Levy, this being Rabbi Shlomo Ha Levy Alkabetz, The 16th century Kabbalist.

Lecho Dodi[1]: **Come my Dodi:**	Come my Dodi, to greet the bride, Let us welcome the Shabbos presence.
Shomor Ve-Zachor: **Protect and remember:**	Protect and remember were said in one word, The unique God mad us hear, God is one, and his name is one, For identity, for glory and for praise.
Likras Shabbos: **To Welcome Shabbos:**	Let us go and welcome Shabbos, Because it is the source of all blessing, It was distinguished from the beginning of time, Last in action, but first in thought.

---

[1]. The word Dodi means my support, my close friend, my loved one and my relative. In this context Dodi refers to God who is our support, our friend and our relative and our loved one. Since Dodi has a broad meaning we will keep the word "Dodi" without translation.

THE RABBI MICHAEL J ELJARRAT LEARNING PROGRAMME – CLASS FIFTY NINE

Midash Melech: **Sanctity of the King:**	Sanctity of the King, Royal city, Rise up and come out from your turmoil, You have stayed in the valley of crying, for too long, And he will pity you.
Hisna-ari: **Wake me up:**	Wake me up, rise up from the dust, Wear your splendid clothes, my people, Through the hand of the son of Yishai the Lachmi, Come close to my soul, Redeem it.
Hisoreri – Hisoreri: **Stir me –Stir me:**	Stir me, stir me, For your light has come, rise and shine, Wake up, wake up, sing a song, The honour of God, has been revealed to you.
Lo Sayvoyshi: **Don't be embarrassed:**	Don't be embarrassed, and don't be ashamed, Why are you fearful, and why are you downcast, The poor people of my nation will find shelter in you, And the city will be built on a hilltop.
Veha-yoo Limshisa: **And your destroyers:**	And your destroyers, will be destroyed, And those that consumed you, will be far away, Your God will be happy over you, Like a groom is happy over his bride.
Yomin oo Semol: **Right and left:**	You will spread out right and left, And you will frighten, with God, Through the hand of a ben Partzi, And we will be happy and rejoice.
Boi-ee BeShalom: **Come in peace:** (This last stanza is said facing the entrance)	Come in peace, crown of her husband, Also with joy and gladness, Among the faithful of your treasured nation, Come in bride, come in bride.

CLASS 60 — PRAYER

THE AMIDA ON SHABBOS

The prayers on Shabbos are somewhat different from the weekday prayers. Firstly the weekday prayers consist of three prayers, namely; Shacharis, Mincha and Mariv, however the Shabbos prayers consist of an additional forth prayer called "Musaf" (Meaning additional). Secondly the prayers on Shabbos do not consist of the regular eighteen (nineteen) blessings, rather something which is unique to Shabbos. In this lesson we will look at the various additional Shabbos prayers which are inserted into the Amida on Shabbos.

The basic framework of all the Shemoneh Esrei's/ Amida's are the same, meaning that the first three and last three blessings are the same in all Amida's; However the part in between changes according to the nature of the prayer.

Amida on Friday night:

Ato Kidashta: **You Sanctified:**	You sanctified the seventh day for your names sake, the purpose of creating Heaven and Earth, and you blessed it from all other days, and you sanctified it from all other times, and so it is written in your Torah:
Va Yechulu: **And it was finished:**	And the Heavens and Earth were completed, and all the constellations, and Hashem completed the work that he made on the seventh day, and he rested on the seventh day, from all his work that he made. And God blessed the seventh day and he made it holy, because on it he rested from all his work that he created to do.
Elo-Kaynu: **Our God:**	Our God and God of our forefathers, may you want our rest. Make us unique with your Mitzvos, and give us our portion in your Torah, sanctify us with your good, and make us happy with your salvation, and purify our hearts so that we can serve you sincerely, and give us our inheritance Hashem our God, with love and with your holy Shabbos, and we will rest in it, the Jews, the sanctifiers of your name. Blessed are you Hashem, who sanctifies Shabbos.

THE RABBI MICHAEL J ELJARRAT LEARNING PROGRAMME – CLASS SIXTY

Amida on Shabbos day:

Yismach Moshe:
Moshe will rejoice:
Moshe will rejoice in the gift of his portion, because he was called a trustworthy servant. A completing of splendour he placed on his head, when he stood in front of you on mount Sinai. And two stone tablets he brought down in his hands, and it was written on them protect the Shabbos, and so it is written in your Torah:

Veshomru:
And they protected:
And the Jews protected Shabbos, to make Shabbos a contract for generations forever.
Between me and the Jews, a sign forever, that in six days Hashem made the Heaven and the earth, and on the seventh day he rested and returned to spiritual repose.

Ve-lo Nosata:
And he did not give:
And Hashem our God did not give to the nations of the land, and our King did not give as an inheritance to idol worshipers, and also in his rest, the uncircumcised cannot dwell.
Because to the Jews, your nation, you gave with love, to the descendants of Yakov, in which you have chosen.
The nation who sanctifies the seventh (day) all of them will be sanctified, and relax in your goodness, and on the seventh you willed in it and made it holy, chosen of days, you called it, to remember the work of creation.

Elokaynu:
Our God:
See above for translation. Notice the word "BOY" instead of "BOH"

Musaf on Shabbos day:

The Musaf prayer is an additional Amida which we say on Shabbos. The word Musaf means additional. The Musaf prayer is structured like the Amida prayer, with the first three blessings, and the last three blessings being the same as found in the Amida. In this lesson we will not be translating the Musaf prayer as it contains many paragraphs.

THE RABBI MICHAEL J ELJARRAT LEARNING PROGRAMME – CLASS SIXTY

Amida on Shabbos afternoon:

Ato Echod:
You are one:
You are one, and your name is one,
And who is like your Jewish nation, one nation in the land,
Magnificent greatness and a crown of salvation,
A day of rest, and holiness, you gave to your nation.

Avraham would rejoice,
Yitzchak would express emotion,
Yakov and his sons would rest in it.

A rest of love and generosity,
A rest of truth and faith,
A rest of peace and tranquillity,

And serenity,
And trust,
A complete rest that you want in it.

Your children will recognize you,
And they will know that their rest comes from you,
And on their rest, they will sanctify your name.

Elokaynu:
Our God:
See above for translation. Notice the word "BOM" instead of "BOY" or "BOH"

 The Machzor Vitri (138):
States that each of the Shabbos Amida's corresponds to an actual Shabbos in history, therefore each Amida is different.

- The Friday Night Amida – The first Shabbos after creation.
- The Shabbos Morning Amida – The Shabbos that the Torah was given.
- The Musaf Amida – The Shabbos that all the Jews kept together (At Moroh).
- The Shabbos Afternoon Amida – The Shabbos in future when Moshiach comes.

THE RABBI MICHAEL J ELJARRAT LEARNING PROGRAMME – CLASS SIXTY ONE

CLASS 61   PRAYER

ROSH CHODESH AND HALLEL

The Jewish calendar follows the lunar cycle, and therefore the new month occurs when there is a new moon. The first day of the new month[1] is called "Rosh Chodesh" (Lit head month), and is considered to be a minor festival.

The prayers on Rosh Chodesh are unique in the following ways:

- Yale- Ve Yavoh is added into all the Shemoneh Esrei's.
- We say Hallel.
- We read a special Rosh Chodesh portion from the Torah.
- We do Musaf (Since Rosh Chodesh is considered a Yomtov[2]).

In this lesson we will look at the prayer of Yale – Ve Yavoh (Added in the blessing of Avoda), as well as certain sections of Hallel.

Yale Ve Yavoh: **May it go up and come:**	Our God, and God of our Forefathers, May it go up and come, may it reach and be seen, May it be wanted and heard, may it be considered and remembered. The remembrance and consideration of ourselves, And the remembrance of our fathers, And the remembrance of Moshiach the son of Dovid your servant, And the remembrance of Yerusholyim your unique city, And the remembrance of your entire Jewish nation, In front of you, for deliverance, for goodness, for grace, for kindness, for mercy, for life and for peace, **On this day of Rosh Chodesh** Remember us Hashem our God, On it for goodness, And consider us on it for blessing, And save us on it for life, And in the matter of salvation and mercy; Have pity on us and be gracious to us, and have mercy on us, and save us, because our eyes are turned to you, because you are a gracious and compassionate King and God.

---

1. When there are two days Rosh Chodesh the first day is the last day of the old month.
2. For this reason we remove our teffilin before davening Musaf – T'amei Minhagim 446.

THE RABBI MICHAEL J ELJARRAT LEARNING PROGRAMME – CLASS SIXTY ONE

Hallel:

Hallel is said on almost every major and minor festival. On some occasions we say the entire Hallel, and on other occasions we leave out certain paragraphs. When we leave out paragraphs we nickname it "Half Hallel".

The Hallel which is said on Rosh Chodesh is a "Half Hallel". There are various customs regarding the blessing which is made before reading Hallel, some have the custom to say as follows:

"Blessed are you Hashem, our God King of the universe, who has made us unique with his Mitzvos…"

- And commanded us to complete ("Ligmor") the Hallel – When the entire Hallel is said.
- And commanded us to read ("Likroh") the Hallel – When "Half Hallel" is said.

In this lesson we will look at the "Half Hallel"

Halleluka: Praise Hashem:

Praise Hashem,
Give praise servants of Hashem,
Praise the name of Hashem,
May the name of Hashem be praised from now until forever.
From the rising of the sun until it sets, Hashem's name is praised.
Hashem is high above all nations, above heaven is his honour.

Who is like Hashem, who sits high above, who lowers himself to see in heaven and on earth.

He rises the poor from the dust,
He lifts up the destitute from rubbish heaps, to sit with noblemen.
Noblemen of his nation.
He transforms a baron woman, into a happy mother of children.

Halleluka.

B'Tzeis Yisroel: When the Jews went out:

When the Jews went out from Mitzryim,
The house of Yakov from a foreign nation,
Yehuda became his holiness, the Jews his rulers,
The sea saw and ran away,
The Jordan turned backwards,
The mountains jumped like rams,
The hills like sheep,
Why do run away sea?
Jordan that turned backwards?
Mountains that jumped like rams?
Hills like sheep?
In front of the Master did the earth shake,
In front of the God of Yakov,
Who turned a rock into a pond of water,
A flint stone into a flowing fountain.

THE RABBI MICHAEL J ELJARRAT LEARNING PROGRAMME – CLASS SIXTY ONE

Psalm 115 is omitted:

Hashem Zocharanu: Hashem who has remembered us:

Hahsem who has remembered us, will bless,
He will bless the Jews, He will bless the house of Aaron (The Kohanim),
He will bless those that fear God,
The small together with the big,

May Hashem give you more,
You and your children,
You are blessed to Hashem, maker of Heaven and Earth,

The Heaven, Heaven for God,
And the land he gave to Man,

The dead cannot praise God,
And neither can those who have descended into silence,
And we bless Hashem, from now until forever,
Halleluka.

Psalm 116 is omitted:

Moh Oshiv: What can I give back:

What can I give back to Hashem, for all his kindness to me,
I will lift up a cup of salvation, and in the name of Hashem I will call.
I will pay my vows to Hashem, in the presence of his entire nation,
The death of his pious ones is precious in the eyes of Hashem,
Please Hashem, because I am your servant,
I am your servant son of your maid servant,

You have released my bonds,

To you I will sacrifice, a thanksgiving offering,
And in the name of Hashem I will call,
I will pay my vows to Hashem, in front of his entire nation,
In the courtyard of the house of Hashem, in Yerusholyim,
Halleluka,

Hallelu Es Hashem: Praise Hashem:

Praise Hashem, all nations,
Give praise to him all the states,
Because his kindness has overwhelmed us,
And the truth of God forvever,
Halleluka

THE RABBI MICHAEL J ELJARRAT LEARNING PROGRAMME – CLASS SIXTY ONE

- Give thanks to Hashem because he is good – Because his kindness is forever.
- Let the Jews say – Because his kindness is forever.
- Let the house of Arron (Kohanim) say – Because his kindness is forever.
- Let those who fear Hahsem say – Because his kindness is forever.

**Min Ha-Maytzar:
From the confounds:**

From the confounds, I called to you Hashem,
And you answered me with expansiveness,
Hashem is with me, I will not fear,

What can man do for me,
Hashem is with me, with my helpers, and I can see my enemies,
It is better to trust in Hashem than to rely on man,
It is better to trust in Hashem than to rely on noblemen,

All the nations surrounded me, with the name of Hashem I cut them down,
They continuously surrounded me, with the name of Hashem I cut them down,
They surrounded me like bees,
They extinguish, like fire to thorns
With the name of Hashem I cut them down,
I was pushed hard to fall, and Hashem helped me,

Hashem is my strength and I will praise, and he will be my salvation,
The sound of rejoicing and salvation in the tents of Tzadikim,

The right hand of Hahsem, does strength,
The right hand of Hashem, is high above,
The right hand of Hashem, does strength,

I will not die, I will live, and I will tell the works of Hashem,
Hashem has made me suffer, but has not given me over to death,

Open for me the gates of the righteous, I will come through them,
And thank Hashem,
This is the gate to Hashem, the righteous come though them,

-
  These verses are repeated when reading the Hallel.
  - I will thank you, because you answered me, and you are to me a salvation,
  - The rock that the builders despised, was for the corner stone,
  - This was from Hashem, it's a wonder in our eyes,
  - This day did Hashem make, we will rejoice and be happy in it.

**Ono Hashem:
Please Hashem:**
- Please Hashem, save (us) now.
- Please hashem, (give us) success now.

THE RABBI MICHAEL J ELJARRAT LEARNING PROGRAMME – CLASS SIXTY ONE

Baruch Ha-Boh:
Blessed is he who comes:

- Blessed is the one who comes in the name of Hashem, we bless you from the house of Hashem,
- "Kel" Hashem, and he lights up for us, tie the "Chag" with cords, until the corners of the Mizbayach,
- You are my God and I will thank you, my God I will exalt you,
- Give thanks to Hashem because he is good, because his kindness is forever.

Yehaleluchah:
They will praise you:

All your creations will praise you Hashem, our God,
And your pious ones
Righteous ones who do your will,
And the entire Jewish nation,

Will thank you in song,
And they will bless you,
And praise you,
And glorify you,
And exalt you,
And they will fear you,
And they will make you unique,
And their King,

Because to you it is good to thank,
And to your name its pleasant to sing,
Because you are God from world to world,
Blessed are you Hashem, King who is praised with praises.

THE RABBI MICHAEL J ELJARRAT LEARNING PROGRAMME – CLASS SIXTY TWO

CLASS 62   PRAYER

THE THREE REGOLIM-FESTIVALS

The Torah states[1] "Three Regolim you must celebrate for me during the year". The word "Regel" in this context is often translated as "festivals", however the root of this word, stems from the word "foot". The reason why these festivals are linked to the "foot" is owing to the fact that, on these festivals (During the time when the temple stood) there was a special Mitzvah to walk up to the temple and offer sacrifices in honour of the festival, and in honour of the pilgrimage. Hence these festivals are "foot/pilgrimage" festivals.

The three Regolim are:

- Pesach – (Passover) Festival of Matzos – Time of freedom.
- Shavuos – Festival of Bikurim – Time of receiving the Torah.
- Succos – Festival of Succos (Booths) – Time of happiness.

The order of prayer on the festivals is as follows:

- Amida (Special Amida for festivals)
- Hallel (Dealt with previously)
- Musaf (Special Musaf for festivals)

In this lesson we will look at the special Amida which we pray on festivals:

Ato Bechartonu:
You chose us:
You chose us from all the nations,
You loved us, and wanted us,
And you raised us above all the languages,
And you made us unique with your Mitzvos,
And you our King, brought us close to your service,
And you called your great and unique name on us.

---

1. Shemos/Exodus 23:14

THE RABBI MICHAEL J ELJARRAT LEARNING PROGRAMME – CLASS SIXTY TWO

Va Teetain Lanu:
And you gave us:
And you gave us, Hashem our God, with love,
[Shabbos to rest and] Festivals, to be happy,
Festivals, and times to rejoice, this day [of Shabbos and this day of]

On Shabbos we add
[Text]

Festival of **Matzos.**	Festival of **Weeks.**	Festival of **Succos.**	Festival of **Shemini Atzeres.**
Time of our freedom.	Time of giving our Torah.	Time of our happiness.	Time of our happiness. (The last day of Succos is a festival in its own right.)

[With love] called "Holy", to remember the coming out of Egypt.

Elokaynu VeElokay Avosaynu:
(See Yale Ve Yavo prayer in class 61)

VehaseeAnu:
And place on us:
And place on us, Hashem our God,
The blessing of your festival,
For life and for peace,
For happiness and rejoicing,
As you want, and said, to bless us,

[Our God, and God of our Fathers, may you want our rest]
Make us unique with your Mitzvos,
And give us our portion in your Torah,
Satisfy us with your goodness,
And make us happy with your salvation,
And purify our hearts, so that we can serve you sincerely,
And give us our inheritance, Hashem, our God,
[With love and with wanting],
With happiness and with rejoicing,
[Shabbos and] Your unique festivals,
And the Jews who sanctify your name will be happy in it,

Blessed are you Hashem,
Who sanctifies [the Shabbos and] the Jews and the times.

THE RABBI MICHAEL J ELJARRAT LEARNING PROGRAMME – CLASS SIXTY THREE

CLASS 63   PRAYER

ROSH HASHANA

The prayers of Rosh HaShana are unique, and the day is significant and filled with many laws and customs. In this lesson we will focus only on the Amida of Rosh HaShana. We will cover the laws and customs in the section dealing with the Jewish calendar.

Oo Ve Chain:
And so too:

And so too,
Give your fear Hashem our God, onto all your creations,
And your awe onto all that you have created,
And all the works will fear you,
And all the creatures will bow in front of you,
And they will all make one group,
To do your will, with a complete heart,
As we know Hashem, our God,
That Rulership is before you,
Power in your hand, and strength in your right (hand),
And your awesome name upon all that you created.

Oo Ve Chain:
And so too:

And so too,
Give honour Hashem, our God, to your nation,
Praise to those who fear you,
And good hope to those that seek you,
And an open mouth to those that rely on you,
Happiness to your land, and gladness to your city,
And sprouting pride, to King David your servant,
And a prepared light to the son of Yishai,
Your Moshiach, quickly in our days.

Oo Ve Chain:
And so too:

And so too,
The righteous will see and be happy,
And the honest people will uplift you,
And the pious people will rejoice in song,
And evil will shut its mouth,
And all the badness will disappear like smoke,
When you remove, the corrupt authority from the world.

THE RABBI MICHAEL J ELJARRAT LEARNING PROGRAMME – CLASS SIXTY THREE

Ve Timloch: **And Rule:**	And you Hashem will rule alone, over all your creations, On Mount Tzion, the temple of your honour, And in Yerusholyim your "Holy" city, As it is written in your "Holy" words, "Hashem will rule forever, God of Tzion, for every generation, Haleluka"
Kodosh Ato: **You are Kodosh:**	You are "Kodosh"(Unique), and your name is awesome, And there is no God besides you, As it is written "And Hashem Tzvos will rise in judgement" "And the "Holy" God will be sanctified with charity" Blessed are you Hashem, the Kodosh King.
Ato Bechartonu: **You chose us:**	You chose us from all the other nations, You loved us, and wanted us, And raised us above all the other languages, And you brought us close to your service, And your great and "Holy" name you called on us.
Va TeTain: **And you gave:** On Shabbos add [Text]	And you gave us Hashem, our God, with love, This day of [Shabbos and this day] of remembrance, Day of Shofar blowing [remembrance of Shofar blowing], [With love] called "Holy", to remember the coming out of Egypt.
Yale Veyavo:	(see class 61 for a translation of Yale Veyavo)
Elokaynu: **Our God:**	Our God, and God of our Fathers, Rule over the entire world with your honour, And rise above the entire land with your uniqueness, And reveal yourself, in your mighty strength, over the inhabitants of the entire world, And every creature will know that that you created it, And every form will know that you formed it, And everything with a soul in its mouth will say, Hashem, God of the Jews is King, and his reign is over everything,

[Our God, and God of our fathers, want our rest]
Make us unique in your Mitzvos,
And give us our portion in your Torah,
Satisfy us with your goodness, and make us happy with your salvation,
[And give us our inheritance, Hashem, our God, with love and desire, your "Holy"
Shabbos, and we will rest in it, the Jewish people, who sanctify your name],
And purify our hearts, to serve you sincerely,
Because you Hashem are sincere and honest,
And your word is sincere, and lasts forever,

Blessed are you Hashem, King of the entire world,
Who sanctifies [the Shabbos and] the Jewish people, and this day of Remembrance.

THE RABBI MICHAEL J ELJARRAT LEARNING PROGRAMME – CLASS SIXTY FOUR

CLASS 64   PRAYER

YOM KIPPUR

The prayers on Yom Kippur are both intense and lengthily, as well as being unique to the day. Yom Kippur is the only day in the year where we pray five Amidos, namely;

1. Mariv
2. Shacharis
3. Musaf
4. Mincha
5. Ne-ela

The significance of the day, as well as the laws and customs, will be dealt with in the section on the Jewish calendar. In this lesson we will focus only on the Amida which is said at Mariv, Shacharis and Mincha.

Oo Ve-Chain – Chanun Ve-Rachum Ato:	See class 63 (Prayer Rosh Ha-Shana)
And so too – You are gracious and merciful:	(The first several paragraphs are identical for both Rosh HaShana and Yom Kippur)
Elokaynu: **Our God:**	Our God, and God of our fathers, Forgive our sins on this day [of Shabbos and on this day] Of Yom Kippur
On Shabbos add [Text]	Erase and remove our sins (done willingly), And our sins (done by mistake), From in front of your eyes,

As it says:

"I and (only) I, am the one who erases your sins (done willingly) for my own sake, and your mistakes I will not remember"

And it says:

"I have erased your sins (done willingly) like a thick cloud, and your mistakes like a (thin) cloud, return to me because I have redeemed you."

And it says:

"Because on this day, he will atone for you, to purify you from all your mistakes, in front of Hashem you will be purified."

THE RABBI MICHAEL J ELJARRAT LEARNING PROGRAMME – CLASS SIXTY FOUR

[Our God and God of our fathers, may you want our rest]
Make us unique with your Mitzvos,
And give us our portion in your Torah,
Make us satisfied with your goodness,
And make us happy with your salvation,
[And give us our inheritance Hashem our God, with love and willingly, your "Holy" Shabbos and the Jews will rest in it, which sanctify your name.]
And purify our hearts, so we can serve you sincerely,
Because you are the forgiver of the Jews,
And the one who pardons the "Shiftey Yeshoroon[1]"
In every generation,
And apart from you, we have no other King,
Who forgives and pardons, except you,

Blessed are you Hashem,
King, who forgives and pardons
Our sins (done willingly),
And the sins (done willingly) of his Jewish nation,
And removes our sins (done in doubt) each and every year,
King of all the land,
Who sanctifies [The Shabbos and],
The Jewish people, and the day of Yom Kippur.

---

1. The Jewish people in their highest state.

PAGE 2

CLASS 65   PRAYER

CHANUKAH AND PURIM

Both Chanukah and Purim are minor festivals, which celebrate miracles which occurred in history.

Chanukah celebrates the miracle which took place in the time where the Greek empire oppressed the Jewish people, in an attempt to force the Jewish people to give up the Torah way of life, and adopt the Greek philosophy.

 However a group of Sages fought against the Greek oppression, and through their uprising were able to preserve the Jewish way of life. In addition during this time, all the oil for the temple was contaminated; all but one jug, which was found with its original seal untouched.

A miracle took place and the one jug of oil, which would have usually lasted for just one day, instead lasted for eight days.

For more details on the laws, customs and significance of Chanukah, see the section on the Jewish calendar.

 Purim celebrates the miracle which took place in the city of "Shushan" (modern day Iraq) in the era between the destruction of the first temple and the rebuilding of the second temple.

During this time, a dictator arose by the name of "Haman". Haman wanted to eradicate the Jewish nation from the world, and had plans to execute men, women and children on one day.

However through miraculous twists of events which transpired, the Jewish people were saved, and Haman was executed on the very day he had planned to annihilate the Jews.

For more details on the laws, customs and significance of Purim, see the section on the Jewish calendar.

On Chanukah and Purim we add the prayer of "Al HaNisim" (For the miracles), into the Amida, in all three services (Shacharis, Mincha and Mariv).

THE RABBI MICHAEL J ELJARRAT LEARNING PROGRAMME – CLASS SIXTY FIVE

On Chanukah we add:

Bee-May Matisyahu:
In the days of
Matisyahu:

In the days of Matisyahu the son of Yochanan, the Kohen Gadol,
The Hasmonian and his sons,
When the evil Greek rule stood up against your Jewish nation,
To make them forget the Torah,
And to remove them from the laws that you desire,
And you in your great mercy, stood up for them in their time of trouble,
You fought their fight, You took up their judgment,
And you took their revenge,

You handed the strong into the hands of the weak,
The many into the hands of the few,
The impure into the hands of the pure,
And the wicked into the hands of the righteous,
And the rebels into the hands of those who were involved in your Torah,

And to you they made a great and holy name in your world,
And to your Jewish nation, you made a great salvation,
And a great redemption, like this day,

And afterwards, your sons came into your special home,
And they cleared out your temple, and they purified your holy site,
And they lit lights in your holy courtyard,
And they fixed these eight days of Chanukah,
To give thanks and praise to your great name.

On Purim we add:

Bee-May Mordechai:
In the days of
Mordechai:

In the days of Mordechai and Ester in the capital of Shushan,
When the wicked Haman stood up against them,
He requested to destroy, kill and eradicate all the Jews,
Young and old, women and children on one day,
On the thirteenth day of the twelfth month,
Which is the month of Adar,
And to cease all their possessions,

And you in your great mercy, annulled his advise,
And ruined his thoughts,
And you returned to him that which was due, on to his head,
And they hung him and his sons on the tree.

THE RABBI MICHAEL J ELJARRAT LEARNING PROGRAMME – CLASS SIXTY SIX

CLASS 66   PRAYER

BROCHOS ON FOODS AND EVENTS

In this lesson we will look at the various blessings which are made on foods, Mitzvos and events.

In general there are three types of blessings:
- Birckas Ha NeNin (Blessings on things we have benefit from – such as food)
- Birckas Ha Shevach (Blessings that we praise Hashem for – such as on thunder)
- Birckas Ha Mitzvos (Blessings over Mitzvos – such as blowing the shofar)

Birckas Ha NeNin: (Blessings of benefit)

Birckas Ha NeNin, are those blessings which me make, which allow us to have benefit from this world. As the commentaries explain:
One verse says "To God is the land and all it occupies"[1]
And yet another verse says "The heavens are God's and the land is given to man"[2]

Thus posing the question: Is the land God's or Man's?

The commentaries answer that, there is no contradiction. Before Man makes a blessing the land and all that is on it belongs to God, however after Man has made a blessing, God gives the land to Man.

From here we see that it is forbidden to have benefit from the world without first making a blessing.

The blessing can be likened to 'Asking permission", meaning God is the "owner" of the world and if we want to take something for ourselves, we must first ask for it.

Birckas Ha NeNin include (but are not limited to) the blessings over food; namely:

- "Ha Motzei" – The blessing which is made on bread.
- "Ha Goffen" – The blessing which is made on wine.
- "Mezonos" – The blessing which is made on cakes and pastries.
- "Ha Eitz" – The blessing which is made on fruits (of the tree)
- "Ha Adama" – The blessing which is made on vegetables (of the land)
- "Shehakol" – The blessing which is made on all other foods (such as meat, fish, eggs)

---

1. Psalms 24
2. Psalms 116

PAGE 1

THE RABBI MICHAEL J ELJARRAT LEARNING PROGRAMME – CLASS SIXTY SIX

The six blessings over food mentioned above are listed in order of priority. Therefore if one has an assortment of foods in front of him/her, one should make the blessing higher up on the list.

There are several exceptions to the above rule, two common applications are:

- If one is eating bread, then one makes a blessing over the bread ("Ha Motzei") after which no further food blessings are required at the meal.
- If one has a preference for a particular food, one can make the appropriate blessing and eat that food even though its blessing is lower on the list than other foods in front of him/her.

Eikar and Tofel:

In general, when one is eating a food which contains two or more foods; for example a cracker with jam, the blessing is made over that food item which is Eikar (Primary) i.e. the cracker and not over that item of food which is Tofel (Secondary) i.e. the jam.

The laws relating to blessings over food are extensive and will be dealt with further in an advanced course.

Birckas Ha Shevach: (Blessings of praise)

Birckas Ha Shevach, are those blessings which we make upon encountering special event, for which we praise God in acknowledgment of God's greatness.

Some examples include: (in no particular order)

- "Oseh Masei Bereishis" (Who makes the work of creation) – said upon seeing lightening.
- "She Kocho oo Gevoroso Molei Olom" (Who's strength and might fill the world) – said upon hearing thunder.
- "She osoh es ha Yam ha Godol" (Who made the Great sea) – said upon seeing the ocean.
- "She Kocho Lo BeOlomo" (Who has such in his world) – said upon seeing beautiful people, trees or fields.
- "Meshaneh HaBreos" (Who changes creatures) – said upon seeing strange looking people or animals.
- "She Nosan MeChochmoso Le Bosor VeDam" (Who gave from his wisdom to human beings) – said upon seeing an outstanding intellectual genius.

These blessings are made upon the first encounter, and are not repeated until a new encounter has occurred. For example when one sees the ocean for the first time, one will make the blessing of "She osoh es ha Yam ha Godol", one would then not be obligated to recite this blessing until 30 days have past without seeing the ocean. After 30 days have past, an encounter with the ocean will be deemed a new experience.

THE RABBI MICHAEL J ELJARRAT LEARNING PROGRAMME – CLASS SIXTY SIX

Birckas Ha Mitzvos: (Blessings on Mitzvos)

Birckas Ha Mitzvos, are those blessings which we recite prior to fulfilling a Mitzvah.

Some examples include:

- "Le HoNeach Tefillin" (To place Tefillin) – said upon the Mitzvah of Tefillin.
- "Likboah Mezuzah" (To affix a Mezuzah) – said upon the Mitzvah of Mezuzah.
- "Al Mitzvas Tzitzis" (On the Mitzvah of Tzitzis) – said upon the Mitzvah of Tzitzis.
- "Likroh es ha Megilah" (To read the Megilah) – said upon the Mitzvah of reading the Megilah.
- "Lishmoah Kol Shofar" (To hear the sound of the Shofar) – said upon the Mitzvah of Shofar.
- "Al Netilas Lulav" (On taking the Lulav) – said upon the Mitzvah of Lulav (and the other of the four species)

When it comes to making blessings over Mitzvos, the general rule is; that the blessing is made "Over Le Asioson" meaning prior to their performance.

For example when one is going to perform the Mitzvah of shaking the four species on Succos, one would first make the blessing of "Al Netilas Lulav" and perform the Mitzvah of shaking.

THE RABBI MICHAEL J ELJARRAT LEARNING PROGRAMME – CLASS SIXTY SEVEN

CLASS 67

TORAH

THE WRITTEN AND ORAL TORAH

In the next several lessons we will explore some of the unique perspectives of the Torah, and some of the common every day Mitzvos. The goal of this section entitled: "Fundamentals of Torah" is for us to gain a love and appreciation for Hashem, the Torah and the unique way in which the Torah helps us to draw closer to Hashem.

The Sefer Ha Yoshor[1] explains that a person's desires and actions are a reflection of their personality.
"Every desire testifies about the one with the desire, and every action sums up the one who performed the action."
This means as follows:
We have all heard the saying "actions speak louder than words"

If we look at the nature of social interactions; they can be broken down into three distinct parts namely;
- Thought
- Speech
- Actions

When we see any of these three elements, we gain an understanding of the person performing that particular element.

Put very simply, if I were to see a man giving charity, I could infer that, that particular man is kind.

1.

But what could I infer, if that man were to merely say that he would give charity?

2.

Could I infer anything at all, if that man were only to think of giving charity?

3.

---
1. Chapter 1

THE RABBI MICHAEL J ELJARRAT LEARNING PROGRAMME – CLASS SIXTY SEVEN

Not being a mind reader, I would have to say that through speech and thought alone I could not possibly infer anything.

It now seems clear why "actions speak louder than words". Actions give a far greater scope of inferable conclusions, than any of the other elements.

Think of the following example: Barry is a postman, earning a very simple salary, and Steven is a destitute beggar and a close friend of Barry's. Barry would love to help his friend Steven, financially, but can barely "make end meet" himself.

Question: Is Barry a kind man?

Based upon what we have said up until now, we could say the following:

- If Barry were merely to think about helping his friend Steven, only he and God would know that he is kind.
- If Barry were to speak about his intentions to help his friend Steven, then he, God and those close to Barry would know that he is kind.
- If Barry were to act upon his intentions, and give to his friend Steven, then it would be clear for all to see that Barry is a kind man.

When we consider Barry's circumstances, and his own financial predicament, it would seem highly unlikely that Barry will give anything to Steven, despite his noble intentions. Therefore only Barry and God would ever know that Barry is in actual fact a kind person.

Or so it would seem.

This is the novel idea, of the Sefer Ha Yoshor; that knowing someone's desires is akin to being a "mind reader". By knowing what Barry wants, we can infer qualities of his personality, long before it becomes apparent to all.

Let us examine this concept further:

We have already said that the desire to give reflects the trait of kindness.
Other desires include:
- The desire for theft – reflects the trait of greed.
- The desire for honour – reflects the trait of arrogance.
- The desire to hurt others – reflects the traits of anger, hate and others.

The Sefer Ha Yoshor continues to say: That out of all the possible desires, which may be displayed;

The desire which reflects one's intelligence is one's desire to draw closer to God. True intelligence is marked by the desire to serve God.

The Sefer Ha Yoshor explains why this is so:

The Human intellect can only comprehend two broad fields of study:

1. The Creator
2. The Created

THE RABBI MICHAEL J ELJARRAT LEARNING PROGRAMME – CLASS SIXTY SEVEN

Let us analyse this statement:

There are various fields of study available in the academic context:

- Humanities – such as Philosophy, Religion
- Social sciences – such as Psychology, Sociology
- Natural sciences – such as Chemistry, Physics
- Formal sciences – such as Mathematics, Statistics
- Professions and Applied sciences – such as Engineering, Law

Think of the following example: You are at a social event, and you meet two new people:
1. A Street cleaner
2. A Physics lecturer

Based upon first impressions alone, which would you say is the more intelligent of the two?

You most likely said the Physics lecturer. The question is why?
You know absolutely nothing about either one of them, other than what they do.

The answer to this question is: Since you know that the "Action" of Physics lecturing requires more intelligence, than the "Action" of Street cleaning, you will be basing your opinion on observable "Actions".

Now what if the two people that you met at the social event were:

1. A Mathematics lecturer
2. A Physics lecturer

Based upon first impressions alone, which would you say is the more intelligent of the two?

You most likely would not be able to say with any certainty, which individual is more intelligent, since the "Actions" of the two, both require high levels of intelligence.

Since "Actions" in this case do not reflect much, any inference which we draw must be from "Speech" and "Thought", hence when these individuals begin to speak we will be able to infer with greater certainty.

But once again, not being a mind reader, how could we possibly know?

The answer to this question is: We need to examine the desires of these individuals to gain a full perspective, and more specifically their desire for knowledge. We can conclude that the individual with the greatest desire for knowledge is the one who is most intelligent.

In the same way as the desire to give reflects the trait of kindness so too, the desire for knowledge reflects a healthy active mind thirty for utilization. This mind can therefore be called an intelligent mind.

THE RABBI MICHAEL J ELJARRAT LEARNING PROGRAMME – CLASS SIXTY SEVEN

 The question now turns to: Which knowledge is the broadest and requires the most utilization of the mind?

The answer to this question: Based on the fact that all knowledge can be broken down into two broad fields namely;

1. The Creator
2. The Created

Studies in the field of the "Created" are finite and limited in their nature; however studies in the field of the "Creator" are infinite, as the "Creator" himself. Thus the study of the "Creator" is the broadest spectrum knowledge that is available to Mankind.

Through further analytical reasoning, and by default may therefore conclude that the desire for knowledge of the "Creator" (i.e. the desire to know everything about everything) infers the greatest intelligence. Hence those with the desire to "Know the Creator" are the most intelligent people.

The connection between Torah and Hashem:

- So how well do you know God?
- How often do you speak to God?
- Have you ever met God?

If one really has the desire to "Know God", then these questions are important questions to have answered.

To phrase this slightly differently, let us ask the following questions about your best friend.

- What is their name?
- Where do they stay?
- How often do you speak to them?
- How often do you meet?

When one has a sincere desire to know God, then one searches for empirical evidence, and displaces myth with fact and fantasy with knowledge.

Before we proceed further let us look at the following concept:

The first letter of the Aleph – Beis is "Aleph"

Spelled: אלף The Aleph has the numerical value of 1, and is symbolic of simplicity.
The word: פלא (The 3 letters of the Aleph placed backwards) means wonder or miracle.

The letters of the Aleph – Beis are divided into 5 categories of vocal pronunciation (See course on Basic Hebrew Skills)

THE RABBI MICHAEL J ELJARRAT LEARNING PROGRAMME – CLASS SIXTY SEVEN

The letters of the Aleph have the following vocal pronunciation:

- Aleph א Guttural sound – Vocalized by the throat.
- Lamed ל Lingual sound – Vocalized by the tongue
- Peh פ Labial sound – Vocalized by the lips

The lips are external, the tongue is internal and the throat is deeply internal. The Sefer Yitzira explains, that when one views objects, people and life itself in a simplistic way, one only sees an external superficial view, to see the wonders however one needs to look deeply, past the superficial into the further depths of understanding.

To know something means to examine it from all sides and perspectives, to turn it inside out and upside down. An individual; who takes his/her surroundings (Including objects, people and life itself) at face value, is indeed extremely far from wisdom.

The Torah:

If one wants to know about God, it would be wise to look at the book which God wrote, namely the Torah. On a superficial level the Torah appears to be a narrative of the lives of Adam and Eve, Avraham, Moses and others. A simple translation leaves the reader misinformed and greatly lacking in the knowledge of God. This would be the outcome of superficial learning of the Written Torah. To unlock the miracles and wonders of the Torah, one needs to plumb the depths of the Torah, and this can only be accomplished by the study of the Oral Torah. If one wants knowledge of God, one has to study and understand all the facets of the Torah.

People:

Similarly if one wants to know a person, a superficial understanding is far from knowledge. To truly know somebody is to plumb the depths of their personality, to know all the facets about them. Once we have knowledge of all these details can we claim to "know them".

THE RABBI MICHAEL J ELJARRAT LEARNING PROGRAMME – CLASS SIXTY EIGHT

CLASS 68   TORAH

THE IMPORTANCE OF FIXING A TIME TO STUDY TORAH

In this lesson we will look at the importance of Torah study, and more specifically the importance of fixing a time for Torah Study.

The Mishna in Ovos says:

"Shamai says: Make your Torah study a fixed practice"[1]
"Hillel says: Do not say when I am free I will study, for perhaps you will not become free"[2]

The Chayai Odom says[3]:

- It is a positive commandment to learn Torah.
- Regardless of ones status, every man is obligated to learn Torah.
- Learning Torah is equivalent to all the Mitzvos.

The definition of learning:

How do we define learning? It would seem relatively simple to define learning as:

"The cognitive process of acquiring skill or knowledge"[4]

Cognitive process: This implies that it is a thoughtful act, requiring thoughtful interactions.
Acquiring skill or knowledge: This implies that this process will lead to the development of a skill or knowledge.

The definition of learning Torah is the same. Unlike the popular misconception, learning Torah is NOT a mind numbing activity, consisting of incoherent ramblings, and being the pass time for incompetent individuals. Learning Torah by definition must engage the mind and require interactive input. Sleeping in a Shiur, sitting in a vegetative state next to one who is learning and mindless flipping of pages are not forms of learning!

---

1. Chapter 1 Mishna 15
2. Chapter 2 Mishna 5
3. Klal 10 (see there for laws of Torah study)
4. Web definition of learning.

Secondly a skill or knowledge must be acquired during the process of learning.
The skill can be "Learning how to learn" and knowledge can even include "an appreciation for the content".

However pointless discussions, non-structured waffling and illogical debates do not assist in building knowledge or in skill acquisition.

Learning Torah; is the occupation of those who are sincere in their Judaism, and have the intellectual capacity to contend with post formal thought processes.

The difference between learning Torah and learning other "Subjects":

There is one fundamental difference between learning Torah and learning other "subjects". Since Torah is the work of God himself, the mere effort taken in engaging in learning, brings one to a higher state of spiritual purity.

Thus unlike other "subjects" where one studies to obtain a specific result, (example: for an exam, furthering ones career etc.) learning Torah can be done purely for the sake of learning itself. Hence one studies to involve oneself in the work of God.

Since the process of learning requires effort, this effort builds spiritual strength, in a similar way that weight training builds muscle strength. The heavier the weight, and the more time spent exercising the stronger the individual will become.

Unfortunately due to the long exile, (which has suppressed honest values in the world today) Torah Scholars have had to "excuse" themselves for studying Torah, by justifying their learning as "Studying to become a Rabbi" or other such "excuses". The truth of the matter is studying Torah for its own sake, is the most noble and worthy cause.

As the Midrash[5] states:

> "You won't find Oral Torah…..Except by one who "kills himself" for it".

The greatness of Torah study:

It is written in the Sefer: Ma-alos HaTorah[6], that the 613 Mitzvos, that we refer to are not a sum total of all the Mitzvos in the Torah, rather these are just the "roots". The sum total of all the Mitzvos in the Torah would be in the range of hundreds of millions, and perhaps even much more. He explains how this idea works:

Using an analogy of a tree: Every tree has roots that lead to its' trunk. The trunk itself splits into branches, and the branches into even smaller branches. These small branches lead to a fruit. The fruit itself contains seeds which have the ability to produce another tree with its own, roots, trunk, branches and fruit, Ad infinitum.

---
5. Midrash Tanchuma – Parshas Noach.
6. Written by the brother of the Vilna Gaon.

THE RABBI MICHAEL J ELJARRAT LEARNING PROGRAMME – CLASS SIXTY EIGHT

The 613 Mitzvos that we speak of are likened to the roots of the tree. Each Mitzvah branches out and contains an infinite number of Mitzvos.

For example the Mitzvah of studying Torah is mentioned in the Torah approximately 30 times, in Nach[7] approximately another 20 times. Each time it is written in the works of the commentaries, this number increases.

Furthermore when the commentators, write on the commentaries yet another branch is created.

Even this very writing, which you are reading which speaks of the Mitzvah of Torah study is yet another branch in the hundreds of times that the Mitzvah of Torah study is spoken of in Jewish literature.

Hence every time one learns Torah, one is really fulfilling each and every source that speaks of learning Torah. So too when we do any Mitzvah, we are in fact lighting up all the "branches" connected and associated with that particular Mitzvah.

The Mitzvah of Tefillin:	Mitzvah itself X number of sources 1 x 30* = 30 Mitzvos	*For illustration purposes
The Mitzvah of Lulav	Mitzvah itself X number of sources 1 x 30* = 30 Mitzvos	

The Vilna Gaon himself explains, that Torah study unlike other Mitzvos is done in "bulk" That means to say that when one shakes the Lulav for example one is doing one Mitzvah per session.

However when one sits down to learn Torah, each and every word is a Mitzvah in its own right. In one session even if one studies just a small paragraph it's bound to contain at least 20 words. Hence Torah study produces the most Mitzvos per session.

The calculation:

When one combines the idea of the Vilna Gaon, together with the idea of the Vilna Gaon's brother, one can make the following calculation:

$$M = \Sigma (ns)$$

- M - Mitzvos.
- n - Number of words studied
- s - Sources referring to Torah study.

If we were to assume that the number of sources, referring to Torah study in Jewish literature were 1000, then every word of Torah study is equal to 1000 Mitzvos. If one could study on average 1000 words per session then:

$$M = \Sigma (ns)$$
$$M = (1000 \times 1000)$$
$$M = 1,000,000 \text{ (One million Mitzvos per session)}$$

Thus proving that; Torah study is the greatest of all the Mitzvos. It is incumbent upon us to use our time productively, and involve ourselves in the greatest of all Mitzvos.

---

[7]. Neveim - Prophets and Kesuvim – Writings

THE RABBI MICHAEL J ELJARRAT LEARNING PROGRAMME – CLASS SIXTY NINE

CLASS 69   TORAH

HOW HALACHAH IS DECIDED

In this lesson we will look at how Halachah is decided. We will explore some of the history behind the writing of the oral Torah and examine the different types of actions that we perform.

The essence of being a Jew is dedicating ones life to the service of God. Serving God is not a way of doing; rather it's a way of being. That means to say, that the actions that one does as a Jew are only effective when ones intentions are to draw closer to God.

As the Ramban says[1], it is possible for one to keep every Mitzvah in the Torah and yet be void of all spirituality. It goes without saying that one who performs Mitzvos, but does not believe in God, is performing meaningless actions.

Had God not given us the Torah, we would be at a loss as how to "serve" or draw close to God. Without the Torah how could we possibly know, what to do with ourselves? We would simply live an animalistic life, scavenging for food and tending to our bodily functions.

With the Torah on the other hand, Man can be more than a glorified animal. Man can be involved in a spiritual quest, trying to draw close to God.

The Torah guides Mankind in the thoughts, speech and actions which bring perfection and closeness to God. As we saw previously the Torah consists of two distinctive components; the written Torah consisting of 24 books, and the oral Torah, the key which is used to unlock the written Torah.

When the Torah was first given, it was taught thoroughly to all the Jews. At that point in history each and every Jew had a clear understanding, what was expected of him/her in terms their obligations and duties. They knew exactly what to do in order to draw close to God.

The body of knowledge or the science dealing with, "knowing what God wants", and deriving that knowledge from the written Torah, is referred to as the oral Torah. The oral Torah decrypts the cryptic message of the written Torah, and transforms the written Torah into a workable user manual. Without the oral Torah (the key) the written Torah is inaccessible.

---

1. Vayikra / Leviticus 19:2

THE RABBI MICHAEL J ELJARRAT LEARNING PROGRAMME – CLASS SIXTY NINE

The oral Torah was taught to every subsequent generation from father to son, as is commanded in the written Torah[2] "And you shall teach your sons". This method proved to be effective, however only several generations later; the Jewish people had strayed from God, and were influenced by cultures foreign to Jewish thinking.

Through out the earlier part of Jewish history, prophets arose who would encourage the Jewish people to observe and maintain the Torah. Some of the prophets were successful, and brought renewed interest in the service of God. Other prophets were less successful, and were unable to change the Jewish nation. During one of the lowest moments in Jewish history, the Jewish people killed one of their own prophets in order to continue unabated in their wrong ways.

Due to the many persecutions, exiles and holocausts that the Jewish nation faced, families were broken up, communities were broken up and the Jewish nation became scattered. Approximately 2000 years ago, the situation became critical, and losing the oral Torah became a stark reality. In an unprecedented situation, a decision was made by the sages of the time; to write down the oral Torah, so that it would not be lost forever. Work soon began writing down the Mishna. (This task was performed by Rebbe Yehudah Ha Nassi)

The Mishna was written in a very concise fashion, and contained the outline for Jewish law. Some time later the Gemorrah was written, which was written in a more elaborate fashion. The Gemorrah contained debates and reasoning, and served to clarify the laws which were stated in the Mishna.

By the time the Gemorrah was completed, the already fragile Jewish nation suffered one of the biggest calamities ever faced by a nation. Namely: The destruction of the second temple. When the second temple was destroyed many hundreds of thousands of Jews were killed. The remaining Jews fled to various parts of the world. For the first time since the giving of the Torah, the Jewish nation was left orphaned without "a father" as God went into "hiding".

Pockets of Jews formed communities in various parts of the world. Each community tried to re-establish Jewish life, and the preservation of the oral Torah. Where ever Jews formed communities they built Shuls and Schools as soon as they were able to.

In some parts of the world communities flourished, and were home to brilliant Torah minds, others were not so fortunate and were continuously persecuted by their hostile neighbours.

Approximately 500 years ago the Jewish people faced yet another dilemma. Owning books had always been a privilege had by very few, until that point in time. However a need arose to have a "Code of Jewish Law" for the layman to grasp. For centuries there had always been many opinions regarding Halachah, and various commentaries wrote responses trying to encapsulate the reasoning's and practical Halachah. One of the most famous works was that of the Rambam (Miamonidies) with his work entitled "Yad Ha Chazakah" (The strong hand) which aimed at giving a guide for practical Halachah in a clear and concise manner. The Yad Ha Chazakah covers all areas of Jewish law and spans across the entire framework of Judaism.

In the 16th century the code of Jewish law named the "Shulchan Aruch" was published. This work was the biggest undertaking since the Yad Ha Chazakah written approximately 500 years earlier.

---

2. Devarim / Deuteronomy 6:7

THE RABBI MICHAEL J ELJARRAT LEARNING PROGRAMME – CLASS SIXTY NINE

The Author of the Shulchan Aruch was Rabbi Yosef Karo, and the laws found within generally follow the Sefardic customs.

Alongside the Shulchan Aruch you will find the works of the R'MA (Rabbi Moshe Isserlis) whose laws generally follow the Ashkenazic customs.

In the 18th century other even more concise books on Halachah were published. Such as the "Chayai Odom" written by Rabbi Avraham Dansig, and more recently the "Mishna Berura" written by Rabbi Yisroel Meir HaKohen the "Chofetz Chaim". These works were intended to give guidance to laymen, who either lacked the time or skills to learn through the laws from their sources.

Today there are many books written in all languages on various Jewish laws, all aimed at giving guidance to the practical application of Jewish law.

How Halachah is decided:

There are two basic approaches when it comes to giving a practical ruling:

- The top down approach
- The bottom up approach

The top down approach:

The top down approach starts by examining the Talmud, earliest source. After which the earlier commentaries are examined (such as the Rosh, Rif and Rambam) to see how the subject was dealt with. After the earlier sources have been examined, later sources are examined typically the Shulchan Aruch with its commentaries (such as the Shach, Taz and Bach). The next step is then to examine later works such as the Chayai Odom and Mishna Berura (where applicable), followed by "Shylos U Teshuvos" (Questions and Answers) of various more recent sages, such as the Chazon Ish and Rav Moshe Feinstein (Igros Moshe) and others. Once this process is complete, the scholar will have a better understanding of the subject matter (as well as the individual where applicable) and then be able to dispense a ruling or refer the individual to a greater Torah scholar.

The bottom up approach:

The bottom up approach, in certain instances such as when dealing with relatively new concepts (such as electricity on Shabbos, organ transplants) the bottom up approach is used. The bottom up approach is the exact opposite of the Top down approach. Therefore the approach starts by examining the most contemporary sources, and working backwards to find its source in the Talmud.

Important Definitions:

- **Halachah** – Jewish Law (Obligation or Right)
- **Minhag** – An area not covered by law but practised by Tradition.
- **Chumra** – Following the opinion of one sage, who is stringent, even though most sages disagree.
- **"Meshugas"** – "Madness" - Practising actions which are unfounded (Not dealt with in any source. i.e. not even one sage is being followed).

THE RABBI MICHAEL J ELJARRAT LEARNING PROGRAMME – CLASS SEVENTY

CLASS 70   TORAH

THE BEN-TORAH AND TALMID CHOCHOM

In this lesson we will look at two terms which are often used in Jewish circles, namely: "Ben Torah" and "Talmid Chochom". We will explain the difference between them, as well as elaborate on the usage of these terms within the context of conversation.

Why these two terms?

The reason for explaining these two terms is owing to the fact that under certain circumstances the two terms are interchangeable. However under other circumstances the two terms can be complete opposites. Therefore one without the knowledge can easily be mislead in conversations, and form incorrect perceptions.

The Ben Torah:

The term Ben Torah literally means "Son of Torah". The term Ben Torah is used as a title of sorts to one who displays all the following qualities: (This is not a complete list, just a general outline.)

- Genuine and sincere belief in God.
- All actions are done for the sake of Heaven.
- Every action is done to draw closer to God.
- Acceptance of the yolk of Torah, and the responsibility of being a Jew.
- Uses every opportunity to learn Torah and do Mitzvos.

The Talmid Chochom:

The term Talmid Chochom literally means "Wise Student". The term is also used as a title of sorts, to one who displays all the following qualities: (This is not a complete list, just a general outline.)

- Has a vast and extensive Torah knowledge
- Has astute critical thinking skills, and highly developed analytical skills.
- Has very advanced learning skills.
- Is exceptionally intelligent.
- Is able to calculate the consequences of actions, several steps in advance.

THE RABBI MICHAEL J ELJARRAT LEARNING PROGRAMME – CLASS SEVENTY

The difference between them:

It should be clear based on the lists that we mentioned above, that a Ben Torah revolves around purity of heart and mind, where as the Talmid Chochom revolves around knowledge and intelligence.

In an ideal world we would expect that the Talmid Chochom – With extensive Torah knowledge is also a Ben Torah – With a pure heart. However the two concepts are mutually exclusive, meaning we can find individuals who are classed as a Talmid Chochom but not a Ben Torah, as well as individuals who are classified as Benei Torah (Plural of Ben Torah), but not Talmiday Chachomim (Plural of Talmid Chochom).

The Talmid Chochom who is not a Ben Torah:

One of the most famous individuals in history is Achisofel. Achisofel was an advisor to King David, and was the one who encouraged Avshalom, King David's son, to rebel against his father. Achisofel was said to have had such an extraordinary Torah knowledge and brilliant mind, that asking a question to him was equilvilant of asking the "Oorim Ve Toomim"[1]. However he used his brilliant mind and Torah knowledge for destructive causes//purposes.

According to the Midrash, Esau, Jacobs's elder brother, was also a tremendous Torah scholar with a brilliant mind. It is thought that Esau's Torah knowledge was equivalent or even greater than his brother's Jacob, and that only Rebecca his mother, and Jacob, his brother knew that Esau was in fact evil. From everyone elses perspective including Esau's own father Isaac, Esau appeared to be righteous and exceptionally learned. This is said to be the reason that Isaac was so shocked to learn that Esau was in fact evil.

Be aware:

Through out time, there has been exceptional Talmiday Chachomim, who managed to fool the public into thinking that they were righteous people, when in actual fact they were extremely evil. People like this are termed "Chamor Nosei Kaylim" (Literally a Donkey carrying vessels). As they carry the knowledge outside of themselves, without internalizing their knowledge, leaving them with the personality of a donkey.

The Ben Torah who is not a Talmid Chochom:

As we said previously one of the characteristics of the Talmid Chochom is having a vast and extensive Torah knowledge. What constitutes a vast and extensive Torah knowledge may be somewhat of a "grey area". In previous generations a sixteen year old Yeshiva student would have known half the Talmud off by heart. The Vilna Gaon was said to have completed the entire Talmud by the age of three! Some may argue that quantity alone does not constitute true knowledge, and that true knowledge can only be measured qualitatively, by the depth of comprehension, and natural wisdom that comes from maturity.

---

[1]. The Oorim Ve Toomim were the stones on the high Priest's breast plate, which would miraculously light up with Torah answers directly from God.

By today's standards, one who has been actively involved in full time learning for a minimum of ten years, and who knows the majority of Talmud, and is able to recall his learning, as well as having profound intelligence may be classified as a Talmid Chochom.

Individuals who don't meet the above criteria, due to lack of learning skills, intellectual abilities or any other reason, may still be classified as "Benei Torah" provided that they meet the criteria mentioned above (Genuine and sincere belief in God etc.).

Not everyone will have the opportunity to become a Talmid Chochom, but everyone has the opportunity to become a Ben Torah. A person who desires to be a Ben Torah and a Talmid Chochom will receive heavenly assistance in his endeavours. As it says

"The testimony of Hashem is trustworthy, making the simple one wise"[2]

Which comes first?

A mistaken question is often asked;

"Which comes first, being a Ben Torah or being a Talmid Chochom?"

The answer is that neither is done first. Focusing on just one of the two tasks almost always results in failure of the second task. When one learns sincerely, one will automatically start developing into a Ben Torah, and one who is developing into a Ben Torah automatically starts to develop a thirst for Torah knowledge. One with a pure heart, who puts in all his effort, will reach his full potential, what ever that may be.

---

[2]. Psalms 19

THE RABBI MICHAEL J ELJARRAT LEARNING PROGRAMME – CLASS SEVENTY ONE

CLASS 71

TORAH

THE LAWS OF TORAH READING

In this lesson we will look at the laws relating to the reading of the Torah, in public settings; as well as the laws regarding honouring a Torah scroll.

This lesson will follow the outline of the Chayai Odom.[1]

Terms used:

1.	Aliya	1.	(Going up) being called to the Torah
2.	Aron HaKodesh	2.	(Lit Holy Ark) closet which the Torah sits in
3.	Bad/Baddim	3.	The wooden poles the Torah parchment is attached to
4.	Bal Koreh	4.	The one reading the Torah
5.	Bima	5.	The table which the Torah is placed on, when being read
6.	Gabai	6.	The one who calls people up to the Torah
7.	Gelila	7.	Rolling the Torah
8.	Haftorah	8.	The verses that are read from the prophets/writings
9.	Hagba	9.	Lifting the Torah
10.	Klaf	10.	The parchment that the words of Torah are written on
11.	Lein	11.	(Yiddish) To read (to read from the Torah)
12.	Maftir	12.	The final few verses of the day's Torah portion
13.	Mantel	13.	(Yiddish) Torah cover
14.	Oleh	14.	(One who goes up) one who is called up to the Torah
15.	Pesee – Cha	15.	Opening the Aron HaKodesh
16.	Sefer Torah	16.	Torah Scroll (Written on parchment according to Halacha)
17.	Tefer	17.	The stitching (The Torah comprises of parchment sheets)
18.	Trop	18.	(Yiddish) Music notes for Torah reading
19.	Yad	19.	(Lit Hand) The ornament the Bal Koreh uses to point with

There are many laws relating to Torah reading; For the purpose of this lesson we will concentrate on the procedures followed regarding Torah reading, in order to make the laws and customs seem familiar.

---

1. Klal 31

THE RABBI MICHAEL J ELJARRAT LEARNING PROGRAMME – CLASS SEVENTY ONE

Day	Portion and procedure
Every Monday and Thursday*	3 Aliyas – 3 people are called up
Shabbos Shacharis	The entire Parsha of the week is read. 7 Aliyas – 7 people +1 Maftir
Shabbos Mincha	3 Aliyas – 3 people are called up
Rosh Chodesh	4 Aliyas – 4 people are called up. Special portion for the day.
Yomtov (Except Yom Kippur)	5 Aliyas – 5 people are called up + 1 Maftir. Special portion for the day.
Yom Kippur Shacharis	6 Aliyas – 6 people are called up + 1 Maftir. Special portion for the day
Public Fast days	3 Aliyas – 3 people are called up. Special portion for the day
Chanukah	3 Aliyas – 3 people are called up. Special portion for each day
Purim	3 Aliyas – 3 people are called up. Special portion for the day
Chol Ha Moed	3 Aliyas – 3 people are called up. Special portion for the day
Tisha B'Av	3 Aliyas – 3 people are called up. Special portion for the day

*Only the first portion of the Parsha is read (i.e. Only Rishon – The First Aliya) See below.

The portion of the week is referred to as the "Parsha of the week". Each Parsha has its own name for example Bereishis, Noach, Lech LeCha etc. The Parsha is divided into 7 Aliyas and the Aliyas are numbered as "First" Aliya (Rishon), "Second" Aliya (Sheini), "Third" Aliya (Shilishi) etc.

Laws of Aliyos:

- "First" Aliya (Rishon) – Is given to a Kohen
- "Second" Aliya (Sheini) – Is given to a Levi
- "Third" Aliya (Shilishi) – Is given to a Yisroel

- On days where there are more than three Aliyos, the remaining Aliyos can be given to anyone.
- We do not call up two brothers one after the other.
- In cases where there is no Kohen available anyone can be called up "In place of the Kohen".
- If there is a Kohen, but no Levi, then the Kohen is called up twice first as a Kohen, and then "In place of the Levi".

Laws for one who is given Pesee-Cha:

One who is given Pesee-Cha (opening the Ark) must do the following:

- Open the Ark
- Take out the Torah, and hold the Torah during the prayer of "Brich Shemay"[2]
- Hand over the Torah to the Chazzan
- Receive the Torah from the Chazzan
- Close the Ark

---

2. This is the Aramaic prayer which we say – "Blessed is the name of the Master of the universe"

THE RABBI MICHAEL J ELJARRAT LEARNING PROGRAMME – CLASS SEVENTY ONE

Laws for one who is given an Aliya:

One who is given the honour of getting an Aliya must do the following:

- Take the shortest route from his seat to the Bima
- Hold the Torah scroll open with both hands (Left hand on left pole and right hand on right pole)
- Close eyes/ look to the side, and say the blessing.
- Follow along with the Bal Koreh until the end of his Aliya. (Keeping left hand on right pole)
- Close the Torah scroll hold the Torah with both hands (Left hand on left pole and right hand on right pole) and raise the Torah slightly while saying the after blessing.
- Remain at the Bima until after the next Oleh has completed his after blessing.
- Take the longest route back from the Bima to his seat.

Laws for one who is given Hagba:

One who is given the honour of Hagba must do the following:

- Roll the Torah scroll until the Tefer is in the Middle
- Lift up the Torah, for the public to see.

Laws for one who is given Gelila:

One who is given the honour of Gelila must do the following:

- Roll the Torah closed
- Dress the Torah with the mantel and other accessories.

THE RABBI MICHAEL J ELJARRAT LEARNING PROGRAMME – CLASS SEVENTY TWO

CLASS 72   TORAH

613 MITZVOS
A CLOSER LOOK AT
TEFILLIN AND MEZUZAH

In this lesson we will look at the concept of Mitzvos in general, as well as the Mitzvos of Tefillin and Mezuzah in more detail.

Mitzvos in the Torah:

We often hear people speaking of the 10 commandments, or the 613 Mitzvos, however when we attempt to count this number we find just 9 commandments, and 600 – 620[1] Mitzvos. The question is then; why have the concepts of there being 10 commandments and 613 Mitzvos become so popular?

The Ten Commandments:

As we have already said in a previous lesson, the statement "I am Hashem your God"[2] is in actual fact not a statement but a commandment, to believe in God. Thus bringing the total count to 10. However the Torah states the 10 Commandments in two places and the wording is slightly different, giving rise to new facets of each commandment.

Thus the 10 commandments are not merely 10 but 10 with subsections. One thing does become apparent, that is: Counting Mitzvos/Commandments in the Torah is a very difficult task, since statements can be commandments and repetitions of Commandments can in certain instances be counted as two separate commandments, and in other circumstances be counted as just one commandment.

613 Mitzvos:

The Talmud[3] states:

> "Rebbe Simlai expounded 613 Mitzvos were said to Moses, 365 negative commandments like the days in the solar year, and 248 positive commandments corresponding the limbs of Man."

Rashi on the above piece of Talmud explains: "248 positive commandments that on each limb we can say go and do a Mitzvah." "365 negative commandments, that on every day we are warned not to transgress.

---

1. Based on the discrepancies of the various counts.
2. Shemos / Exodus 20:2 , Devarim / Deuteronomy 5:6
3. Makkos 23b

PAGE 1

THE RABBI MICHAEL J ELJARRAT LEARNING PROGRAMME – CLASS SEVENTY TWO

From this it would seem that the concept of having 613 Mitzvos is for us to be surrounded with Mitzvos with every part of our body all the time.

As we have seen earlier[4] the concept of a Mitzvah, is a means through which we can perfect ourselves and become closer to God. One who completes and fulfils all the Mitzvos, all the time, and with all his/her being can be considered "Complete" or "Perfect" and thus close to God.

As we use the expression 24/7 to mean all the time (24 hours a day, 7 days a week) so too we use the expression 613 Mitzvos to mean, constantly involved in Mitzvos. (365 days a year, with 248 limbs of the body)

This is what the Talmud[5] means when it says that King David established 11 Mitzvos. When King David saw that every generation was spiritually weaker than the preceding generation, he established 11 qualities which would insure a person was surrounded with Mitzvos all the time.

This means, that originally people were able to fulfil all 613 Mitzvos (all the Mitzvos all the time) with complete devotion. Later generation however could only fulfil 11 qualities (all the time) with complete devotion. Thus the Torah is a complete unit consisting of all the Mitzvos within, what ever than number may be. That number of Mitzvos is the entire Torah, no more and no less and one who wants to obtain perfection must fulfil the entire Torah.

The Marsha[6] explains that all the positive and negative commandments are collapsible into their roots. The root of all positive commandments stem from "I am Hashem your God" (which is the Mitzvah of faith), and the root of all negative commandments stem from "Do not have any other Gods". The numerical value of "The Satan" = 364 as the Talmud in Yuma explains that, the Satan influences Man every day except for the Day of Atonement (Yom Kippur). This corresponds to: 365 days/negative commandments.

Summary:

In summary, we can say that there are 613 Mitzvos in the Torah, but these are just roots Mitzvos which are expandable ad infinitum. As well as being collapsible into roots of 11 as was stated by King David, and ultimately collapsible into 2 primary roots (as explained by the Marsha). Thus perfection is attained by fulfilling the 2 roots Mitzvos, which are 11, which are 613, which are infinite.

The Mitzvos of Tefillin and Mezuzah:

Keeping within the theme of 613 Mitzvos, as meaning surrounded by Mitzvos all the time. Two Mitzvos play an important role in surrounding ourselves with Mitzvos all the time. These are the Mitzvos of Tefillin (which were worn all day in previous generations) and the Mitzvah of Mezuzah, which fills ones surroundings with the presence of Hashem.

---

4. Fundamentals course –Lesson on reward and punishment.
5. Makkos 24a
6. On the Talmud cited above.

THE RABBI MICHAEL J ELJARRAT LEARNING PROGRAMME – CLASS SEVENTY TWO

Tefillin:

For the purpose of this lesson we will just outline several laws of the Mitzvah of Tefillin. The laws of Tefillin are vast and include everything from making Tefillin and wearing them, to the laws of repairing them when broken.

We will look at just a few laws.

- The outside of the boxes of the Tefillin must be perfectly square (That is length = width, however height can vary)
- The rectangle base of the Tefillin is called the "Titoora"
- The outside boxes (called the "Batim") must be completely black.
- The straps (called "Retzuos") must be completely black.
- Tefillin made from the leather of oxen are called "Gasos" and those made from the leather of sheep and goats are called "Dakos".

For more on the laws of Tefillin, please see the lesson entitled "The laws of Tefillin"

Mezuzah:

The laws of Mezuzah are equally vast to the laws of Tefillin. Once again we will just mention a few laws.

- Each and every room, in ones house requires a Mezuzah (except bathrooms and toilets)
- In order to make a blessing the following conditions must be met:
    - The room must be 4 by 4 Amos (approximately 2m x 2m)
    - The entrance must have 2 posts and a lintel
    - The room must have a roof
    - There must be doors in the entrance.
- The Mezuzah is placed on the top third of the post, slanting inwards towards the entrance.

For more on the laws of Mezuzah, please see the lesson entitled "The laws of Mezuzah"

THE RABBI MICHAEL J ELJARRAT LEARNING PROGRAMME – CLASS SEVENTY THREE

CLASS 73   TORAH

THE NEED TO STUDY MUSSAR

In this lesson we will look at the concept of "Mussar" and why the study of Mussar is an integral part of leading a Torah life style. We will also briefly examine the goals of Rav Yisroel Salanter Zt'l known to be the father of the modern day Mussar movement.

What is Mussar?

The word Mussar has its roots in the word "Mossar" (M.S.R) which means to transfer[1]. The word is also used in the root form, to mean tradition as in "Mesora". However the closer description of the word "Mussar" has its roots in the word "Yossar" (Y.S.R) which means to restrain, set limits and influence towards a goal. The common root letters are "Sar" (S.R) which means to move or turn aside.

We may therefore describe Mussar as: That which moves us, influencing us towards a goal and brings us closer to the original Torah values.

The need to study Mussar:

The verse in Psalms[2] says as follows:

- "Praise worthy is the man who did not **go** with the council of the wicked
- And in the ways of the sinners he did not **stand**.
- And amongst scoffers he did not **sit**"

The Chofetz Chaim asks the following question:

It would seem that the order of the verse is incorrect: If one were to praise an individual for not mixing with evil people, then we should first praise one who does not sit, then one who does not stand, and finally one who does not even go?

The Chofetz Chaim answers:

A person's attitude can change very subtlety over time, and this attitude change can be so subtle that the person him/her self is not even aware that this is taking place. A person may find him/her self being righteous today and yet several years later being completely wicked.

---

1. Etymological Dictionary S. R Hirsh – M. Clark.
2. Psalms 1:1

This marked change in personality can happen very gradually, and the character change can only be noted by contrasting the old self with the new self.

In the context of the verse stated above, the Chofetz Chaim explains as follows:

- A person starts off by saying to him/her self that they would like to be far removed from wicked people and that they will never "go" and mix with them.
- Over time the person's attitude changes and they begin to feel left out. They then rationalize that they will "go" (not to feel left out), however they will not "stand" with them. (in order to keep the distance)
- Once again a new attitude develops, whereby the person then thinks to themselves; I can't just stand around like a tea pot, I need to mingle and be social. In order to satisfy this new attitude the person compromises and "sits" quietly in the crowd.
- However the person soon starts to feel self conscious, and begins to voice his/her opinions.
- When he/she begins to feel acknowledged, the urge then develops to be the leader of the crowd.
- Before long this person becomes the very thing which was once despised.

Thus the true test of character and the one who is most praiseworthy is the one who does not go in the first instance, and maintains his/her good values.

The inner and outer self:

What seems apparent is that a person's "inner" self (i.e. his/her attitudes and belief's) are strongly influenced by the external environment.

This gives rise to the following problems:

- A person may have good morals and values, and not be socially acceptable.
- A lack of social acceptance, may lead to an erosion of good morals and values.

Since the dawn of time, Mankind has struggled with this dilemma, and Mankind's solution to this ongoing problem is to develop something called "Social Skills". Those with the best developed "Social Skills" are always given positions of power and authority.

What is the meaning of "Social Skills"?

Social Skills can be defined as: The ability to maintain one's personal set of values in private intimate settings, and hold a different set of values in public social settings. (A set of values that is socially acceptable)

One who possesses "Social Skills" effectively has two parts to themselves:

1. The "Inner self" – For private intimate settings.
2. The "Outer self" – For public social settings.

THE RABBI MICHAEL J ELJARRAT LEARNING PROGRAMME – CLASS SEVENTY THREE

The historical development of Social Skills:

As we know every generation is spiritually weaker than the preceding generation. The resulting consequence is that every generation is morally weaker than the preceding generation.

As society descends into moral weakness, maintaining morals and values becomes an increasingly difficult task.

The way in which society in general has dealt with this moral dilemma, is by giving power and authority to individuals with "Social Skills" (i.e. individuals who are 'good" on the inside and "socially acceptable" on the outside). This helps society to rid themselves of feelings of "guilt" for not maintaining their own set of moral values; by placing "Social" people in positions of power, and using them as role models for behaviour.

These "Socially acceptable" people were responsible for policy legislation and governing the public.

The first set of individuals in history to govern and rule society, were members of the Clergy. Up until not that long ago, countries were controlled and governed by the Church.

As society progressed, and social norms deviated too far from religion, members of the Clergy were replaced by Politicians.

As society descended even further into moral decline, society needed skilled professionals who were able to change from "Inside" to "Outside" personalities with absolute ease. These skilled professionals were placed on a pedestal and used as the new role models.

Who are these skilled professionals?

Actors and actresses are the current social benchmark for moral behaviour. Society's inability to deal with the moral dilemma, has placed actors and actresses who are able to "Fake it" with ease on the pedestal.

Celebrity culture:

Celebrities show the public that it's "Ok" to fake it, its "Ok" to be one thing on the inside and another thing on the outside. This intern comforts society's feelings of guilt, and turmoil which comes from inner/outer inconsistencies and conflict.

For this reason celebrities are lorded, for they bring "tranquillity" to the world. By placing celebrities on a pedestal, society fulfils its secret desire to possess the ability to "Change Personalities" like changing clothes, seamlessly and without feelings of guilt.

The Torah approach:

As we have seen above, our external environment influences our inner world. Therefore being one person on the inside and another person on the outside is not a viable solution, since the "Outside" will damage the "Inside" leaving a person without morals and values, both "inside" and "outside".

THE RABBI MICHAEL J ELJARRAT LEARNING PROGRAMME – CLASS SEVENTY THREE

What is the solution?

Studying Mussar is the solution to this problem. By studying those parts of Torah that move us, motivate us and directs us towards upholding our morals and values, we strengthen our "Inner" self to the point whereby we are able to maintain our morals and values, regardless of the external environment.

Rav Yisroel Lipkin (Known as Reb Yisroel Salanter) founded a Yeshiva in around 1842 in the town Zarechya, in Vilna Lithuania. Reb Yisroel Lipkin was known to be a profound Talmudic scholar and was one of the first people in history who attempted to translate the entire Talmud into another language.

Reb Yisroel Lipkin emphasised the need to study Mussar as part of ones daily Torah learning. In his writings he refers to the conscious as the "Chitzonius" (Outside) and the subconscious as the "Penimius" (Inside) he stresses the need for an individual to know and understand both their Penimius and Chitzonius.

When an individual has consistency between the "Inside" and the "Outside" the resultant effect is inner peace and tranquillity.

It is for this reason that the sages say:

"Torah scholars increase peace in the world"[3]

It is the Torah scholars, not celebrities that hold the solution to the moral dilemma. The only viable solution to slow our descent into moral decline is to strengthen our "Inner" self. The study of Mussar is all about building that "Inner" self and developing self esteem, self worth and self respect. One who has a healthy self concept does not fear and is not intimidated by social pressure and conformity. One who has a healthy self concept can stand on his/her own two feet and make life decisions in a purely objective way, free from defective social constructs.

In the days of Moshiach it will be Torah scholars that are placed on a pedestal to be role models for moral behaviour. It will then be apparent for even the unscholarly to see, that tranquillity lies in internal/external consistency.

---

[3]. Talmud Brachos 64a

THE RABBI MICHAEL J ELJARRAT LEARNING PROGRAMME – CLASS SEVENTY FOUR

CLASS 74   TORAH

RABBINICAL RULINGS AND CONTEMPORARY HALACHAH

In this lesson we will look at Rabbinical rulings and how halachah is dealt with on a practical day to day basis. As we have already seen in a previous lesson (dealing with how halachah is decided), the purpose of halachah is in essence to "do what God wants".

Having said that; a point which often gets raised by people from all walks of life is, something along the lines of:

"I'm happy to do what God wants, but not what the Rabbi's want".

People often feel that Rabbinical rulings both past and present, are not a part of the Torah and "What God wants", rather it is something man made which has been imposed onto the Torah, and perhaps deviating from "What God wants".

For this reason it is critical for us to understand the relationship between God, the Torah and Rabbinical rulings. It is important for us to gain an understanding of how these three elements work together.

> **"And you shall do according to everything they teach you"**
> (Devarim / Deuteronomy 17: 10-11)

From the above verse we clearly see that God does in fact want us to listen to our teachers.

Question: Why does God want us to listen to our teachers?

To examine this Mitzvah, we will look at the Sefer Ha Chinuch (Mitzvah 496).

The Chinuch explains that everyone has their own views and perceptions, and if everyone were left to interpret the Torah as they saw fit, the Torah would become so fragmented, that further dissemination to future generations would become impossible.

For this reason God instructs us to listen to the "Balei Ha-Kabolah" (A term the Chinuch uses to describe Torah authorities) and not to deviate from their rulings, in order to maintain a form of structure within Torah rulings and Torah Authority.

PAGE 1

THE RABBI MICHAEL J ELJARRAT LEARNING PROGRAMME – CLASS SEVENTY FOUR

Why the "Balei Ha-Kabolah"?

Perhaps we can think of the "Balei Ha-Kabolah" as the professionals in the "Torah Industry" These are the people who have dedicated their entire being to Torah study.

We could not find anyone more suitable to interpret the Torah, other than those who have made it their life goal to understand the Torah.

People readily accept medical opinions from medical professionals such as doctors, and financial opinions from financial professionals such as economists. One would hardly consider the economist's medical opinions, and the doctor's stock tips and financial advice.

However for some unknown reason; nearly every layman and novice feels that: They have the "right" to interpret the Torah, and impose their Torah opinions on to others, without much regard for the opinions given by the "Professionals in the industry". Something akin to the economist imposing his/her medical opinions onto others, despite his/her lack of knowledge and evidence to the contrary.

Thus the essence of this Mitzvah is to:

> Listen to those "who know what they are talking about".

The Chinuch goes on to say, that it is so important to maintain a structure within Jewish authority, that even if a Sage were to instruct the masses to do something which is blatantly incorrect, it is still a Mitzvah to listen to the Sage, and follow his command, in order to maintain this structure within Jewish Authority.

Understanding this Mitzvah:

On the surface, this Mitzvah seems contrary to all forms of logic, and seems to be in direct conflict with Judaism as we know it. As we have seen many times, the role of a Jewish human being is: To perfect oneself and become Godlike. This is accomplished through exercising our free will, and making decisions to do what is good.

> "The bigger the decision, the greater the individual"

Following the will of another individual seems the furthest thing from being "Godlike". Being a follower and not a leader seems to be the very opposite of greatness.

Therefore this Mitzvah needs a great deal of explanation, subjugating our will to another human being, is to deny free will itself.

Furthermore the Chinuch says that it is a Mitzvah to listen to a sage, even when he is clearly making a mistake. How can any God loving Jew, follow the wishes of a human being, when it is in direct conflict with the will of God himself?

Before we answer this question, let us look at a story which is found in the Talmud[1]. Regarding an argument which transpired between the Sages and Rebbe Eliezer, regarding the status of purity concerning a "Tanoor Achsenai" (lit the oven of a snake).

---

1. Baba Metzeah 59b

THE RABBI MICHAEL J ELJARRAT LEARNING PROGRAMME – CLASS SEVENTY FOUR

On day the sages argued with Rebbe Eliezer: The Sages said that the oven is impure and Rebbe Eliezer said it's pure.

Rebbe Eliezer brought all the proofs in the world, but the sages did not listen to him.

- Rebbe Eliezer then said, "If the law is like me, this carob tree will prove it" immediately the carob tree moved one hundred Amos away.
- To that the sages replied "We don't bring proofs from carob trees".

- Rebbe Eliezer then said "If the law is like me let the water canal prove it" immediately the water began flowing backwards.
- To that the Sages replied "We don't bring proofs from water canals"

- Rebbe Eliezer then said "If the law is like me let the walls prove it" immediately the walls of the study hall began collapsing.

- Rebbe Eliezer then said "If the law is like me Heaven will prove it" immediately a Heavenly voice proclaimed "The Law is like Rebbe Eliezer"

- To that the Sages replied "The law is not (made) in heaven" (I.e. What ever miraculous proofs, you may bring we will not budge from our opinion.)

What does God want?

The Talmud cited above continues to say, that at the time this argument between Rebbe Eliezer and the Sages was taking place, God was "smiling".

This story seems confusing, on the one hand, the opinion of Rebbe Eliezer seemed to be what God wanted, but on the other hand, God seemed to want the Sages opinion to prevail, as indicated by God's "smiling".

The Chinuch explains, that although regarding the law itself, Rebbe Eliezer was correct, and God's desire was in line with the opinion of Rebbe Eliezer, never the less God also wants structure and authority amongst the Jewish people, and was therefore "Happy" that the Sages stood their ground and maintained their authority over the Jewish law, despite any proof to the contrary.

Structural system versus Independent thought:

The Chinuch explains further that the Torah commandment and its violation thereof is applicable to any interpretation of the words of the Torah itself, or any law considered "Halachah Le Moshe M'Sinai". However the Torah violation is not broken regarding Rabbinical rulings to guard the Torah.

To understand this fully, we can look at the laws of the Torah as "Core elements" and "Outside coverings".

Core elements:	Outside coverings
<ul><li>The written Torah</li><li>The Prophets and Writings</li><li>The Laws of Halachah Le Moshe M'Sinai</li><li>Laws instituted by the Sages in the Talmud: Such as Chanukah and Purim</li></ul>	<ul><li>Customs</li><li>Idiosyncratic cultural adaptations</li></ul>

THE RABBI MICHAEL J ELJARRAT LEARNING PROGRAMME – CLASS SEVENTY FOUR

One who ignores Rabbinical Rulings in the "Core elements", ruins the essence of the Torah and its values, however changing the "Outside coverings" is subject to independent thought.

Inner Core: Not to be changed.
Outer Covering: Subject to independent thought.

Balance:
- Humility to do exactly like the core Prescribes.
- Creativeness to exercise free will, without bias.

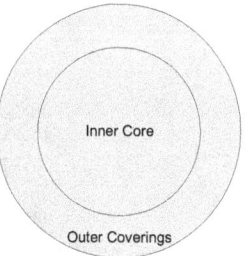

In Summary:

The only way to insure that the Torah can be passed on from one generation to the next is by protecting the "Core" of the Torah. Maintaining the "Core" of the Torah is so important that the system must prevail, regardless of opinions (As was indicated by the story with Rebbe Eliezer and the Sages). One who does not conform to the "Core elements" of the Torah, cannot be said to be a practising Jew. One has to be humble and subjugate oneself to the "Core elements", there is no room for choice. The only choice is "Do you accept the Torah or not?" One who wants to practise Judaism must comply with the "Core elements", one who does not comply with the "Core elements" is not a practising Jew period.

On the other hand the non-essential outer parts; such as cultural norms and practises are not a part of the "Core" Torah, and is therefore a matter of individual choice. One who practises the "Core elements" of the Torah is considered a practising Jew, regardless of any outer coverings, and idiosyncratic cultural adaptations.

Being a good Jew; lies in the balance of being humble and subjugating oneself to the "Core" values and elements of the Torah, as well as being open and adaptive to express free will, without any prejudice or bias.

On the one side of the scale, one who is a "Cowboy" and does everything contrary to the Torah, is out of balance and far from perfection. On the other hand, one who is like a "Robot" subjugating his will to everyone's but his own, is also out of balance and far from perfection. One who knows when to subjugate himself and when to be independent is a balanced individual, who is well on the way to perfection.

THE RABBI MICHAEL J ELJARRAT LEARNING PROGRAMME – CLASS SEVENTY FIVE

CLASS 75

TORAH

KABBALAH AND MYSTICISM

In this lesson we will explore the concept of Kabbalah, and define the terms which are frequently used when dealing with mysticism.

Before we begin, let us first define several words.

Ho-Kum[1]

1. Something apparently impressive or legitimate, but actually untrue or insincere; nonsense.
2. A stock technique for eliciting a desired response from an audience.

Kabbalah: A Branch of Torah study. (Comprising of three categories)

1. Theoretical Kabbalah
2. Medetative Kabbalah
3. Magical Kabbalah

All three types of Kabbalah will be explained in further detail below[2]

Throughout time, trickery and deceit were the common tools used by Con Artists, to prey upon the weak and vulnerable.

However in recent times, Torah itself is used by Con Artists to give a false sense of hope to people in unfortunate situations. The word used to capture the attention of the unwise[3] is "Kabbalah" or variations of this word such as "Kabbalistic", "Kabbalah tools", "Kabbalah skills" etc.

It would seem that when ever a topic fails to draw in an audience, the word "Kabbalah" (or one of its variations) is used as a prefix or suffix to the topic at hand.

Such as: "Marriage and Kabbalah", "Job hunting and Kabbalah" and "Golf and Kabbalah" etc.

What is advertised today as "Kabbalah" is the very definition of Ho-Kum, i.e. using a true concept in a nonsensical fashion, in order to elicit a desired response from an audience.

---

1. The free online dictionary
2. Based upon the introduction to Sefer Yetzeira translated by: Rabbi Aryeh Kaplan.
3. The ignorant and the stupid.

PAGE 1

THE RABBI MICHAEL J ELJARRAT LEARNING PROGRAMME – CLASS SEVENTY FIVE

Theoretical Kabbalah:

As we know and believe, God created the universe.
Theoretical Kabbalah deals with the dynamics of the spiritual domain.
Such as:
- "How did God create the universe?"
- "How does God run the world?"
- "What are Souls?"
- "What are Angels?" etc.

Theoretical Kabbalah can be thought of as "Spiritual Science" just as "Physical Science" explores the laws and dynamics of the physical world, so too theoretical Kabbalah explores the laws and dynamics of the spiritual world.

Most of the published works on Kabbalah belong to this category.

Meditative Kabbalah:

Meditative Kabbalah deals with using the names of God, and permutations of words and letters as a "Mantra" to meditate to higher states of consciousness.

In essence one uses this form of Kabbalah to unleash the power of the Soul, and to "Travel" into different dimensions of reality.

Such techniques are used for "Astral Travel"[4] and other out-of-body experiences, where one would not be bound to the constraints of physicality.

There are various states of higher consciousness, and depending on the "Matra", technique, spiritual level and knowledge of the individual partaking in the meditation, different outcomes can be achieved; all the way from understanding physical reality to conversing with Angels.

These states of higher consciousness are an "Unmasking" of reality as we know it. A person, who uses this form of Kabbalah, is able to perceive the depths of reality to its full extent.

Most of the main texts of this form of Kabbalah, have never been published, but exist in the form of manuscripts and can only be found in museums and great libraries.

Magical Kabbalah:

Magical Kabbalah is similar to meditative Kabbalah, in that it uses names of God and special signs to change natural events.

As the Ramchal explains in Derech Hashem: Just as the physical world is bound by laws of "Nature" (Such as: Gravity, Laws of motion, etc.) so too the Spiritual world is also bound by the laws of "Super Nature" (Super Natural).

To put this in simple terms: Just as the laws of physics are not haphazard and unstructured, the force of gravity for example does not change from one day to the next, rather the laws are stable and work within very specific parameters, so too the laws of the spiritual are defined and stable.

---

4. Sometimes referred to as "Remote viewing"

THE RABBI MICHAEL J ELJARRAT LEARNING PROGRAMME – CLASS SEVENTY FIVE

The laws of Spirituality are equally if not more structured than the laws of Physicality. We often tend to think that spirituality is some sort of unstructured combination of esoteric "Mumbo-Jumbo", but in truth spirituality couldn't be further from that.

As we know, everything which presents itself in the physical world has its origins and source of existence in the spiritual world. The spiritual laws pertaining to a particular object; determine the physical laws that, the particular object will display in nature. For example the spiritual laws pertaining to water, do not allow for fire and water to co-exist physically.

The Talmud tells us:
That once a Sage did not have money to buy oil to light Shabbos candles, so he filled his candelabra with water and said.

>"He who makes oil flammable, should also make water flammable."

He then lit Shabbos candles using water instead of oil, thus he changed natural events. This is Magical Kabbalah.

Who can learn Kabbalah?

According to Halachah, only one who has learnt all of the revealed Torah and is above the age of 40 may learn Kabbalah.

This halachah is used as a gauge, to determine one's overall knowledge, and intellectual maturity and sophistication.

Kabbalah is a field of Torah study, for the very advanced Torah learner. Just as one cannot learn fifth year medicine in isolation, and without all the knowledge learnt in years 1 – 4, so too one cannot learn Kabbalah in isolation and without the prior knowledge of a substantial amount of revealed Torah.

Needless to say, one has to be a Talmid Chochom[5] and a Ben Torah to even think about learning Kabbalah. Any Kabbalah being taught to laymen is in all likelihood Hokum.

For more information: Listen to "Kabbalah explained CTC Class 75".

Found at – www.beejewish.org

Recommended reading:

- Derech Hashem – The way of God. (Written by the Ramchal – Translated by Rabbi Aryeh Kaplan)
- Meditation and Kabbalah – Written by Rabbi Aryeh Kaplan.

---

5. See previous classes for definition of Talmid Chochom and Ben Torah.

THE RABBI MICHAEL J ELJARRAT LEARNING PROGRAMME – CLASS SEVENTY SIX

CLASS 76   HISTORY

FROM ADAM - AVRAHAM

This lesson begins a new section which deals with Jewish history. We will look at the history of the world, from the creation of the universe up until the present day. We will try and explore some of the major turning points in Jewish history, such as the birth of the Jewish nation, the exodus from Egypt and the giving of the Torah.

An introduction to Jewish history:

Before we begin our journey through time, let us first understand the concept of "History".

What is History?

Every day events transpire, around the world. Some events are brief and short lasting; others are longer and transpire over days, weeks, months and even years. Some events change people's lives, while others go by almost unnoticed. Some events make "headline news", while others are barely reported.

All of these events are a part of history. If we look back to the beginning of time, many trillions of trillions of events have transpired.

The events which are recorded as "history" vary drastically depending upon who is telling the story. For example if we think of any great war or battle, where one nation was victorious, and another nation was defeated; depending on who is telling the story the very same events can be told from two very different perspectives.

Thus history is very seldom an objective study. Facts are often distorted or supported with opinion, and knowing the true events which transpired, is often a difficult task.

Furthermore before the days of Television and Radio, the main source of documenting and recording history was through eye witness accounts, thus leaving room for misinterpretations.

Even today with our "modern technology", media reporting is far from holistic. As media reporting is often bias, and riddled with political agenda's.

For example: 3000 people dying in Mogadishu in Africa would get far less coverage than would; say 3000 people dying in down-town New York.

THE RABBI MICHAEL J ELJARRAT LEARNING PROGRAMME – CLASS SEVENTY SIX

In many ways Jewish history is the same, events are not all holistically recorded, and rely on various cultural perspectives. However in other ways Jewish history is very different from any other history which one may encounter. This is due to the fact that the source of the history is like none other, and the people (the Jewish people) are like no other nation on earth.

We will now look at these two unique properties of Jewish history in greater detail. Our goal is to gain a better understanding of world events both past and present.

While some history lessons focus on "What happened", these lessons will try and make sense of "Why it happened".

The Ramchal explains in Derech Hashem[1] that one of the deepest concepts relating to the Jewish Nation is the fact that on the outside and in terms of nature, the Jewish Human Being looks just like any other Human Being from any other nation. However in Torah law, the two are treated as two entirely different species. This is the starting point when it comes to understanding the Jewish nation. We will explore this in greater detail shortly.

Unlike the history of other nations, Jewish history for the most part is not just documented and recorded from eye witness accounts, but rather from the Torah and the prophets. Thus the source of Jewish history is more comprehensive and reliable.

Based on the above let us now begin our journey through time.

Jewish history explored:

As we have learnt previously, all the events which transpire in reality, transpire in a five dimensional plane.

The five dimensions of reality are:

1. Length (North, South / Forward, Backward)
2. Breadth (West, East / Left, Right)
3. Height (Up, Down)
4. Time (Future, Past)
5. Spirituality (Good, Evil)

Hence every event which transpires will transpire in a specific location within the world, given by co-ordinates of:

1. Longitude
2. Latitude
3. Altitude
4. In a specific time given by Date and Time,
5. And with a specific spiritual cause or outcome given by Good / Evil.

---

1. Part 2 Chapter 1

THE RABBI MICHAEL J ELJARRAT LEARNING PROGRAMME – CLASS SEVENTY SIX

In other words, take an event such as one which would be reported in a news headline as:

"50 People died this weekend, in a train accident in Paris, France."

This could be said as follows:

1. Longitude: 2° 19' 60 E
2. Latitude: 48° 52' 0 N
3. Altitude: 66m (216 feet) above sea level.
4. Date[2] and Time: Year 5771. Month: Shvat. Day: Friday. Time: 16:42pm.
5. Spiritual element: Bad / Evil event[3]

The fact that God controls the universe means that each one of the details mentioned above, is specifically co-ordinated to transpire exactly as is. (Longitude: 2° 19' 60 E and not, Longitude: 2° 20' 61 E etc.)

Adam and the creation of the world:

At a specific period God created space, time and spirituality. It was at this moment that history began.

The creation of the universe was a deliberate action taken by God, for a very specific purpose.

The purpose:

- Creating a "Being" which would be capable of attaining perfection through decision making.
- Creating an environment for this "Being" which would facilitate decision making.

This "Being" is the "Human Being" and the world was thus created to facilitate this goal and purpose.

Adam and Eve: The world begins:

1. Longitude: Unknown
2. Latitude: Unknown
3. Altitude: Unknown
4. Date and Time: Year 0. Month: 1 Tishrei. Day: Friday. Time: Morning.
5. Spiritual element: Good (High influx of God's presence)

---

2. We use the Jewish calendar, when plotting dates as the Jewish calendar cycle is intertwined in the fifth dimension of reality.
3. We are calling this an "Evil" or "Bad" event since 50 people died, although technically speaking this event may be positively or negatively spiritually charged.

THE RABBI MICHAEL J ELJARRAT LEARNING PROGRAMME – CLASS SEVENTY SIX

The plan:

The "original" plan was to create a "Human Being" and to give this "Human Being" just a single decision to make.

- The commandment was: "Do not eat from the tree of knowledge" [4]
- The decision that "Man" had to make: "I choose not to eat from the tree of knowledge".
- The outcome: Doing the will of God, and through that choice attain perfection and closeness to God.

"Man" would have then enjoyed "Olam HaBah" / Shabbos for eternity and in those few hours he would have achieved the "World Goal".

However as we know "Man" made the wrong choice, and ate from the tree of knowledge. This not only affected Adam himself, but changed the course of history for the entire world. The "Moment" that "Man" ate from the tree of knowledge, was one of the greatest moments in the history of the universe.

Although the goal and purpose of the world did not change; namely for "Man" to attain perfection through decision making never the less the method in which this would be accomplished did change.

A new "Man" is needed:

Once the original "Man" failed at his task, the species of "Man" changed. "Good" and "Evil" were no longer found solely in "Mans" external environment, but as composites of his very being. Thus attaining perfection became a far more difficult task.

The Mishna in Ovos[5] says that there were ten generations from Adam to Noach, and ten generations from Noach to Avraham.

During this period in history spanning twenty generations, God was searching for a new "Man" one who would pass the test and attain perfection.

The Derech Hashem explains that for the first twenty generations, God was looking for a candidate to name "Man". Afterwards the next period would be dedicated to establishing "Man" and his descendants culminating in the nation of "Man".

As the Mishna in Ovos says, from creation until Noach, every generation angered Hashem and did not produce a single worthy candidate.

---

4. Bereishis / Genesis 2:17
5. Chapter 5 Mishna 2-3

THE RABBI MICHAEL J ELJARRAT LEARNING PROGRAMME – CLASS SEVENTY SIX

Noach as "Man":

The Torah tells us that Noach was "Ish, Tzadik, Tamim be Dorosov" (a righteous man, perfect in his generation). Noach was the greatest man which lived in the first ten generations from creation. However the population of the world was entirely evil at that time. Therefore God brought a flood to destroy everyone except Noach and his family.

Thus although Noach did not reach the state of "Man" he was however great enough to be the source of the world's population today. God made a special convenient with Noach, and from that time the seven Noach laws acted as a symbol between God and the descendants of Noach to mark the status which Noach reached.

The seven Noach laws:

1. Do not commit idolatry.
2. Do not murder.
3. Do not steal.
4. Do not be sexually immoral.
5. Do not eat a limb from a living animal.
6. Do not curse God.
7. Set up a court justice system.

Avram as "Man":

Another ten generations past; until finally a "Man" was "born". The "Man" was Avraham, who at first was known as Avram. (Meaning father of Aram)

Avram reached the highest state of perfection, and spiritual purity, therefore God chose Avram to be "Man"; Thus ending the period of searching for "Man" and beginning a new period in history, focused on the development of "Man".

God tested Avram to insure that he was in fact worthy of the title "Man", after which God gave Avram a "stamp of approval" as it were and added the letter "Hey" to his name.

Thus from that point onwards Avram was to be called Avraham. This symbolic act was also marked by a special covenant between Avraham and God, and so began a new era which would change the course of world history.

The descendants of Avraham would later receive a far greater bond with God, than did Noach and his descendants. This would be in the form of receiving the Torah, the honorary prize or "Gold Medal" as it were, for the one who attained the status of "Man".

Although God's search for "Man" had ended with the choosing of Avraham. Still every participant in the race i.e. every other Human Being, could still chose to join Avraham in his quest and thus "Join" the higher purpose. Thus converts to Judaism would later be titled "Ben Avraham" (Son of Avraham).

THE RABBI MICHAEL J ELJARRAT LEARNING PROGRAMME – CLASS SEVENTY SEVEN

CLASS 77   HISTORY

THE PATRIARCHS

In this lesson we will explore the next period of history, the period which I have termed "The Patriarchs".

The Patriarchs namely: Avraham, Yitzchak and Yakov set the course for the Jewish nation that would later follow.

By examining the life and times of the Patriarchs, we will gain a better understanding of Jewish history. As our Sages tell us:

The actions of the Fathers, (are a) sign for (the) children.

Meaning: The Patriarchs formed the "Prototype" of all Jews which would follow. Their lives, and events which occurred in their lifetime, would later occur to the Jewish Nation itself later on in history.

Avraham:

As we saw in the previous lesson, the first twenty generations of the world held the goal of finding a suitable "Man". Once Avraham was chosen as "Man", the world goal shifted, to establish Avrahams descendants in order to create a nation from this "Man".

The process of making a nation required various "Filtering" stages.

- Avraham perfected the trait of kindness.

But more was needed for the nation of "Man".
Avraham had two sons, one son would possess the "Filtered" or refined trait of kindness, the other son would possess the "By Product" or "bad elements" of kindness.

- Yitzchak perfected the trait of "Fear" (order, structure and self discipline)

But once again more was needed for the nation of "Man".
Yitzchak had two sons, one son would possess the "Filtered" or refined trait of fear, the other son would possess the "By Product" or the "bad elements" of fear.

- Yakov perfected the trait of "Truth" (honesty, balance and mercy)

From him the nation of "Man" could begin to take root and prosper in its refined state of being.

THE RABBI MICHAEL J ELJARRAT LEARNING PROGRAMME – CLASS SEVENTY SEVEN

The family tree of "Man" would appear as follows:

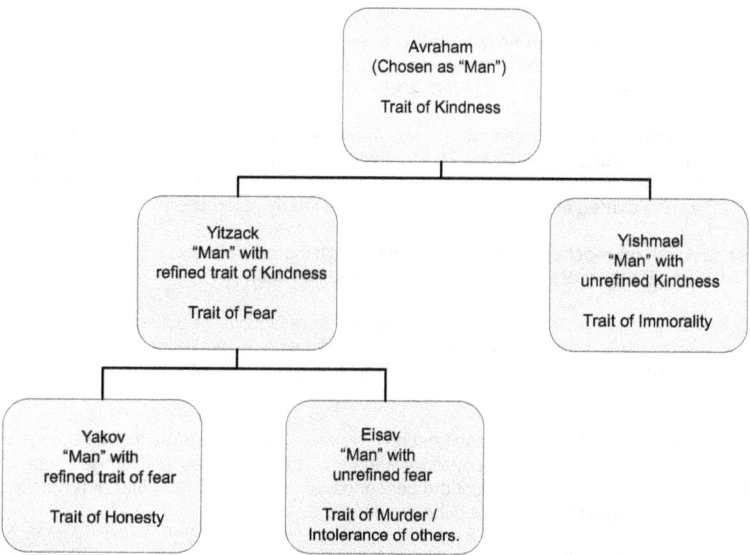

We will now look at how this refinement process unfolded into what would later become the foundation of the Jewish Nation.

Avraham – "Man" of kindness:

Avraham	
Born: 1948 Parents: Father – Terach. Mother – Amaslai Siblings: Nachor – Brother Horon - Brother	In the year 1948 from the beginning of creation, in the city of "Oor Kastim" (possibly the city of Ur or Uruk) in Mesopotamia (Modern day Iraq) Avraham was born. Originally called: Avram (Meaning: Av – Father, Aram – Nation of Aram) He was so called the "Father of Aram" as he was the teacher of the inhabitants of Aram.

The first 75 years of Avraham's life were somewhat ordinary in the sense that no "Super natural" events occurred.

During that period in history, in Mesopotamia, Mono-Theism (Belief in a single God) was unheard of; although other belief systems were very popular. Avraham recognized the true, one and only God, and during those first 75 years he dedicated his time to teach people about Hashem. Avraham did the opposite of everyone around him and was nick-named "Avram Ha-Ivri" (Avram the opposite). Avraham was exceptionally warm and loving, and he welcomed people into his home.

THE RABBI MICHAEL J ELJARRAT LEARNING PROGRAMME – CLASS SEVENTY SEVEN

The Torah refers to Avraham's students as members of his family, as he brought people into his home, taught them and made them feel like members of his family.

Avraham excelled at what he did, and as a result, God chose him to be the "Man". However owing to the great consequences of selecting a "Man", God had to test Avraham to insure that he was in fact worthy of being the "Chosen one".

When Avraham was 75 years old, he was imprisoned by King Nimrod (who hated Avraham for spreading his Mono-Theistic belief system) and thrown into a burning furnace. Miraculously an Angel sent by God came and saved him, and this started Avraham's elevated status, whereby he would regularly communicate with God.

Since Avraham reached his belief system through logical deduction, God tested Avraham with several tests that were contrary to all logic.

Even though the instructions Avraham received from God, were difficult to carry out and hard to understand, nevertheless Avraham did exactly as God commanded, even when it was contrary to every fibre in his being, such as when God commanded Avraham to slaughter his own son Yitzchak.

Once Avraham had proven himself entirely, he was "inaugurated" as the "Chosen one" and God made a special covenant with him. This treaty was a "Promise" from God that he would always protect the descendants of Avraham, and that Avraham's descendants would become the "Chosen people"

Yitzack – "Man" with refined kindness / fear:

Yitzack
Born: 2048
Parents:
Father – Avraham.
Mother – Sarah
Siblings:
Yishmael – Half Brother

Yitzack was born in the Jewish year 2048, in the land of K'nan (Israel).

Unlike his father Avraham, Yitzack's life was totally miraculous from the very beginning.

Yitzack was born to his parents, at a very old age; Avraham was 100 years old and Sarah (his mother) was 90 years old.

Avraham was a person capable of conversing with God, and his mother Sarah was a prophetess, therefore the home environment in which Yitzack grew up, would have been very far from ordinary.

The turning point in Yitzack's life came when he was 38 years old. In the Jewish year 2086, Avraham was tested with his final test; to sacrifice his son Yitzack and to burn his body on a Mizbayach (Alter).

Yitzack who would be the sacrifice, willingly bound himself to the alter and stretched out his neck, for his father to slaughter him.

In literally the last second an Angel called out to Avraham, and told him not to slaughter Yitzack. It was at that moment that Yitzack instilled the quality of "fear" into the Jewish nation that would follow.

THE RABBI MICHAEL J ELJARRAT LEARNING PROGRAMME – CLASS SEVENTY SEVEN

Yakov – "Man" with refined fear / honesty:

> Yakov
> Born: 2108
> Parents:
> Father – Yitzack.
> Mother – Rivka
> Siblings:
> Eisav – Brother

In the Jewish year 2108, Yakov was born to Yitzack and Rivka.

Although Yakov grew up in a home, where both his parents were able to communicate with God, Yakov had an exceptionally difficult life from start to finish.

Yakov had many significant and life changing events in his lifetime.

The first major event in Yakov's life was his feud with his brother Eisav, who wanted to kill Yakov for having "stolen" his birth right.

Yakov fled and stayed with his uncle Lovon a notorious liar and thief. Lovon manipulated, deceived and stole from Yakov for 14 years.

The turning point in Yakov's life came when he was escaping from his uncle's house and left behind some of his belongings.

Yakov went back alone to fetch his belongings, and was accosted by Satan himself. Satan attacked Yakov and after a great struggle Yakov won the fight, at which point the refinement of "Man" was completed, and the "Nation" was born.

> "And he said, you shall not be called Yakov, but Israel"
> (Bereishis / Genesis 32:29)

The newly formed nation would be known as the "Nation of Israel" and its descendants would encapsulate all the qualities of the Patriarchs.

The existence of the "Nation of Israel" would follow the same course as the Patriarchs themselves.

At this point in history the "world goal" shifted once again. The new "world goal" would be the building of the "Nation of Israel".

THE RABBI MICHAEL J ELJARRAT LEARNING PROGRAMME – CLASS SEVENTY EIGHT

CLASS 78   HISTORY

FROM MOSES TO DAVID

In this lesson we will look at the next period of Jewish History from Moses until King David. This period marks the next shift in the "world goal", from building the "Nation of Israel" to establishing leaders of the Nation.

As we said in the previous lesson, the lives of the Patriarchs set the precedent for the Jewish nation which would follow.

Just like a Human being goes through various stages of development: from conception to embryo, and then from fetus to birth so too the Jewish nation went from conception to embryo, and then from fetus to birth.

- The "D.N.A" of the nation of Israel was developed by the Patriarchs.
- The birth of the 12 tribes – could be viewed as conception (splitting of the cells)
- The slavery in Egypt – could be viewed as the "womb" in which the nation of Israel developed into a fetus.
- The redemption – could be viewed as the birth of the Nation of Israel.

A Nation is born:

Just as a new born baby is weak and vulnerable, and heavily dependant on its parents, so too the nation of Israel was weak and on the lowest spiritual level, and heavily dependant on God for miraculous protection.

Just as a baby cries and complains, so too the Jewish nation cried and complained in their journey through the desert.

Just as a baby soils itself, so too the nation of Israel soiled itself with the sin of the golden calf.

Moshe Rabeinu – The first leader of the Nation of Israel:

Just as all the leaders of the Jewish Nation were "hand picked" by God, so too was Moshe (Moses) "hand picked" by God.

The Torah tells us that Yosef (the son of Yakov) was sold as a slave, and then transported to Egypt. Yosef had the skill of being able to interpret dreams, and through several miraculous events became the viceroy of Egypt (A position of second in command to Pharaoh).

THE RABBI MICHAEL J ELJARRAT LEARNING PROGRAMME – CLASS SEVENTY EIGHT

During this era in history, Egypt was the "Super Power" of the world, and was the heart of the world's economy. Yosef was responsible for Egypt's national treasury, and through a system of taxes, Yosef made Egypt the wealthiest nation in the world. The commentaries explain that during the great famine which effected the entire world in the years 2236 -2238 (On the Jewish calendar) Egypt was the only country which had a supply of grain and other consumables.

The reason why Egypt had the "upper hand" was owing to a successful interpretation of a dream.

The Torah tells us (Bereishis / Genesis 41:1-8) that Pharaoh had a dream in which he saw "Seven fat cows and seven thin cows" following that the "Seven thin cows consumed the seven fat cows" Pharaoh went back to sleep thinking that this was just a dream, however upon falling back asleep his dream was repeated, this time he saw "Seven fat ears of grain" and "Seven thin ears of grain" following that the "Seven thin ears consumed the seven fat ears".

Pharaoh was greatly disturbed and knew that this was more than just a dream. It was in fact a mild form of prophecy. No one but Yosef was able to correctly interpret the dream, which was interpreted by Yosef to mean:

- "Seven fat cows" / "Seven fat ears of grain" – Seven years of abundance (During the years 2228 – 2235)
- "Seven thin cows" / "Seven thin ears of grain" – Seven years of famine (During the years 2236 – 2238/9[1])

As a result of his correct interpretation, Yosef was appointed "Finance Minister" of Egypt. Yosef then began implementing measures to store and safe keep grain during the seven years of abundance. Outside of Egypt no one was aware that the abundance would be followed by a famine, thus outside of Egypt no one stock pilled grains and consumables.

When the famine began, the world almost came to a complete stop, with mass starvation worldwide. It was then that Egypt began selling grain to the rest of the world. As the population outside of Egypt had no form of income, they sold their personal belongings to buy food. When they had sold all their movable assets to Egypt, they then sold their fixed assets, and finally their own bodies as "slaves to Egypt". As the famine continued even Egyptian farmers fell prey to the "assets for grain" system. By the year 2239 Egypt effectively "owned" the entire world and its population, and was the greatest "Super Power" ever to be seen in the history of the world. Even until today no single country has had such a grip on the entire world population.

The Torah tells us that shortly after Yakov's death in the year 2255 (3516 BCE) a new Pharaoh arose in Egypt. This period is most likely the start of the "Early dynasty" period in Egyptian history, where the northern and southern regions combined, and were ruled by Pharaohs. The new Pharaoh took advantage of Egypt's great power and enslaved the population. The "Jewish" people were especially oppressed, and this slavery and oppression went from bad to worse. Pharaoh ruled that all "Jewish" males shall be killed at birth. Pharaoh did this to try and control the rapid growth of the "Jewish" population, as he feared that there would soon be more "Jews" than Egyptians in Egypt.

---

1. When Yakov / Jacob came to Egypt the famine ended in his merit.

THE RABBI MICHAEL J ELJARRAT LEARNING PROGRAMME – CLASS SEVENTY EIGHT

When one calculates the rate at which the "Jewish" population increased, we can understand why Pharaoh was concerned with the state of affairs in Egypt.

We know that the "Jewish" population that went into Egypt was 70, we also know that the "Jewish" population which went out of Egypt was 600,000 (excluding children) the Talmud tells us that the number of people who left Egypt was in the region of 3,000,000. We are also told that only 20% of the Jewish population left Egypt, which translates to a total population of 15,000,000 just prior to the exodus. Considering that the "Jewish" people were enslaved in Egypt for 210 years, the growth rate from 70 – 15,000,000 in such a short space of time is enormous.

The pain and suffering of the "Jewish" people was likened to "birth pains", as this was the start of "labour" and the birth of the Jewish Nation, which was soon to emerge from the contracted state of Egypt.

Born from miraculous events and guided with divine providence "Moshe" (Moses) was born. The name "Moshe" (Moses) was given by the daughter of Pharaoh, who saved "Moshe" (Moses) from drowning in the Nile River. The name comes from the word "Mishisehu" (Which in context means "drew him [from the water]) Moshe (Moses) had several other names one of them being "Avigdor"[2] (Father of the generation).

Moshe (Moses) – Leader of the Jewish Nation:

| Moshe
Born: In Egypt
Parents:
Father – Amram.
Mother – Yochevet
Siblings:
Aaron – Brother
Miriam - Sister | After being saved by the daughter of Pharaoh, Moshe was taken to the palace of Pharaoh where he grew up. At the age of 40 (approximately) Moshe became the ruler of the land of Midyan, and remained a ruler for 40 years. At the age of 80 (approximately) Moshe returned to Egypt, where he became the leader of the Jewish people. Moshe was the greatest prophet ever to live (both before and after his time). |

Moshe carried out the will of God, and after many miraculous events led the Jewish nation out of Egypt, and took the Jewish nation to the highest state of spirituality. The nation was "crowned", and bore a special pact with God, this event was symbolized by God giving the Torah to the Jewish Nation, and thus concluded the final step in "Building" the Jewish Nation.

| Yehoshuah
Born: In Egypt
Parents:
Father – Nun
Mother – Unknown
Siblings:
Unknown | After the Jewish Nation had received the Torah, the world goal shifted to occupying the land/territory for the Jewish Nation. The reason for this new goal was two fold. Firstly several of the Mitzvos given in the Torah required occupation of the land, and secondly the Jewish Nation required a temple to fulfil their role in the world. |

---

2. Talmud Megila 13a

THE RABBI MICHAEL J ELJARRAT LEARNING PROGRAMME – CLASS SEVENTY EIGHT

The role of the Jewish Nation – "Avraham Stage"

Just as the Patriarchs required "Filtering Stages" in order to perfect the family roots of "Man", so too the Jewish Nation required (and still does require) filtering.

- The role of the Jewish Nation is to bring Godliness into the world, and thus bring Mankind to a higher state of being.
- This role is accomplished by bringing the presence of God into the world through having a "House of God".

Thus the Jewish Nation could only function to serve its purpose through having a Beis Ha Mikdash (Holy Temple). To accomplish this goal various steps had to be taken by the leaders of the Jewish Nation.

- Yehoshuah – Conquer the land and divide it into territories.
- Judges / Prophets – The next stage was to bring order and guidance to the Jewish Nation.
- Kings – King Saul was the first Jewish King (Jewish history continued with a series of Kings which served as leaders)

King David – A Royal Line is established:

> **David**
> Born: In Israel
> Parents:
> Father – Yishai
> Mother – Nitzevet
> Siblings:
> 6 Brothers
> Eliov, Avinodov, Shima, Nisanel, Radai, Otzem

The final stage in establishing a leader for the Jewish Nation was to establish a Royal Line, this could be thought of as finding a "Man" from the "Nation of Man".

This role was given to King David, and thus King David's rule would continue until the coming of Moshiach, who will come from the blood line of King David.

As we say "David, King of the Jews, lives and is established.

From all the Jewish Leaders, King David had the most difficult life. King David was a descendant of Ruth, a convert to Judaism. King David was oppressed by his contemporaries, as a child he was excluded from his own family, and thought of as being an illegitimate child. For most of King David's life he was "hunted" by people who wanted to kill him, even his own son tried to kill him. King David withstood every trial and was true to God his entire life.

Based upon his unique qualities God selected King David to be the eternal King of the Jewish Nation.

As it is written in Psalms
"The rock that the builders cast aside was for the corner stone."

This is King David who was persecuted by all, but chosen by God as the "corner stone" of the Jewish Nation. (Yalkut Shimoni)

CLASS 79

HISTORY

FROM TANOYIM TO GEONIM

In the year 2448 the Jewish nation received the Torah. This event marked the end of one period and the start of another. The new "world goal" became the building of the Beis Ha Mikdash (The Holy Temple). However due to the actions of the Jewish people, they were punished and remained in the desert for 40 years instead of perhaps 1 year. This delayed their entry into the land designated for the "Nation of Man", as well as the building of the Beis Ha Mikdash, the very tool needed for the Jewish Nation to fulfil their purpose.

The Jewish Nation was then lead by various leaders, as Moshe (Moses) was restricted from entering the land of Israel.

The leaders were:

- Yehoshuah - 28 years
- Othniel – 40 years
- Ehud – 80 years
- Devorah and Barak – 40 years
- Gideon – 40 years
- Abimelech – 3 years
- Tola – 23 years
- Yair – 22 years
- Ammonite's then ruled for 18 years
- Jephthah – 6 years
- Ibzan – 7 years
- Elon – 10 years
- Abdon – 8 years
- Samson – 20 years
- Eli – 39 years
- Samuel – 11 years

This takes us to the Jewish year: 2880. The Jewish Nation was then lead by various Jewish Kings.

The Kings were:

- Saul Ben Kish – 2 years
- Ishboshes Ben Saul – 2 years
- David Ben Yishai (King David) – 40 years
- Solomon Ben David – 40 years

THE RABBI MICHAEL J ELJARRAT LEARNING PROGRAMME – CLASS SEVENTY NINE

The first Beis Ha Mikdash was built by King Solomon in the year 2928 and stood for 410 years. In the year 3338 the first Beis Ha Mikdash was destroyed. This was followed by a period of exile which lasted for 70 years. In the year 3408 authorization was given to build the second Beis Ha Mikdash.

The second Beis Ha Mikdash was built by Darius the Persian King believed to be the son of Achashverosh and Ester (Found in the story of Purim) in the year 3410. In the year 3830 the second Beis ha Mikdash was destroyed, some 420 years after it had been built. This was followed by an exile which has already lasted almost 2000 years.

The Tanoyim:

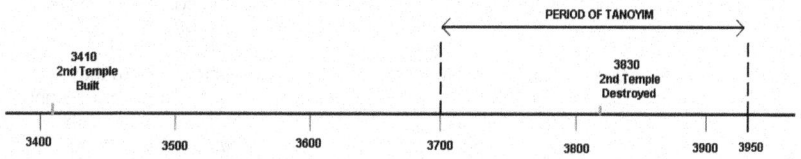

Up until this point in history, the Written Torah (consisting of the Prophets and Writings) was not yet "complete", as the works of the Writings had not yet been written.

Writings such as the books of "Ester" written in the year 3408 (approximately), "Daniel" written in the year 3408 (approximately) and "Ezra / Nechemiah" written in the year 3420 (approximately) as well as the book of "Chronicles" written by Ezra in the same time period, concluded the period of "Holy Writings".

The Tanoyim followed directly after the period of the "Holy Writings". The Tanoyim were the founding sages whose teachings, views and opinions are found in the Mishna.

The Tanoyim built the works of the Oral Torah, the very fabric which holds the Jewish people together even until today. The discussions of these sages, which would later be written in the Mishna, formed the foundation of Jewish law in practice.
Our sages tell us, that every generation is spiritually weaker than the preceding generation. To give us an understanding of the calibre of the Tanoyim, the Talmud tells us that every person listed by name in the Talmud, was able to resurrect the dead. If this is said about the Amorayim of the later generation, how much greater were the Tanoyim who lived several hundred years earlier. As the Talmud relates to the difference between Tanoyim and Amorayim: "If they (the Tanoyim) are people then we (the Amorayim) are like animals, and if we (the Amorayim) are people then they (the Tanoyim) are like Angels" We can barley fathom the spiritual greatness of these individuals, all we can say is, we were privileged to have such individuals shape our history.

The Amorayim:

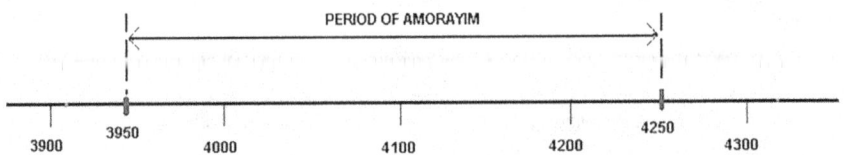

The period of Amorayim began shortly after the destruction of the second Beis Ha Mikdash, and ended in the year 4250 (approximately) with the completion of the Talmud.

The sages known as Amorayim, lived mainly in Bavel (Babylonia) where they established several large Yeshivos, such as: Neharda, Sura, Mechuza, Shilhe and Pumpedisa. It was in these cities that the Amorayim discussed and studied the Mishna of the Tanoyim, and compiled their own works known as "Gemorrah", coming from the Aramaic word "Gmor" meaning study. The Gemorrah was written in Aramaic, the common language spoken in Bavel (Babylonia), unlike the Mishna which was written in Hebrew, the common language spoken by the Tanoyim. The Mishna (written in Hebrew) and the Gemorrah (written in Aramaic) together form what is known as the "Talmud". The Talmud with the works of the sages of Bavel (Babylonia) is called the "Talmud Bavli" (Babylonian Talmud), and the Talmud with the works of the sages of Israel is called the "Talmud Yerushalmi" Jerusalem Talmud.

The Tzavaroyim:

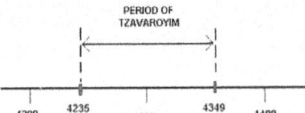

The Tzavaroyim were a group of sages in Bavel (Babylonia) during the period between the Amorayim and the Geonim. This period was very chaotic for the Jews in Bavel, as the Persian rule governing that area was especially harsh on the Jewish population. The Tzavaroyim were responsible for keeping Torah study strong in Bavel during that period in history.

The Geonim:

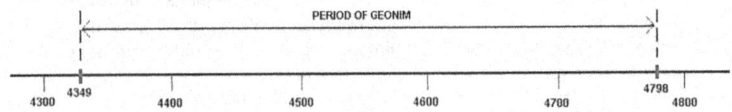

With a change of government from Persian to Arab in the city of Bavel, new challenges arose as Islam became widespread in the Middle East. During this period in history the Jewish nation was graced by the Geonim (lit Geniuses). These sages developed Torah and enlightened the world. Through them Torah in Bavel was maintained.

THE RABBI MICHAEL J ELJARRAT LEARNING PROGRAMME – CLASS EIGHTY

CLASS 80   HISTORY

FROM RISHONIM TO ACHRONIM

In this lesson we will look at the next period of Jewish history, and the sages that influenced and inspired the Jewish people of their time. This period spans almost 1000 years, and brings us to modern day Judaism. We will explore some of the trials and tribulations faced by the Jewish nation during period, and how Judaism became what it is today.

After the destruction of the second Beis Ha Mikdash (Holy Temple) in the year 3828 (approximately) the Jewish nation began spreading to all parts of the world and settling in their new countries. The circumstances which caused the Jewish people to disperse, was in fact a hidden blessing from Hashem. Without a homeland and without a Holy Temple the Jewish people were extremely vulnerable, and as history has shown; the Jewish people were never short of enemies who wanted to attack and destroy the Jewish nation, and take advantage of their vulnerable state. Had the Jewish people been concentrated into one specific area, total annihilation of the Jewish people would have been almost certain. However owing to the fact that the Jewish nation was spread all over the world, the enemies of the Jewish nation were never able to eradicate the entire Jewish population, and as such the Jewish people managed to re-populate several times after various calamities.

From the period of the Geonim, Jews from Bavel began settling in Europe in countries such as Italy. The Jews in these European countries would often send their questions to the Geonim, who were still in their homeland Bavel. Although most of the works written by the Geonim were never published, never the less they still became a part of Jewish culture and were later published by the Rishonim who studied them.

The Rishonim 4288 – 4863 (Jewish calendar year)

For a period lasting almost 600 years, the Jewish sages known as the Rishonim graced the Jewish nation, with many works in all areas of Jewish study. During that period the Jewish population had settled mainly in Western Europe and Northern Africa. It was at this period that two groups formed within Jewish society; The Ashkenazi Jews who settled mainly in France and Italy, and the Sephardi Jews who settled mainly in Spain and Northern Africa. The life and culture of these two groups differed greatly in terms of their adaptation into general society. For Sephardic Jewry, who spoke Spanish and Arabic, gaining a secular education was somewhat easier, and as such the Sephardic Rishonim, were financially independent, and did not require support from their perspective communities. The leaders of the Sephardic communities were mainly professionals such as the Rambam (Maimonides) who was a noted doctor of his time.

THE RABBI MICHAEL J ELJARRAT LEARNING PROGRAMME – CLASS EIGHTY

For Ashkenazic Rishonim, who settled in Western Europe, life was difficult. Not only did they face the challenge of learning a new language, but also through circumstances and by choice they did not acquire any secular education. This meant that the Ashkenazic Rishonim were for the most part dependant on their respective communities for financial aid and support. The "Rosh" an Ashkenazic Rishon had an exceptionally difficult time earning a living, when he moved from the regions of the Ashkenazic community to the regions of the Sephardic community.

The world during the period of the Rishonim:
The period of the Rishonim 4288 – 4863 (528 – 1103 CE)

The middle ages began after the Western Roman Empire had fallen. During the early Middle-Ages, Northern Africa and the Middle East were governed by Islam, however during the high and late Middle-Ages, Christian rule had gained a strong position over these territories, as a result of the Crusades (who intended to capture the "Holy Land"). For the Jewish nation, life in these territories depended greatly upon who was in rule at the time, and the rulers attitude towards Jews.

Rashi: (22 February 1040 – 13 July 1105)

Rabbi Shlomo Yitzaki was a French Rabbi, born in the French town of Troyes, Champagne. It is believed that Rashi was a direct descendant of King David (Although Rashi himself never made such a claim). Rashi studied under Rabbinu Gershom (Known as the M'ohr Ha Godol – The Great Light) who was one of the first to establish France as a place of Torah, and was one of the first who moved from Bavel (Babylon) to France.

The work of Rashi may be the most used commentary studied by the Jewish people until the present day. The commentary of Rashi can be found on the entire written Torah, as well as almost the entire Talmud. There are to date approximately 300 super commentaries on Rashi's commentary. What makes the commentary of Rashi so unique is the fact that it can be studied on a simple level as an explanation to the text at hand, as well as on a much deeper level with many hidden meanings.

Rashi had three daughters, his eldest daughter Yochevet married Meir Ben Shamuel and they had four sons: Shamuel (Rashbam), Yitzack (Rivam), Jacob (Rabbinu Tam) and Shlomo. These four Talmudic scholars were amongst the most prolific of the Baalei – Tosfos. When the Talmud was typeset to be printed it was the commentaries of Rashi and Tosfos which appeared alongside the Talmud. (Rashi on the side of the page closest to the binding, and Tosfos highlighted in bold at the far end of the page).

Rabbinu Tam: (1100 – 1171)

Rabbi Jacob Ben Meir, grandson of Rashi was born in France. His primary teaches were his father and his older brother. He attained world renowned greatness, and is one of the most cited of the Balei Tosfos.

THE RABBI MICHAEL J ELJARRAT LEARNING PROGRAMME – CLASS EIGHTY

Rambam – Maimonides (1135 – 1204)

Rabbi Moses Ben Maimon known as the Rambam was born in Cordova, Spain. Despite the fact that his life was filled with many personal hardships, never the less the Rambam single handily achieved unprecedented greatness in all areas of life. His most famous work was the Mishna Torah also called the "Yad Ha Chazakah" (the "Strong Hand" Hand – in Hebrew having the numerical value of 14, the number of volumes in the Mishna Torah) Apart from the mammoth size of the Mishna Torah (an encyclopaedia of Jewish Law) the Rambam also wrote many other works both on Torah and on secular subjects. The Rambam also was a doctor, mathematician, astronomer and philosopher and was world renowned in all the fields he pursued.

There were of course many great sages that lived through out the Middle Ages (One who is interested in Jewish History should study the works on Jewish History in further detail – as this course will not cover Jewish History in great detail.)

By the year 1478 the Jews of Spain who had enjoyed much success and comfort in their homeland, were expelled in what would later become known as the Spanish Inquisition. Sephardic Jews, who were living in Spain, moved to other parts of the world and started new communities in such places as Greece, Morocco and other North African countries. The end of the medieval period also marks the end of the period of the Rishonim, and the start of a new period. The sages of this new period were called Achronim, and it is in this period that we find ourselves today.

The Achronim 4863 – Present day (Jewish calendar year)

After the printing press was invented in 1452 many historians believe that the age of the renaissance began. The period of the renaissance was a liberating time for Mankind as a whole, and sparked a new age of scientific discovery and creativity. This was followed by the age of discovery, a period in which the continents of the world were discovered and explored. This was followed by various periods expressed by different names in different parts of the world. (Victorian era, Machine era, Modern era) The greatest changes occurred in the last 200 years, with the industrial revolution, electricity, computers and space travel.

Some Achronim of the time:

Rabbi Yosef Karo (1488 – 1575)
Author of the Shulchan Aruch – (code of Jewish law), which covers all areas of Jewish law. In addition he wrote a commentary on the Yad Ha Chazakah of the Rambam known as the Kesef Mishna, as well as a commentary on the Tur, known as the Beis Yosef.

Maharshal (1510 -1573)
Rabbi Shlomo Luria, author of the Yam Shel Shlomo a commentary on the Talmud.

Rabbi Moshe Isserles (1530 – 1572)
Author of the "R'MA" commentary on the Shulchan Aruch as well as being the main halachic authority for Ashkenazic Jews.

Maharsha (1555 – 1632)
Rabbi Shmuel Eliezer Ben Yehuda Ha Levy Adels, author of the Maharsha commentary on the Talmud.

THE RABBI MICHAEL J ELJARRAT LEARNING PROGRAMME – CLASS EIGHTY

Taz (1586 -1667)
Rabbinu David Ha Levy, author of the Turei Zahav commentary on the Shulchan Aruch.

Magen Avraham (1633 – 1683)
Rabbi Avraham Avli Ben Chaim Ha Levy Gombiner, author of the commentary "Magen Avraham" on the Shulchan Aruch.

Gr'A (1720 – 1798)
Rav Eliyahu Ben Shlomo Zalman of Vilna, known as the Vilna Gaon. Author of the Gr'A commentary on the Torah, Mishna, Talmud, Mishna Torah and Shulchan Aruch.

Rabbi Avraham Danzig (1748 – 1821)
Author of the "Chayei Odom" and the "Chochmas Odom" a halachic guide.

Ramchal (1707 – 1746)
Rabbi Moshe Chaim Luzzatto, author of "Derech Hashem", "Da'as uTevunos" and "Mesilas Yesharim".

Minchas Chinuch (1801 – 1874)
Rav Yosef Ben Moshe Babad, author of the Minchas Chinuch.

Rav Naftali Tzvi Yehuda Berlin (1816 – 1893)
Known as the "Netziv", author of Ha'emek Davar a commentary on the Torah as well as many other works. He was also the Rosh Yeshiva of the Volozhin yeshiva.

Rav Yisroel Meir Ha Cohen (1839 – 1933)
Known as the Chofetz Chaim, author of the Mishna Berura a commentary on Jewish law, as well as the Chofetz Chaim and Shemiras HaLoshon a compendium on the laws of Loshon Harah.

Rav Moshe Feinstein (1895 – 1986)
Author of Dibros Moshe a commentary on the Talmud, and Igros Moshe a collection of response on Jewish law.

Chazon Ish (1878 – 1953)
Rabbi Avraham Yeshaya Karelitz, author of the Chazon Ish a commentary on Jewish law.

Rabbi Yakov Yisroel Kanievsky (1899 – 1985)
Know as the Steipler, author of Sharei Tevunah and Kehilas Yakov a commentary on the Talmud.

There were of course many sages during this period spanning almost 1000 years, this list is in no way comprehensive nor are the names which appear greater than those that do not.
It is highly recommended that one studies the life and times of the individuals listed above, as the one or two lines, hardly does justice to the great impact that these sages made on Jewish History.
God willing I will write an advanced course on Jewish History with greater detail on the last 200 years.
I highly recommend reading: Triumph for survival by Rabbi Berel Wine as well as The History of the Jewish people from Nechemeya to the present by Rabbi Rabinowitz.

THE RABBI MICHAEL J ELJARRAT LEARNING PROGRAMME – CLASS EIGHTY ONE

CLASS 81   HISTORY

ISRAEL AND JERUSALEM

In this lesson we will look at the history of Israel and Jerusalem, and the significance this land holds for the Jewish people. We will pay special attention to the events leading up to the founding of the modern state of Israel and contrast the biblical versus the modern concepts of Israel and Jerusalem.

The Promised Land:
In the year 2023 (On the Jewish Calendar) Avraham was selected to be "Man", and subsequently God made a covenant with Avraham. God promised Avraham the following:
- And I (God) will make you into a great nation. (Bereishis / Genesis 12:2)
- And He (God) said to your children, I will give this land. (Bereishis / Genesis 12:5-7)
- And I (God) will give you, and your children after you, the land which you travel on, the entire land of Canaan as an everlasting possession; and I shall be a God to them (Bereishis / Genesis 17:6-8)
- And My (God) promise, I (God) will uphold through Isaac which Sarah will give birth to. (Bereishis / Genesis 17:6-8)

From the versus quoted above, we see that it was God's will to give the land of Canaan to Avraham and Yitzack and their descendants provided that "I shall be a God to them".

As we saw in a previous lesson Avraham had two children:

1. Yishmael (Modern day descendants are the Arab Nations)
2. Yitzack

Yitzack also had two children:

1. Eisav (Modern day descendants are the European Nations)
2. Yakov

As we can see above, the land of Israel has always been occupied (and ruled) by one of the descendants of Avraham. The Jewish Nation when Jews are fulfilling "I shall be a God to them", the Roman (European Nations) when the Jewish people is less deserving, and the Arab Nations when the Jewish Nation is unworthy. Since this is a "God Given" land, when the Jewish Nation is worthy, no one can take it away from them, and when the Jewish Nation is not worthy no one can give it to them. Thus as many nations have learnt in the past, the land of Israel is not a land for conquering, the land of Israel was and always will be "God Given", the ones that God Chooses to settle in the land, will settle in the land, and the ones not chosen by God will be driven out. Each individual that lives in Israel is selected by God according to merit and lineage.

The inhabitants of Israel:

During the days of Avraham, Israel was inhabited by the Cananite Nations, and was then called the land of Canaan. After the Jewish Nation left Egypt they were instructed to settle in the land of Canaan, and wage war with the local inhabitants if necessary. In the days of King Solomon the land of Canaan / Israel was finally occupied and in the hands of the Jewish Nation, this was the state for almost 900 years. After the destruction of the second Temple, (When the Jewish Nation was less worthy) Israel fell into the hands of the Romans (descendants of Eisav /Esau) and into the hands of the Arab Nations (Descendants of Yishmael)

Where is Israel?
Modern day Israel and Canaan (Biblical Israel) are not the same place in terms of their coordinates on a map. Biblical Israel extents far out into the Middle East (past the borders of Jordan and Syria); where as Modern day Israel is found within Biblical Israel and overlapping in areas to the south.

Europe in the year 1900:

As we saw previously, the lives of the Patriarchs were the blue print for their descendants which would follow. Never do we see this maxim unfold so clearly, as it did in the period before world war two. Ever since the period of the Rishonim almost 1000 years ago, a divide existed between the life of the Sephardic Jewry and the life of the Ashkenazic Jewry. The Rishonim emanating from Sephardic Jewry, were financially independent and well educated, they were able to achieve unfathomable Torah greatness, as well as being able to integrate into their surrounding societies simultaneously, without difficulty. The Rishonim emanating from Ashkenazic Jewry, were dependant greatly on their respective communities, however for the most part the communities themselves were not financially independent. This was due to circumstances and choice. Europe was mainly governed by Christian authorities, and the atmosphere was not in the slightest conducive to Jewish life, never mind Torah greatness. However the Ashkenazic Jewry still managed to not only maintain a Torah lifestyle but even to produce exceptional Torah giants. This was accomplished by isolation and fortification from their surrounding societies. Therefore one can say: that circumstances created their predicament, and choice determined their survival.

This isolation from general society had its many advantages. For those pure of heart and soul there were no "distractions", and Torah was the only focus of life, as it was in Bavel (Babylon). Up until the industrial revolution in the 1800's integrations into mainstream society was not essential, in the sense that for a Jew, complete dedication to God could be accomplished as is befitting a Jew, and integration or non-integration would only have bearing on financial independence or financial survival.

However after the industrial revolution, the world changed dramatically. Those who were integrated into society kept abreast of the current changes and were thus able to survive, and even prosper. However those that had not integrated into society got left behind, with little chance for survival. For Ashkenazic Jewry who had isolated themselves, times were tough. Although they maintained their Torah greatness, they lacked the skills and education needed to survive in the world. This caused huge pressure on the Ashkenazic community at large.

THE RABBI MICHAEL J ELJARRAT LEARNING PROGRAMME – CLASS EIGHTY ONE

The first split to occur in the Ashkenazic community was between the Ashkenazic Jews of Western Europe and Ashkenazic Jews of Eastern Europe. Western Europe unlike communist Eastern Europe and Asia was more liberal, and Ashkenazic Jews of Western Europe slowly started integrating into their anti-Semitic societies.

For Western European Jews integrating into society must have been nothing less than uncomfortable. Society was quite happy for the Jews to keep to themselves, and Jews would have felt out of place amongst their society. The Jews of Western Europe tried different ways to blend into their hostile society, from changing their clothes to changing their beliefs, however apart from a few individuals, integration always came at a price, it was a choice between integrating into society and abandoning Torah and Judaism, or maintaining Torah and Judaism and being impoverished.

For Eastern European Jews, financial struggle and impoverishment was a way of life.[1] Apart from the lack of integration into society, Eastern European Jewry was governed by Authoritarian dictators. This resulted in wide spread poverty. Most of the Jews in Eastern Europe were peasants who were constantly on the verge of starvation. Eastern European Jewry was tempted by the prospect of integration, and to follow suite of the Western European brothers. As they were looking to end their starvation and have a better life, Eastern European Jews were far more desperate, and abandoning Torah and Judaism was a real prospect if it meant putting an end to their starvation. It was out of this desperation that many fractions began to form within the Ashkenazic community of Europe.

Although politics has absolutely nothing to do with Judaism, for the Jews in Europe, forming political parties was a means to form new "types" of Jews in what appeared to be a legitimate construct. Each "type" of Jew was represented by the political party, each with its own ideals and values. The aim of these political parties was to create a "modern" Jew that would fit into "modern" society, this modern Jew would still carry the label of "Jew" but for all intents and purposes would be just like everyone else.

By the year 1899 two political movements had formed, both offering Jews a chance to abandon Torah Judaism, normalize into society and earn a good living, while at the same time holding onto Jewish "culture". What was to be considered Jewish "culture" depended on the view of the political movement.

- Yiddishist Movement: Jewish "culture" meant speaking Yiddish.
- Zionist Movement: Jewish "culture" meant governing a Jewish homeland.

The Yiddishist Movement soon faded away and the Zionist movement (secular in nature) gained strong popularity. For religious, Torah observing Jews having a political party which was secular in nature but recognized as legitimate in the "world's eyes" created a new dilemma. Torah observant Jews realized that the only way to be recognized in the "world's eyes" as a legitimate opposition to secular parties, was to form their own political parties, and thus two new parties soon formed each with its own ideals and values.

---

1. Gefilta Fish is one of the many traditional Eastern European Jewish foods – made from entrails and off-cuts as could be afforded. (Other cheap foods include: Chulent, Kugel and Tzimas)

- Mizrachi (1902): worked with the Zionist movement, as having a homeland would be beneficial to Torah observant Jews as well.
- Aggudas Yisroel (1912): Worked against the Zionist movement to show opposition against their (Zionist) secular views.

Needless to say, since politics isn't a part of Judaism, the formation of the many political parties just brought hatred and divide amongst the Jews. These divides have in essence crippled the Ashkenazic community until this very day.

As we said earlier this parallels the events of the Patriarch Jacob. On the way to meet his brother Esav (Esau), Jacob went back alone to fetch some small jugs, he had left behind. He was accosted and attacked by Satan, who crippled his one leg (Bereishis / Genesis 32:25-33)

So too the Ashkenazic Jews went in alone into Europe the hostile territory of Esav (Esau) Motivated to get "small jugs" / financial independence, the Ashkenazic Jews were accosted and attacked by the forces of Satan (Anti Jewish sentiment) and were left fragmented and "crippled". The other leg of Jews namely the Sephardic Jews, had long since learnt how to integrate and maintain Torah Judaism, for this leg fragmentation and divide never occurred and thus was not crippled.

The Jewish nation is likened to a Human Body; each generation from Sinai is a lower limb of the body. I.e. Moses' generation is the head; the generation of the Judges is the chest etc. The divide between Sephardim and Ashkenazim occurred in the middle of the time line (the waist) and the two legs can therefore be likened to these two "Legs" of the Jewish population. Today we are at the "Feet" of the Human Body, as today we are divided like the Toes, each Toe does not cooperate with the other, as do fingers. However the entire Human Body is resting on us.

The land of Israel:

The land of Israel was under the Ottoman Empire (1841 -1917) then under British Mandate (1920 – 1948) and in 1948 the modern state of Israel was formed.

CLASS 82

HISTORY

MITZVOS OF THE LAND

In the previous lesson we looked at the significance of Israel and Jerusalem, and the events in history leading up to the current state of affairs. In the next lesson we will look at the current situation in Israel, and the events leading up to the various conflicts which now take place in Israel. However in this lesson we will look at Israel and its history from a purely spiritual point of view.

We saw previously that when God chose a "Man", God also promised two other things:

1. "Man" would become an entire Nation, driven by a single purpose.
2. "Man" would inherit a particular piece of land, from which he would be able to fulfill his purpose.

What does land have to do with Judaism?
When one analyses the events in history concerning the history of the Jewish people, one question often remains unanswered namely "What does land have to do with Judaism?" The answer to this question holds the key to understanding the very fundamental concept of: What does it mean to be a Jew?

Let us begin by asking two questions:

1. Why did God promise to give land to Avraham?
2. Why did God want to give the land of Canaan in particular?

To answer the first question let us recap the purpose of a Jew in this world, namely: To attain perfection (closeness) to God through making good decisions and to show the world that God is the creator.

On the surface it would seem that all that is needed for attainment / fulfillment of this goal is: A variety of choices to choose from, and a means of expression to show the world that God is the creator. To achieve this, God placed good and bad into the world in all shapes and forms, thus giving rise to free choice. God also imbued speech and action into man, and thus man can express what ever he so desires.

Therefore the question remains, why does a Jew need land? The answer is: Being a Jew requires more than attaining spiritual greatness, if God wanted "Man" to be entirely spiritual, God would have made "Man" as an angel. The purpose of "Man" is to be immersed in physicality, and to transform the mundane into something meaningful and spiritual. As the sages explain, the structure of a being shows its purpose. Let us examine three different creatures that God created, and through their form we will gain insight into their purpose.

THE RABBI MICHAEL J ELJARRAT LEARNING PROGRAMME – CLASS EIGHTY TWO

Three creatures we will examine are:

1. The Animal
2. The Human Being
3. The Angel

The Animal:

The animal we will look at is the domesticated animal, such as the cow, sheep or goat. What these three animals have in common is that they all have four legs, and they walk on all four. Thus the sages tell us that an animal is rooted entirely in the physical.

The Human Being:

The Human Being has two legs and two arms; the legs are grounded and used for walking, were as the arms are flexible and used for a variety of functions. Thus the sages tell us that a Human Being is partly rooted in the physical and partly rooted in the spiritual.

The Angel:

The Angel (not being physical, does not have arms and legs as we know it, but it) has "Wings" which it used to complete its functional tasks, and has no earthly component. Thus the sages tell us that an Angel is rooted entirely in the spiritual.

Therefore the "Human Being" is an entirely unique creature. The Human Being is a mix of two entirely opposite things. A great Human Being therefore is one that is "down to earth" in a literal and metaphorical sense and incredibly spiritual at the same time. Thus the Human Being has the most difficult task of all the creatures that God created. All the other creatures can focus on one area of development, but Human Beings must focus on two areas of development simultaneously.

It is for this reason that the Jew needs land, or at least a root in physicality. Since the primary job of a Jew is to transform physicality into something meaningful and spiritual, the Jew needs physical things to transform.

Without ownership of physical items a Jew runs the risk of either becoming like an animal who is immersed entirely in the physical or like an Angel with no roots in the physical, and although the latter seems noble, it is neither the purpose of "Man" nor is it a sustainable solution. It is for this reason that God promised to give land to Avraham and his descendants as this is an important element, or a tool which is needed in order to fulfill the purpose.

Why the land of Canaan?

As we saw in a previous lesson, all events which occur, do so in a five dimensional plane namely:

1. Longitude
2. Latitude
3. Altitude
4. Time
5. Spiritually

The sages tell us that "Tzion"/ Zion is the place where the Temple was built, and the place where the Third Temple will be built in future. The word "Tzion"/ Zion in Hebrew means the mark / spot, this land in fact marks the spot on earth that contains the highest spiritual energy.

Our sages tell us that in terms of spiritual radiation; the centre of the world is Israel / The land of Canaan, the centre of Israel is Jerusalem, the centre of Jerusalem is the Temple mount, the centre of the Temple mount is the Temple, the centre of the Temple is the holy of holies.

Thus God gave land to Avraham as we saw above, and specifically the land of Canaan as it is the most spiritually energized.

Making use of this spirituality:

Although superficially, the land of Israel looks just like any other land, in reality this land is spiritually infused like no other land. This additional spirituality is manifested in the special laws which apply only to the land of Israel. Any produce which grows within this Holy Land of Israel, contains within it a certain type of spirituality, and various procedures need to be performed prior to their consumption.

Some of these laws include:
- **Teruma** – Giving between 1/40 – 1/60 to the Cohen.
- **Mei'ser** –
    1. Giving 10% to the Levy in the first and forth year of the Shemita cycle (Known as Mei'ser Rishon)
    2. Giving 10% to consecration in the second and fifth year of the Shemita cycle (Known as Mei'ser Sheini – Eaten by the owners in Jerusalem)
    3. Giving 10% to the poor in the third and sixth year of the Shemita cycle (Known as Mei'ser Oni)
- **Shemita** – A Law requiring all agricultural activity to stop in the seventh year of the Shemita cycle.
- **Yovel** – A law requiring all agricultural activity to stop in the seventh cycle of the Shemita (i.e. year 50)

Some of these laws apply only when the Temple is standing, while others apply at all times. The above are just a few examples of Mitzvos of Israel. It is the spiritual energy of the land of Israel which makes it a desired land for the Jewish people.

THE RABBI MICHAEL J ELJARRAT LEARNING PROGRAMME – CLASS EIGHTY THREE

CLASS 83   HISTORY

CURRENT SITUATION IN ISRAEL

To write a lesson about the current situation in Israel, is like striking at a moving target, in a sense that Israel is forever changing on almost a daily basis. Therefore in stead of looking at "what" the current situation is, we will look at "why" Israel is so volatile and the reasons that Israel is forever changing.

As we said previously, the land of Israel is very unique in the following ways:

- It's a "God – Given" land – Meaning it is a land, whose inhabitants are "hand – picked" by God, those who don't merit staying in the land of Israel, are thrown out one way or another.
- It's a spiritually unique land – meaning that it is a land which is very intense, and spiritually charged.

The Promised Land:

Israel must be one of the smallest countries in the world, and yet it makes "Headline news" as often as any of the world's super power nations. The question is why? What makes Israel the focus of the world's attention? The answer is, as we said above Israel is a unique land, which belongs to the descendants of Avraham (Jews, Arabs and Europeans) and because it's spiritually super charged, all the descendants are drawn to it in an inexplicable way. Whether it was the Christian Europeans in the days of the Crusades, or the Islamic Arabs at various other times or the Jewish Jews at other points in history, all the descendants want it, and are willing to fight for it.

Therefore more often than not, Israel is at war. It is for this reason that Israel continuously makes "Headline news" as a new conflict erupts on a daily basis. There is no reason why there couldn't be peace in the Middle East, but since each one of Avrahams descendants has full entitlement to the land (when they deserve) forming any sort of compromise is a futile exercise.

In order for there to be peace in the Middle East, the Jews must occupy the land of Israel, and in order for the Jews to occupy the land of Israel, the Jews must be worthy, and the cold hard truth is that they are not. The Jewish nation today, is probably at the weakest spiritual point it has been in history. Idol worship in the form of idealizing money is prolific, and thinking has been replaced with pointless superficial externalities. It is purely by the grace of God that the Jewish Nation has not been destroyed. Even though God gives special treatment to the Jewish Nation,

THE RABBI MICHAEL J ELJARRAT LEARNING PROGRAMME – CLASS EIGHTY THREE

this is a kindness which we should not take for granted. Those who occupy Israel must do so humbly, carrying the yolk of responsibility that goes with the territory.

The opposite can also be said, that is: When the Jewish Nation is worthy, they will inherit the land as God promised Avraham, and absolutely no nation will be able to push them out or terrorize them.

By way of parable we can think of the land of Israel as an "executive office" in a corporate environment. The executive office comes with a large expensive desk and state of the art equipment. This office is reserved for the C.E.O. of the company. The C.E.O. has a functional role to play within the organization, and so long as the C.E.O. is doing his/her job right; he/she deserves the perks. However if the C.E.O. is dysfunctional and incompetent, he/she no longer belongs in the "executive office", and the board of directors and shareholders will quickly have him/her removed from office.

So too the Jewish Nation is the "C.E.O." of the world, when we are serving God and making God's name great in the world, we belong in the "executive office" of Israel, and we'll hold the most powerful position. However when we disgrace Hashem's name in the world, and we abandon and disgrace the Torah and those who study Torah, then we must abdicate, until we are worthy and God calls us back in.

Israel in the year 1900:

As we saw previously the situation of the Jewish people in Europe was far from perfect, and as a result several movements began with the hope of starting a new "type" of Jewish community either in Europe or elsewhere. It is estimated that the Jewish population in the world at the turn of the 20th century was 16 million, with the vast majority of Jews living in both Western and Eastern Europe. The Zionist movement wanted to create a "Modern" Jew who was not bound by the Torah or its values, but rather would be bound to a land which would maintain "Jewish culture".

As we have stated above, the land of Israel comes with the condition of true and faithful Torah observance. It is almost ironic that the Zionist Movement chose the land of Israel to start a new Jewish community being void of Torah values, for that is the single place on earth that Judaism without Torah would be rejected. Had the Zionist Movement chosen any other place on earth (such as Uganda as was offered by the UN prior to 1948) to start a new form of Judaism, they would have been entirely successful, despite the fact that they were uprooting Judaism altogether. Since God helps man to achieve his goals for both good and bad.[1] However the land of Israel is entirely unique, and does not conform to the general laws of providence.

At that time the land of Israel was under the control of the Ottoman Empire, after which it was ruled by British Mandate. The land of Israel remained under British Mandate up until the forming of the State of Israel in 1948.

The early years:

With the rise of Nazism in Europe in the 1930's, approximately 250,000 Jews moved to Israel to escape the Nazi regime. This influx of new settlers caused the Arab revolt (1936 – 1939). This intern led to the issue of the white paper of 1939 which curtailed the immigration of Jews around the world, as many countries closed their "doors" to escaping Jewish refugees.

---

1. Talmud Makos 10b

THE RABBI MICHAEL J ELJARRAT LEARNING PROGRAMME – CLASS EIGHTY THREE

After the Holocaust in 1945, the British faced a great conflict with the Jewish community, and in 1947 the British withdrew their mandate over Palestine, stating that they cannot find a solution that would be acceptable to both the Arabs and the Jews living in Palestine. Later that same year the UN sought to divide Palestine into two states, one for the Arabs and one for the Jews. This plan was accepted by the Jewish community, but rejected by the Arab community. This sparked a civil war within Palestine, the Palestinian economy collapsed and 250,000 Palestinian Arabs were expelled from Palestine.

The State of Israel:

In the late afternoon on the 14th of May 1948, David Ben-Gurion proclaimed independence and the State of Israel was born. The very next day Egypt, Syria, Lebanon and Iraq waged war against Israel. The war lasted for a year and an Israeli border was marked, which is known as the "Green Line".

Between the years 1948 and 1958 the population of Israel rose from 800,000 to 2,000,000. By the year 1966 Israeli – Arab relations were at an all time low, and in 1967 a war broke out in Israel, this was known later as the 6 day war. On October 6 1973 Israel was launched into yet another war, this war was later to become known as the Yom Kippur war.

In 1982 Israel went to war against Lebanon, this was followed by other conflicts which occurred in 1987, 1992 and 1995. In the year 2000 the first "Intafada" began which included recurring waves of terrorist attacks. In 2006 Israel went to war with Lebanon for the second time and in 2008 Israel entered into a new conflict with Hamas, this conflict has continued until the present day, and seems to be an ongoing situation.

As we can see above, Israel has barely gone a single decade without a war. Israel remains a volatile and fragile state, and will in all likelihood continue in its current state until the coming of Moshiach, when the Third Beis Ha Mikdash (Temple) will be built and peace will fill the world, Amen.

THE RABBI MICHAEL J ELJARRAT LEARNING PROGRAMME – CLASS EIGHTY FOUR

CLASS 84

HISTORY

THE JEWISH COMMUNITY IN SOUTH AFRICA

In this lesson we will look at the history of South African Jewry, over the past 200 years or so. South Africa is a rich country, with beautiful seas, magnificent forests and several bustling metropolitan city centers. The diversity of South Africa is truly unique, and its history is filled with many complexities. To explore the history of South Africa in its own right is a grand task, more over to explore the unique Jewish people is an equally grand task, and thus to explore the history of the Jewish people in South Africa is a task which requires years of research and perhaps thousands of interviews. As this is a course merely on the fundamentals concepts, we will explore this topic in the same manner as we have done previously with other complex topics, namely glancing over the important points, and their significance with regards to Judaism. If you have a particular interest in this subject, I recommend that you do further research.

1652 – 1820:

In the year 1448, Bartholomew Dias and Vasco da Gama first sailed around the Cape of Good Hope. Originally set up as a stopping point for ships and their crew to rest and re-stock, and later set up by the Dutch East India Company as a settlement, the Cape of Good Hope was a major destination for all explorers.

In the year 1652 the Dutch East India Company sent its representative Jan Van Riebeeck to establish the Cape of Good Hope as a permanent settlement. Although there may have been Jews on board when Jan Van Riebeeck first set foot in South Africa, Jewish settlement did not occur in great numbers until the year 1820.

1820 – 1880:

At the start of the 1800"s Jewish people began settling in Cape Town. The first Shul was built in the year 1841. This Shul was called the Gardens Shul. In the early days of Jewish South Africa, many Jews were involved in the diamond industry, shipping, fishing and ostrich farming.

THE RABBI MICHAEL J ELJARRAT LEARNING PROGRAMME – CLASS EIGHTY FOUR

The Volksraad (Parliament) of the time had strict rules about who could occupy positions of power, and as of such Jews could not hold military posts, state secretary, president or any position in Parliament. Their rules stated that these positions could only be occupied by persons above the age of 30 with permanent property. The Boer (Farming Community) only established themselves in the year 1857, and as a result they were also excluded from high power positions. This situation caused strife between the early Dutch settlers and the Boer, with Jews taking both sides. The Jews that settled amongst the Boer were later known as Boerejode (Boer Jews).

The Witwatersrand Gold Rush:

In the year 1886, large gold deposits were discovered in the area stretching from Johannesburg to Welkom. It is believed that the Australian gold miner George Harrison was the first to make this discovery. Soon after the discovery many people flooded to Johannesburg, in the hope of making a fortune. Within 10 years the population of Johannesburg outgrew the population of Cape Town, giving rise to the "Rand Lords" (a group of wealthy miners and industrialists who made their fortune from gold mining) Johannesburg was nick named "The City of Gold". The great posterity that came with the discovery of gold also had its down side, with the great influx of foreigners, heavy taxes were made and a great deal of resentment was felt between the local Boer and the British mine owners.

1880 -1939:

The first Anglo – Boer war, also known as the "Transvaal War" was a short war that occurred between the Boer and the British who governed Transvaal. The war took place from 1880 -1881, and the Boer regained their independence.

The second Anglo – Boer war lasted from 1899 – 1902. In this war the British Empire defeated the Boer, and turned the Boer republic into British colonies. This was a long and bloody war with great casualties sustained on both sides. The great human atrocities that took place in the British concentration camps sparked a world outcry and the British were forced to make a treaty with the Boer. It is ironic that Germany protested the ill treatment of the Boer in British concentration camps, and yet several years later they would be responsible for a far greater human atrocity, in which the world kept silent. It is believed that approximately 300 Jews fought along side the Boer in the second Anglo – Boer war.

In 1902 a Boer union was formed, which gave the Boer a certain level of independence. From 1902 – 1930 the Jews lived in relative harmony with the Boer. However in 1930, the South African government put a clamp on Jewish emigration. With the rise of Nazism and general Anti Semitism in Europe, many Jews were emigrating from Eastern Europe (Mainly Lithuania) and heading for South Africa. In 1886 it is believed that the South African Jewish population was just 4000, however by the year 1916 it had grown to over 40,000.

By 1939 the migration of Jews from Europe had come to a complete halt. Many Afrikaaner Boer were pro Nazi, and banned Jews from becoming permanent residence of South Africa. In 1948 the National Party come to power, and many Afrikaans politicians publicly apologized to the South African Jewish community for their earlier Anti Semitic actions. The South African government of the time created an Apartheid state, whereby complete segregation between various races was enforced.

THE RABBI MICHAEL J ELJARRAT LEARNING PROGRAMME – CLASS EIGHTY FOUR

1948 – 1994 (Apartheid South Africa):

Apartheid South Africa, sometimes referred to as the "Old South Africa" had various advantages and disadvantages for the Jews living in South Africa. Under Apartheid rule Blacks, Coloreds and Indians were marginalized, and denied basic human rights such as education, employment and housing. The full extent of the damage caused by the Apartheid era will never be known, but there is no doubt that the current fall of South Africa was partly caused by the mistakes of the past. Although the laws of Apartheid were unjust, it brought a level of discipline to the governance of the country. Jews were lucky in the sense that they were white, and as a result they benefited from the unjust laws. During the 1950's and 1960's large Jewish communities were established in the Johannesburg central business district and the surrounding areas. In the 1970's and 1980's the Jewish community shifted away from the city centre into the nearby areas of Hilbrow, Yeoville and Berea.

Pressurized by world opinion and trade embargos, South Africa started relaxing its Apartheid laws by the mid 1980's. The South African Jewish community reached its peak in the 1980's with a population estimated at 120,000. By the start of the 1990's negotiations were underway to end the Apartheid era, this intern caused much anxiety and uncertainty within the South African Jewish community, and within the South African society as a whole. In the year 1994 Nelson Mandela was released from prison, and the "Old South Africa" formally came to a close.

1994 – Present (Modern South Africa)

With the change of government from white to black in 1994, fears arose that South Africa would follow suite of the other failed African countries that quite literally fell apart soon after they had gained independence. These fears sparked mass immigration out of South Africa, by Jews and non Jews alike. Over the next twenty years the Jewish population fell from 120,000 to approximately 70,000 with many orthodox Jews leaving the Jewish community. The Jewish community shifted once again to areas such as Glenhazel and its surrounding areas.

The "New South Africa" has developed in a unique way, and has become a land of latent opportunity. Today the state of the world in general is chaotic; this intern has worked to South Africa's advantage as it has masked the underlying problems of South Africa such as corruption and disservice. South Africa has become a progressive country, and the Jewish community within, has to a large extent followed the trends of the Jewish communities around the world. (With commercialized Judaism and "Kiruv" franchises such as Chabad, Ohr Somayach, Arachim and Aish Ha Torah).

For an intelligent individual, the point is clear that regardless of where in the world a Jew finds him/her self, the duty remains the same i.e. to attain perfection and closeness to God. May Hashem bring us out of the darkness into the light and build the Third Beis Ha Mikdash speedily in our days, Amen.

CLASS 85   HISTORY

THE DIFFERENCE BETWEEN JUDAISM AND OTHER RELIGIONS

In this lesson we will look at the history and development of several religions found in the world today. We will then explore the fundamental differences between Judaism and other religions.

The starting point of this lesson, is to dispel the popular misconception that Judaism is a religion. Religion can be defined as: A belief in a Super Natural power or powers that control man's destiny[1]. When you first see this definition the problem is not at all apparent, however upon further investigation we will see that this very definition is what separates Judaism from other religions.

The Ramchal in Derech Hashem[2] begins by saying "Every Jew must believe and know that there exists a first being, without beginning or end, who brought all things into existence and continues to sustain them. This being is God" This opening statement of the Ramchal is in actual fact a very precise definition of what Judaism is.

At first glance there doesn't seem to be much difference between our definition of religion and our definition of Judaism, however on closer inspection the two are worlds apart.

As the Ramchal explains "Every Jew must belief and know"; The concept of knowing is foreign to all religions, but an integral part of Judaism. In Judaism one's life journey is a process of "Getting to know God". To understand this concept fully we need to first understand the difference between belief and knowledge. Belief implies trust as in "I believe what I read in the newspaper yesterday, but I wasn't there to see it for myself, I therefore trust that the journalist was reporting truthfully". Where as knowledge is not dependant on trust, as in "I don't believe what I read in the newspaper yesterday, I was there and I know what happened". When one knows something, one doesn't need to believe or trust anyone, knowledge is powerful, it creates independence. In Judaism we need to believe and know God. This implies two distinctive tasks; one to believe what we are told and trust the ones who told us, the second to "distrust" what we have been told and to base our actions on knowledge. We will now explore these two tasks further.

---

[1]. Web Definitions
[2]. Part 1 Chapter 1

THE RABBI MICHAEL J ELJARRAT LEARNING PROGRAMME – CLASS EIGHTY FIVE

Belief:

As we stated above the concept of belief requires trust. With regards to Judaism this means as follows: we need to trust the prophets and the sages who told us about the nature of God, and how God runs the world. Since we are not prophets or sages, we are dependant on the teachings of our forefathers for guidance in the ways of God.

Therefore if we want to be closer to God; we must be believers. We must believe what we have been told despite the fact that we don't know or understand. We must believe with faith that all the words of the Torah, prophets, writings and sages are true, despite the fact that we may not understand.

Belief is something which is found in religion as well, whether it is believing that Jesus will be a saviour or Mohamed being a prophet sent by God, believers place their faith in what they have been told, whether they understand it or not.

Knowledge:

In Judaism we have an added task of knowing God, this means to say: we are responsible for verifying everything that we have been told. We have to ask questions, we have to study and we must build our own reservoir of knowledge. What makes Judaism unique, is the fact that we say: Believe all the teachings to be true and at the same time test it for yourself, and you will come to the same conclusion. This is the meaning behind the words which we say daily:

"Our God and God of our Forefathers"

- "Our God" – meaning the God that we have come to know personally, through life experience, study and self gained knowledge.
- "God of our Forefathers" – meaning the God that we have been taught about; the God who our Forefathers knew and the God we believe in even though our knowledge is incomplete.

It is only with believe and knowledge that one can gain an understanding of the ultimate reality, and attain closeness to God.

Knowledge is something foreign to other "religions". Other religions frown upon those who ask questions. People who ask questions are considered to be "non-believers". We find this concept in history with regards to Christianity, the "New Testament" remained un-translated for many years, in order that only clergy members would have access to the knowledge. The Christian authorities feared that should the masses gain knowledge, they would upset the power and authority of the Church, and this is exactly what happened when the "New Testament" was translated. The fundamental flaw with religion is that if the religion is not based on truth, then the only way to keep the religion intact is by convincing other people to "believe", knowledge on the other hand can be seen as poison to religion, as knowledge has the power to reveal the underlying concepts. Should religion be "selling" untruths "Knower's" as apposed to "Believers" are the biggest threat to that religion.

Salesmen:

Based upon what we have seen above, we can now understand an interesting phenomenon. In Judaism the concept of "converting the masses" is forbidden, in fact Jewish law states that one should discourage people from converting to Judaism. (And observe the seven Noachite laws, as apposed to converting) In almost all religions on the other hand "converting the masses" is not only not forbidden but encouraged. For many of the world's religions, those who do not believe and accept the said faith are doomed and destined for hell, and it is the life mission of "Believers" to convert as many people as possible to the said religion.

As we said above religion is based on believe, and believe that is not supported by knowledge is short lived. If one person was to believe, and all those around him/her did not believe, the single believer would soon question his/her own beliefs. Thus the only way to sustain belief without knowledge is to increase the number of believers, and in that way a support group is formed.

The more fragile a belief is, and the more unfounded or untruthful the belief is; the stronger the "need" to create believers. In this sense the litmus test of a religion, is the level of enthusiasm to convert others, the greater the need/desire to convert the masses, the further away from truth that religion is.

This concept is easily understood with regards to sales and marketing. Drug dealers are not the greatest salesmen, they don't come with a convincing presentation or an articulated speech, and nevertheless they manage to sell their product. How? Simple, the product sells itself. Users get addicted, and they come running to the dealer. Recruiters for pyramid schemes on the other hand, are amongst the world's greatest salesmen. They dress well, present well and know how to deliver the most articulate speech. When it comes to pyramid schemes only the best salesmen are successful, why? Simple the product is worthless; making a sale is dependant solely on the skills of the salesman.

Truth does not need marketing; it is a "product" that sells itself. However today we live in a world of lies and corruption, and unfortunately many people fall for the "pyramid schemes" and fall prey to shrewd salesmen.

Some of the world's religions:

Christianity:
- Catholic – founded in the 1st century.
- Protestant – founded in the 16th century.

Islam:
- Sunni – founded in the 7th century.
- Shia - founded in the 7th century.
- Wahhabi - founded in the 7th century

In the world today there are literally hundreds of religions some include:
- Bahai
- Rastafari
- Druze
- Hinduism
- Jainism
- Buddhism

THE RABBI MICHAEL J ELJARRAT LEARNING PROGRAMME – CLASS EIGHTY SIX

CLASS 86   HISTORY

DIFFERENT PHILOSOPHICAL APPROACHES IN JUDAISM

This lesson brings us to the end of our short course on Jewish History. In this lesson we will look at the different philosophical approaches to Judaism, and some of the history associated with the development of several of these approaches.

The verse[1] states:
"The end matter, everything is heard, God should be feared, and his Mitzvos should be kept because this is all of Man."

In other words:
"All that matters, is everything is heard, and God should be feared and his Mitzvos should be kept, because this is what Man is all about."

Before we branch off into the different philosophical approaches, it is important to establish, that a philosophical approach is only considered a valid approach in Judaism if it adheres to the two items stated in the verse above, namely:

1. Fear of God (Implied belief)
2. Observance of the Mitzvos

A way of life which does not include fear of God, and observance of the Mitzvos is not classified as Judaism. Many people through out history have attempted to created variations of Judaism which did not include these items. Although some of these new variations gained popularity and have large followings, even to this day, this in no way changes the definition of Judaism. Christianity and Islam also have big followings, but Christianity is not Islam and Islam is not Christianity and neither one is Judaism.

At the same time a way of life which does include fear of God and observance of Mitzvos is classified as Judaism; Regardless of clothing, external appearance and geographical location. There is only one Judaism; and it is based solely on thoughts, actions and speech, not on childish externalities. Unfortunately due to the lethal combination of ignorance and arrogance, this issue has become clouded when in actual fact it is as clear as day.

---

1. Koheles / Ecclesiastes 12:13

THE RABBI MICHAEL J ELJARRAT LEARNING PROGRAMME – CLASS EIGHTY SIX

Philosophy:

Philosophy can be defined as[2]

1. Doctrine: A belief (or system of beliefs) accepted as authoritative by some group or school.
2. Any personal belief about how to live or how to deal with a situation.

A parable:

A wise man once received four different letters from four different people. Each letter contained a single question, and the question was absolutely identical in each one of the four letters.

The wise man replied to each one of the four letters, giving a completely different answer to each writer.

Several weeks past and the wise man once again received four different letters; it was from the same four people that had written earlier. This time the letters contained a single sentence "Thank you for your advice, I was successful"

The townsfolk were in awe of the wise man…."How could the wise man, give four different answers to the identical question, and be correct on all four counts."

The townsfolk asked the wise man to explain:
The wise man answered: Each one of the four individuals asked me

"How do I get to the city centre from where I live?"

Although they all asked the same question, I could see from the postage stamps that they were living in different locations.

To the person coming from the north I said "Travel south…"
To the person coming from the south I said "Travel north…" etc…. (Parables of Rabbi Eljarrat)

Philosophy can be understood in the same manner. When the question which is being asked can be understood from various perspectives, there may be many view points but in essence, everyone is saying the same thing.

Should the four people in our parable above argue with one another, regarding which way is the correct way to travel, they would indeed be foolish; but sometimes this is exactly what happens, the man from the south will argue that the only way to get to the city centre is to travel north, he'll bring his experience as a proof "I tried it, and I was successful" and he'll appeal to authority to substantiate his claim "This is what the wise man told me to do". The man from the north will argue likewise, that the only way to get to the city centre is to travel south. Those who lack wisdom see inconsistency; however those with intelligence see the grander picture and find consistency.

---

2. Online definition

PAGE 2

THE RABBI MICHAEL J ELJARRAT LEARNING PROGRAMME – CLASS EIGHTY SIX

Jewish Philosophy:

As we said above, all Jews (Jews with a valid philosophy) believe that one should fear God and perform all the Mitzvos found in the Torah. By way of our parable; all Jews want to get to the "city centre", however each person is coming from a different "Place", and therefore needs to head in the direction that is most suitable.

So long as the philosophy is valid, the net result will be fear of God and observance of all the Mitzvos, and thus the argument of which philosophy is best, is a mute point. A great Jew can and should be able to reach the "city centre" from all directions.

The list below contains some of the philosophies found within Judaism: (There are approximately 100 additional Chasidic Sects not listed). This list is not comprehensive there are many other philosophies some valid, and some not.

THE RABBI MICHAEL J ELJARRAT LEARNING PROGRAMME – CLASS EIGHTY SEVEN

CLASS 87 THE JEWISH CALENDAR

LAWS AND SIGNIFICANCE OF ROSH HA SHANA PART ONE

This lesson starts a new section dealing with all the major and minor festivals, found in the Jewish calendar. This is the final section in the course dealing with the fundamentals of Judaism. In the course to follow we will build upon the fundamental concepts covered in this course, and revisit some of the topics which were previously covered.

The structure of this section is such; that each festival is covered in 2 parts. The first part will deal with the significance of the festival, while the second part will focus mainly on the laws and customs of that particular festival.

What is Rosh Ha Shana?
Rosh Ha Shana is often referred to as the start of the "High Holidays". The literal translation of Rosh Ha Shana is "Head of the Year", but a less literal translation is "New Year". Hence the festival of Rosh Ha Shana, is a festival celebrating the Jewish New Year. The Mishna[1] tells us that there are four "New Years" in the Jewish calendar; Rosh Ha Shana marks the new year for Man, meaning that Rosh Ha Shana marks the anniversary of Adam (the first Man), and his first footsteps on planet Earth.

So how do we celebrate the New Year?
Not with fireworks and all night parties, but rather we spend most of our time in Shul praying.
Why? This is because the Jewish New-Year, also marks Judgment Day.
The question which is often asked is: If Rosh Ha Shana is Judgment Day, then why is the focus of the prayers on Rosh Ha Shana primarily on Gods kingship of the universe, and not about judgment as one would expect?

Assessment Day

The answer to the question above is: Rosh Ha Shana is not Judgment Day in the traditional sense, but rather "Assessment Day". On Rosh Ha Shana, God carries out an "Audit" of the world. God looks at the world to see what changes need to occur in the world during the coming year, in order for the world to attain its purpose.

---

1. Rosh Ha Shana 2a

THE RABBI MICHAEL J ELJARRAT LEARNING PROGRAMME – CLASS EIGHTY SEVEN

On Rosh Ha Shana God performs a "Stock Take"; the old, obsolete and stale products are removed, the new products are re-shelved and the "best sellers" are moved to the front of the store. God looks at the world, to see who should stay and who needs to go.

The Audit Procedure

Rosh Ha Shana is a two day festival (even in Israel), and our Sages tell us that these two days are different from one another. On the first day God judges the world with "Din" (Judgment), and on the second day God judges the world with "Rachamim" (Mercy).

Rav Dessler explains how this procedure works:
On the first day when God does a "Stock Take", God looks at each individual in the world separately. God then enquires about this individual: "If this was the only person in the world, would it be worthwhile to continue and sustain the universe just for this person alone?" This is a very intensive judgment, since the question which is really being asked is: "What's the use of this person in the world? Does he/she have any purpose?" Very few people can say "If I was the only person in the world, the continuation of the world will be worth it" or "If everyone in the world behaved like me, the world would be a perfect place".

On the second day of Rosh Ha Shana, God judges with mercy. The question which is being asked is slightly different; on the second day God enquires about this individual: "Is this individual contributing or assisting those individuals who are worthy in their own right?"

Thus if individual A is a righteous individual, who carries enough merit to exist in his/her own right, and individual B doesn't have enough merit to exist in his/her own right, but plays a role in the life of individual A. Then on the first day of Rosh Ha Shana, individual A will have a favourable judgment, and on the second day of Rosh Ha Shana individual B will have a favourable judgment, because of his association to individual A.

Social Network:

The full extent of the social network is something which is known only by God. However our Sages tell us that, even those indirectly associated with helping the righteous have merit. For example the righteous individual needs food to eat, clothes to wear, a dwelling to live in etc. Therefore all the people that are involved in manufacturing and producing the food, clothes and dwelling etc are all indirectly needed for the maintenance of the righteous individual. Thus a simple factory worker who is far removed from spirituality may in fact merit to life on the second day of Rosh Ha Shana even though he/she is not worthy in his/her own right, simply because he/she contributes in some way to the maintenance of the righteous individual. It goes without say that one who directly assists a righteous individual will have merit on the second day of Rosh Ha Shana.

THE RABBI MICHAEL J ELJARRAT LEARNING PROGRAMME – CLASS EIGHTY SEVEN

The Rosh Ha Shana Prayers:
The main theme of the prayers on Rosh Ha Shana deal with God's sovereignty over the universe. Now that we understand what Rosh Ha Shana is all about, we can better understand the theme of the Rosh Ha Shana prayers. Since we are being judged on Rosh Ha Shana as to whether or not we are useful in "God's plan", and we know that our purpose on earth is to perfect ourselves and bring Godliness into the world, the first place to start is with our acknowledgement of God's sovereignty. If we are doing our job on earth properly, then God will give us everything we need, if however we are wasting time and not doing our job, then God is forced to remove us. Thus Rosh Ha Shana is one of the most powerful days in the year, since our fate is being decided and our actions audited.

As we say in the prayer "Ovinu Malkenu – Our Father, Our King" There are two ways of approaching God, either as our "Father" or as our "King". For those who have a real relationship with God, and love God every day of the year, then God is the "Father", and if Rosh Ha Shana is the day when we inaugurate God as the king, then by default we are being inaugurated as princes' and princesses', hence Rosh Ha Shana is a happy day. If however one does not have a relationship with God, then God is just the king, a complete stranger, and Rosh Ha Shana is a terrifying day, where the strange king deals with life and death.

The Mitzvah of Shofar:
On Rosh Ha Shana, we have a special Mitzvah to blow the Shofar (The horn of a ram), this is a Torah Mitzvah as its written in the verse[2] "And on the seventh month (from Nissan) on the first day of the month, there will be a holy calling for you, all work you shall not do, a day of Teruah will be for you".

The word Teruah means blowing of the Shofar, and the Shofar is blown for several reasons. One of the reasons given for blowing the Shofar, is to awaken us to do introspection and to reflect on our relationship with God. The Sages also tell us that the blowing of the Shofar arouses God to deal with us with mercy and not harsh judgment. The sounding of the Shofar makes God "Remember" the sacrifice of Isaac, who was willing to give up his life when it was commanded, but who was replaced by a ram, that became the sacrifice in his place. Based on all of the above we can understand the three components of Rosh Ha Shana, namely:

1. Making God the King
2. Asking God to "Remember" our merits

And how is this accomplished? Through,

3. Blowing the Shofar

---

2. Numbers/ Bamidbar 29:1

THE RABBI MICHAEL J ELJARRAT LEARNING PROGRAMME – CLASS EIGHTY EIGHT

CLASS 88 — THE JEWISH CALENDAR

LAWS AND SIGNIFICANCE OF ROSH HA SHANA PART TWO

The days leading up to Rosh Ha Shana:

There are two main customs relating to the days leading up to Rosh Ha Shana. The custom is to say Selichos (Special prayers of supplication) prior to Rosh Ha Shana. The month before Rosh Ha Shana is Elul, and Elul is a special time designated for Teshuva.

1. The Sephardic custom is to say Selichos from the first day of the month of Elul.
2. The Ashkenazic custom is to say Selichos from 4 days[1] before Rosh Ha Shana and to start on the Motzei Shabbos in which Rosh Ha Shana falls.

- There is a custom to blow the Shofar after Shacharis every day in the month of Elul.
- There is a custom to say Psalm 27 after Shacharis and (Mincha / Mariv) each day from the start of Elul until the end of the Chagim (Shemini Atzeres).

Erev Rosh Ha Shana (The day before Rosh Ha Shana):

- On Erev Rosh Ha Shana we get up early and say lengthily Selichos.
- There is a custom to fast on Erev Rosh Ha Shana from sunrise until midday.
- There is a custom to ask for forgiveness, from those whom one might have wronged during the year.
- There is a custom to do "Hatoras Nedorim" (annulment of vows) on Erev Rosh Ha Shana.

The night of Rosh Ha Shana:

- We pray a special Amida – these prayers can be found in a Rosh Ha Shana Machzor (Machzor – Special prayer book).
- When Rosh Ha Shana falls on Shabbos we add "Zichron Teruah" in place of "Yom Teruah".
- The custom is to greet one's friends with a greeting wishing them blessing and success in their judgment. (See Machzor for wording)

---

[1]. When Rosh Ha Shana falls on Monday or Tuesday, Selichos starts a week earlier.

- The custom is to eat a variety of special foods which are symbolic of blessing. (See Machzor for details)

Rosh Ha Shana Day:

- One should get up early on Rosh Ha Shana day in order to daven all the prayers of Rosh Ha Shana together with the congregation from start to finish.
- The Prayers for Shacharis are the same as for all festivals; however the Amida for Rosh Ha Shana is unique. (See Machzor)
- After the special prayers included in the Chazzan's repetition of the Amida, we say the prayer of "Ovinu Malkinu".
- When Rosh Ha Shana falls on Shabbos we do not say the prayer of "Ovinu Malkinu".
- We read a special portion from the Torah on Rosh Ha Shana. (See Machzor for details)
- After the Torah reading, we perform the Torah Mitzvah of blowing the Shofar.
- One is obligated to hear 100 Shofar blasts on each day of Rosh Ha Shana.
- On Rosh Ha Shana we Daven a special Musaf which contains there distinctive parts:
    1. Malkeus – Dealing with God's rule over the universe.
    2. Zichronos – Dealing with God remembering the inhabitants of earth.
    3. Shofros – Dealing with various verses stating the importance of the Shofar.

Rosh Ha Shana Afternoon:

- We Daven a special Amida for Mincha on Rosh Ha Shana afternoon (the same as for Shacharis and Mariv)
- Many have the custom to say "Tashlich" on Rosh Ha Shana by a pond of water that has fish.

Other customs of Rosh Ha Shana:

There is a custom to have a new fruit or new clothes on the second day of Rosh Ha Shana. The reason for this custom is as follows: Rosh Ha Shana even in Israel is celebrated for two days, however these two days are considered as one long day. Because of this consideration a doubt arises on the second night of Rosh Ha Shana, as to whether or not to recite the blessing of "Shechiyanu" – the blessing for a "New" festival (i.e. is the second day of Rosh Ha Shana "New" or not?) Thus to remove ourselves from doubt, we make the blessing of "Shechiyanu" over a new fruit or clothes, whilst having in mind that should the second day of Rosh Ha Shana in fact need a blessing of "Shechiyanu", the blessing over the fruit / clothes should cover this obligation.

As we saw above there is a custom to eat special foods on the night of Rosh Ha Shana that signifies blessing. There are various customs related to this. Some eat these special foods on both nights of Rosh Ha Shana and some even make their own special foods and blessings not found in the standard Machzor. The reason for the latter; is that the actions of eating these foods together with a prayer forms a strong request/petition towards God to bestow blessing.

THE RABBI MICHAEL J ELJARRAT LEARNING PROGRAMME – CLASS EIGHTY NINE

CLASS 89 — THE JEWISH CALENDAR

LAWS AND SIGNIFICANCE OF YOM KIPPUR PART ONE

Yom Kippur is often referred to as the holiest day in the Jewish Calendar, and is termed the most important day of the days of awe (Yomim Na-Royim). The question which we will address in this lesson is: What makes Yom Kippur so special?

To answer this question let us first look at the translation of the words "Yom Kippur", Yom Kippur is often translated as "Day of Atonement", as the verse states[1]

"For on this day he shall provide atonement for you to cleanse you; from all your sins before Hashem shall you be cleansed."

To understand this concept fully we need to examine three concepts namely:

1. Sin
2. Atonement
3. Cleansing

What is a Sin?

As we have seen numerous times, the purpose of Man in this world is to achieve closeness to God, by means of perfection. To accomplish this task God gave us the Torah, which contains specific instructions of "do's" and "don'ts". Each time we do an instruction we take a step closer to attaining perfection, each time we do a negative instruction (i.e. a "don't") we take a step further away from attaining perfection. The journey of life consists of taking small steps, hopefully in the right direction. Therefore in essence a "Sin" is a step in the wrong direction.

So what makes a person Sin?

To answer this question "What makes a person Sin?" we would need to know the complexities of each individual as well as the complexities that motivate all forms of behaviour good and bad. The only being that has this answer is God himself. Thus in order to Judge man and his associated level of perfection one would need an infinite amount of information and the only being which is in possession of this information is God himself.

---

[1]. Vayikra / Leviticus 16:30

THE RABBI MICHAEL J ELJARRAT LEARNING PROGRAMME – CLASS EIGHTY NINE

However, despite our lack of knowledge, we do nevertheless know that several broad concepts motivate human behaviour. We know this from our personal experiences and from research into this topic. Therefore although we can never know with certainty, what motivated a particular person to do a particular action; we can however know that a particular action was motivated by one or more general factors.

Our sages classify three types of Sin:

1. A "Chait" (Mistake) – Motivated by ignorance.
2. A "Ovon" (Wrong Doing) – Motivated by self gratification.
3. A "Peshah" (Violation) – Motivated by rebellion.

The general rule is, the greater the motivation to Sin; the bigger the "Step" in the wrong direction. Thus if one were to Sin "Be – Shogaiag" (Meaning he/she was ignorant of the fact that their action is a Sin) the step in the wrong direction is less that say, if one were to Sin "Be – Maizid" (willingly – for self gratification or to rebel against God).

This is all true from Man's perspective; however this is not the only equation to be solved. We also know that different Sins carry different weights as the Talmud[2] tells us: There are four different levels of Sin: (In ascending order of severity)

1. Not fulfilling a positive commandment
2. Transgressing a negative commandment – that carries the punishment of lashes.
3. Transgressing a negative commandment – that carries the punishment of "Kores" (being cut off)
4. Disgracing God (in public)

We can understand the human condition in the following way: An intelligent individual will soon discover that this world has a creator (See Class 1), he/she will be motivated to learn about the creator. He/she will then be faced with a life choice, namely:

1. Further study of the creator and its subsequent outcomes.
2. Denial of the creator.

One who chooses the path of getting to know the creator, will initially make mistakes and act to fulfil self gratifying ends, but will make fewer mistakes as time goes on and his/her knowledge increases. One who chooses to deny God however will live a life of self gratification and rebellion against God. Hence the path leading towards or away from perfection is largely determined by one's attitude towards God.

What is atonement?

To understand the concept of atonement let us use a parable: Imagine you were driving and were trying to reach destination A, however along the way, you took the wrong turn off by mistake. To make matters worse you take yet another wrong turn, and before long you were completely lost. Without navigation the prospect of reaching destination A is grim, and even if you do eventually find the right road you will certainly not reach your destination in time.

---

2. Yoma 86a

THE RABBI MICHAEL J ELJARRAT LEARNING PROGRAMME – CLASS EIGHTY NINE

In the journey of life, taking the wrong turn or making a mistake and taking a step in the wrong direction can get you lost. Essentially what atonement is is a "Magical Road" linking your current position to destination A. In the parable mentioned above, it's as if a new road suddenly appears before you, called the "Your – Name – Here Motorway to destination A" Taking this special motorway, built just for you, will get you there, and it will get you there on time as well.

Roads are not built for nothing:

These "Magical Roads" are not built for free; it costs spiritual currency, namely a yearning heart. Only those who truly desire to reach destination A, and regret getting lost in the first place, merit to having a road built especially for them. For ten days between Rosh Ha Shana and Yom Kippur, God gives us a ten day free trial period, where we can easily merit having a "Magical Road" built just for us. On Yom Kippur itself, God makes it even easier to merit to the "Magical Road". Even those who have made a life choice to deny God can merit to having a "Magical Road" built for them, should they have a change of heart.

What is cleansing?

Using the same parable as above, of getting lost on the motorway; Imagine the joy one has when one sees the sign "Your – Name – Here Motorway to destination A", all is well but there's just one small problem, taking the wrong road has used up more than half a tank of fuel, even with the "Magical Road", there's just not enough fuel left to make it to destination A.

But what if, the same people who built the "Magical Road" also fill up your car with a full tank of fuel, now everything is all set, all that needs to be done is for you to drive.

In the journey of life, taking the wrong turns; drains us mentally, emotionally and physically. On Yom Kippur, God not only builds the "Magical Road" for us, God also "Re-sets" us and gives us the strength to carry on, and continue our journey as if we had never gotten lost in the first place.

For on this day "He shall provide a "Road" for you" and "give you energy" from being lost you will find your way. Yom Kippur is a life changing day – it truly is a day of awe.

THE RABBI MICHAEL J ELJARRAT LEARNING PROGRAMME – CLASS NINETY

CLASS 90 THE JEWISH CALENDAR

LAWS AND SIGNIFICANCE OF YOM KIPPUR PART TWO

The days leading up to Yom Kippur:

- The days between Rosh Ha Shana and Yom Kippur are known as the "Aseres Yemei Teshuvah".
- During this period we say Selichos.
- In the Amida prayer we add/change the following:
    1. In the blessing of Ovos we add – "Zochraynu LeChaim" (Remember us for life)
    2. In the blessing of Ovos we add – "Me – Chamocha" (Who is like you)
    3. In the blessing of Kedushas Hashem we change from "Ha Kel HaKadosh" to "Ha Melech Ha Kadosh"
    4. In the blessing of Din we change from "Tzedaka O Mishpat" to "Ha Melech Ha Mishpat"
    5. In the blessing of Hodah we add – "Oketov LeChaim" (Write for life)
    6. In the blessing of Shalom we add – "Be Sefer Chaim" (In the book of life)

Erev Yom Kippur (The day before Yom Kippur):

- There is a special Mitzvah to eat on Erev Yom Kippur.
- The Selichos on Erev Yom Kippur are relatively short.
- There is a custom to do "Kaporos" on Erev Yom Kippur. That is we take a chicken/money and raise it above our heads, and say this should be my "Replacement" (See Yom Kippur Machzor for variations)
- It is fitting for one to ask forgiveness from anyone he may have wronged through out the year.
- It is a Mitzvah for men to go to the Mikveh on Erev Yom Kippur, but without a blessing.
- On Erev Yom Kippur we Daven Mincha early and we add "Vidoi" (Confession) at the end of the Amida.
- An hour or two before Yom Kippur we have a special meal called a "Suda – Ha Mafsekes".
- There is a custom to bless one's children on Erev Yom Kippur.

PAGE 1

THE RABBI MICHAEL J ELJARRAT LEARNING PROGRAMME – CLASS NINETY

- There is a custom to dress in white clothes for Yom Kippur; Men wear their "Kitel" (White Robe).
- There is a custom to give extra charity on Erev Yom Kippur.
- After the "Suda – Ha Mafsekes", we go to Shul wearing non-leather shoes.
- When we get to Shul, we wear a Talis (We keep it on until after Mariv).
- The Torah is taken out of the Ark, and we say the prayer of "Kol Nidrei" (See Yom Kippur Machzor)

The Night of Yom Kippur:

From the time Yom Kippur comes in until the time Yom Kippur goes out (Roughly 25 Hours) the following is absolutely forbidden. (*The prohibitions carry "Koreis" (being cut off) see previous lesson).

1. Eating and drinking.*
2. Bathing and washing.
3. Rubbing creams and oils on one's body.
4. Wearing leather shoes.
5. Sexual Intercourse.

Yom Kippur Day:

The day of Yom Kippur, is a day dedicated primarily to prayer. On Yom Kippur we pray an extra Amida after the prayer of Mincha, this special prayer is called "Ne-ila" (Meaning "Closing"). It is said that on Yom Kippur the gates of prayer (which are usually closed) are opened, just for the day. Thus "Ne-ila" the "Closing" prayer is said just before the gates of heaven are closed. The prayer of "Ne-ila" is the last chance for our prayers to be answered. The five prayers of Yom Kippur are:

1. Mariv
2. Shacharis
3. Musaf
4. Mincha
5. Ne-ila

Other customs of Yom Kippur:

- After the fast of Yom Kippur there is a custom to have a "Yom Tov" like meal in celebration of God having cleansed us from our Sins.
- It is a Mitzvah to start working on building the Succah after the Motzei Yom Kippur meal mentioned above. (If one is not too tired)
- We make Havdalah on Motzei Yom Kippur using:
    1. Wine/grape juice (As on Motzei Shabbos)
    2. Without Besomim (Spices)
    3. But with "Ner" (Candle) even when Yom Kippur falls on a weekday.

THE RABBI MICHAEL J ELJARRAT LEARNING PROGRAMME – CLASS NINETY ONE

CLASS 91
THE JEWISH CALENDAR

LAWS AND SIGNIFICANCE OF SUCCOS
PART ONE

On the fifteenth of Tishrei just five days after Yom Kippur, we celebrate the festival of Succos. Succos is the festival which commemorates the clouds of glory which surrounded the Jewish people when they came out of Egypt. When the Jewish Nation left Egypt they wondered into the desert without food and shelter, ordinarily speaking they wouldn't have been able to survive, being exposed to the elements. However God performed a miracle for the Jewish people, and surrounded them with clouds of glory, which would shield them from the hot desert sun, and pillars of fire at night to provide them with light and warmth. These clouds of glory and pillars of fire also protected the Jewish Nation from enemies, as well as providing the Jewish Nation with manna.

The verse states[1]
"And you shall sit in Succos for seven days, etc
In order for the generations to know that I placed the Jewish Nation in Succos, when I took them out the land of Egypt".

Succos is referred to as the "time of our happiness"; in this lesson we will explore the connection between happiness and Succos, and through this derive the significance of Succos.

What is happiness?

The word "Happy" appears all over, in our daily context. We see "Happy Birthday", "Happy New-Year" etc. In the media we see the word "Happy" used in sorts of contexts. However despite the frequent use of the word, only a few know its meaning, and even fewer experience it.

So what exactly is this emotion called "Happiness"? We know instinctively that "Happiness" is an emotion which makes us feel good inside, but not all "good" feelings are "Happiness". What we can say though is that, the feeling of "Happiness" cannot co-exist with the feeling of "Unhappiness". Therefore any feeling/emotion which does not remove "Unhappiness" cannot be called "Happiness" in the true sense of the word.

---
1. Vayikra / Leviticus 23:42

THE RABBI MICHAEL J ELJARRAT LEARNING PROGRAMME – CLASS NINETY ONE

Is "Happiness" the same as "Excitement"?

The answer is most definitely not. Many people mistake the feeling of "Excitement" for the feeling of "Happiness"; the feeling of "Excitement" can be defined as: "an elevated level of joy".

 We experience the feeling of "Excitement" when something "good" happens. For example when we hear good news, experience something pleasant or look forward to a pleasant event.

Excitement however, is not happiness. Even though "Excitement" makes us feel good inside, "Excitement" can co-exist with "Unhappiness". This is because the feeling of "Excitement" fades away very quickly; when the feeling of "Excitement" has dissipated, the underlying original feeling of unhappiness returns.

Is "Happiness" the same as "Relaxation"?

Once again the answer is no. Although many people fanaticize the ultimate relaxation, (e.g. lying on the beech all day in Hawaii) and imagine themselves feeling "Happy" as a result of that relaxation, however in truth "Relaxation" and "Happiness" are two entirely different "feel good" sensations.

The feeling of "Relaxation" can be defined as "Being free from all burdens". We experience the feeling of "Relaxation" when we have no responsibilities.

However "Relaxation" is not "Happiness", this is because "Relaxation" can co-exist with "Unhappiness" we can find ourselves being responsibility free, but still dry inside.

Only "Happiness" is the same as "Happiness":

There may be many "feel good" emotions which can temporarily mask the horrible feelings of "Unhappiness", but all these other "feel good" emotions are only a temporary fix. The only emotion which can displace "Unhappiness" entirely is "Happiness" itself.

The Orchas Tzadikim writes[2]:

> **"Happiness comes to a person**
> **Who experiences few "upsets" in his/her life"**

From this we see the following:
1. Happiness comes to a person; the person cannot come to happiness.
2. "Upsets" prevent happiness from coming to a person.

Let us examine these two points above:

- Firstly happiness is a feeling that cannot be perused; a person cannot do anything to become happy. This means that if "Happiness" doesn't come to you, you will feel "Unhappy".
- Secondly "Upsets" such as worry, anxiety and problems prevent "Happiness" from resting on a person, thus only when everything is good, will "Happiness" be able to come.

---

2. Gate of Happiness

THE RABBI MICHAEL J ELJARRAT LEARNING PROGRAMME – CLASS NINETY ONE

From what we have said above, it would seem that "Happiness" is a feeling which is almost impossible to find. How many people having everything going smoothly all the time? Furthermore those who are "Unhappy" cannot chase "Happiness" as "Happiness" is a feeling which has to come on it own.

The good news:

The Orchas Tzadikim writes further that "Happiness" is tied into "Trust in God". So how are the two connected?

Above we said "Upsets" prevent happiness from coming to a person, the term "Upsets" has a relative definition, meaning that what upsets one person may not upset another. Even when an "Upset" is felt by all, we each experience it in a unique way.

So why are "Upsets" relative?
Upsets are relative to ones attitude towards the crises at hand. If one believes that one has a solution to the crises, or that the crises will soon dissipate, then the crises at hand seems manageable. This attitude usually has no bearing on the crises itself, but ones associated attitude plays a vital role in dealing with the crises. Thus although one cannot avoid having "Upsets" all together, one can nevertheless acquire a positive attitude which can deflect the small "Upsets".

Therefore if one does not experience major "Upsets" frequently, and one has the tools to deal with the minor "Upsets" then "Happiness" is far more attainable.

The connection between "Happiness" and Succos:

Since happiness is largely determined on having a positive attitude, acquiring a positive attitude is a subject which must be addressed. One of the biggest obstacles which stand in the way of having a positive attitude, is our natural tendency to take what we have for granted. This always sounds cliché, and we've all heard the saying "Don't take what you have for granted" in one form or another, or "You don't know what you have till its gone" so many times before, however despite the fact that hearing this again now is probably nauseating, nevertheless it is true and perhaps a fresh perspective on this concept will refresh one's attitude.

Reality:

Anyone who has experienced "Not Having" will know that putting a smile on your face and pretending that everything is "Ok" when it's not, only goes so far. A "Happy Face" doesn't pay the bills, cure cancer or revive the dead. When things are not "Ok" the last thing one needs to hear is "Don't take what you have for granted" as the Mishna in Ovos[3] says "Do not appease your fellow in the time of his anger, do not console him while his dead lies before him etc" One who has experienced "Not Having" finds it laughable when he/she hears someone who "Does Have" complain about their seemingly petty problems.

---

3. Chapter 4 Mishna 23

THE RABBI MICHAEL J ELJARRAT LEARNING PROGRAMME – CLASS NINETY ONE

What belongs to you is yours:

Due to Man's competitive nature, we seem to always compare "what I have" with "what they have". When things are going great and "what I have" is equal or exceeds "what they have" this competitive nature doesn't bother us. However when tragedy strikes this comparative nature of ours, magnifies and exacerbates our hurt, it adds pain to injury. The concept of "Don't take what you have for granted" really means stop comparing yourself to others! Instead focus on what belongs to you, the good and the bad together, "keep your eyes on the road" and focus inward. The feeling "I don't have, and he/she does have" is a lot worse than "I don't have" alone.

How clever is God?

Let us take a step back for a moment, and think about the following from a purely logical perspective: I'm sure we (God believing Jews) all would agree, that the design of the "Human Body" is "Clever" in that it is highly complex, it's definitely not the design of a fool! The same can be said about nature, the solar system, marine system and many others of God's creations. Just by looking at these systems on the most basic level, it is clear for us to see that God is infinitely "Clever".

We also know that God is not "sadistic" (God Forbid), and God gains absolutely no pleasure in Human Suffering. This concept can be proven logically, through the attribute of God's perfection (However we will not elaborate on this proof here). Thus we can say:

1. God is "Clever" (In our terms of intelligence – His wisdom is in fact infinite)
2. God has no benefit from Human Suffering.

With the above two points in mind, let us address the concept of "Not Having", "Comparing ourselves to others" and "Happiness" we will begin by examining why comparing ourselves to others is fundamentally flawed.

The Uniqueness of Man:

As we have seen in previous lessons, "Man" as a species as a whole is unique, and very different from all the other creatures on Planet Earth. Within the species of "Man" each person is completely unique as is apparent from our faces (see previous lessons for details). The magnitude of difference that is found between "Man" and the other creatures is equal to the magnitude of difference between each individual "Man" and another.

> Thus we may say: Each person is a unique species.
>
> We can further state: that just as every species on earth has a unique role to play (e.g. Birds and Lions each serve a different goal) so too each person (which is its own species) has a unique role to play.

Comparing ourselves to others is every bit as absurd as comparing ourselves to a Lion, Frog or Monkey, and then wondering why we can't roar, leap or swing from trees. So too each person is absolutely unique; each person has a unique role to play and each person will be given a different set of life circumstances.

God is "clever" and knows what each one of us needs; God takes no pleasure in seeing us suffering.

PAGE 4

Therefore when tragedy strikes we must remember our uniqueness and make the best of what we have. Hidden in our tangible and intangible assets is the ability to survive the challenge and complete our role on earth.

Succos

Succos is the time where we reflect on "Not Having" we sit in a Succah and expose ourselves to the elements, just as the Jews faced exposure to the elements in the desert, but survived the ordeal through the kindness of God. So too we can have faith in God's kindness, develop the positive attitude needed, and allow happiness to make its way into our lives.

Based on the above discussion, we can understand why we read "Koheles" (The book of Ecclesiastes) on Succos, as "Koheles" is an elaborate discussion of the points covered in this class.

THE RABBI MICHAEL J ELJARRAT LEARNING PROGRAMME – CLASS NINETY TWO

CLASS 92 — THE JEWISH CALENDAR

LAWS AND SIGNIFICANCE OF SUCCOS PART TWO

In this lesson we will look at some of the laws and customs of the special Mitzvos which are connected to the festival of Succos, namely:

- The Mitzvah of Succah
- The Mitzvah of the four species
    1. Esrog
    2. Luluv
    3. Hadasim
    4. Arovos

The Mitzvah of Succah:

"Succah" gets its name from "Scach" (Pronounced Sgag – with a guttural "G") the leafy covering on top of the structure. The walls are not called "Succah" we will therefore just deal with a few laws pertaining to the covering. (I.e. the "Scach")

There are six things which invalidate the Scach: (and can therefore not be used as a roof covering)

1. Something which is susceptible to Tumah (spiritual impurity)
2. Something which does not grow from the ground.
3. Something which is still attached to the ground.
4. If there is more sun then shade.
5. If it is made on its own, and not built. (such as hollowing out a pile of leaves)
6. If it is higher than 20 Amos. (approximately 12m)

It is customary to decorate one's Succah to show love for the Mitzvah, however one should be careful not to place posters in the Succah which contain verses from the Torah, since these posters containing verses will be mishandled, and come to be desecrated (See: Shulchan Aruch Yoreh Dayeh 283 in the Taz and Chayai Odom 146-45)

PAGE 1

THE RABBI MICHAEL J ELJARRAT LEARNING PROGRAMME – CLASS NINETY TWO

The Mitzvah of Succah is to live in the Succah as one lives in one's home. This includes:

1. Eating meals.
2. Learning Torah.
3. Sleeping in the Succah.

However in extreme weather conditions, that cause discomfort one is exempt from sitting in the Succah.

Therefore when it rains into the Succah, one should not sit in the Succah, as the Talmud tells us "One who sits in the Succah when it rains is called a fool". It is for this reason that we don't pray for rain until after Succos. (See: Chayai Odom 147-11)

The Four Species – The Arbah Minim[1]:

The laws of Esrog – Citron:

- The Esrog represents the true Tzadik namely one with Torah and Good Deeds.
- The Esrog is called a "Pri Eitz Hadar" – A Beautiful Fruit.

From the four species the Esrog has the most criteria concerning its laws and validations. Because the laws are numerous, we will not cover the laws of Esrog in this course, but will God willing cover these laws in an advanced class.

(For the laws of Esrog see "The Four Species" Published by Artscroll)

The laws of Lulav – Young Palm Branch:

- The Lulav represents one with Torah but without Good Deeds.
- The Lulav is called a "Kapos Temarim" – The branch of the Palm Tree
- The Lulav must be complete in its entirety; it must be fresh and moist.
- The Lulav must be 4 Tefachim in length (1 Tefach = 10cm) – Minimum requirement.

The laws of Hadas – The Myrtle Leaf: (Know by its plural since we take 3)

- The Hadas (Plural – Hadassim) represents one with Good Deeds but without Torah.
- The Hadassim are called "Anaf Eitz Ovos" – Twigs of a Plaited Tree.
- The Hadassim must be complete in its entirety; it must be fresh and moist.
- The Hadassim must 3 Tefachim in length (1 Tefach = 10cm) – Minimum requirement.

---

[1]. Vayikra / Leviticus 23:40

THE RABBI MICHAEL J ELJARRAT LEARNING PROGRAMME – CLASS NINETY TWO

The laws of Arovos – The Willow Leaf: (Know by its plural Arovos since we take 2)

- The Arovah (Plural – Arovos) represent one with neither Torah nor Good Deeds.
- The Arovos are called "Arvei Nachal" – Brook Willows.
- The Arovos must be complete in its entirety; it must be fresh and moist.
- The Arovos must 3 Tefachim in length (1 Tefach = 10cm) – Minimum requirement.

The minimum requirement of the four species:
The following invalidate all four species:
- Incomplete set[2]
- Unknown Species[3]
- If it is missing a part[4]
- If it has a blemish
- If it was taken in Sin[5]
- If it is dry.

---

[2]. One must take all four species together – taking only some and not others invalidates the Mitzvah.
[3]. The species must conform to its name-sake.
[4]. For example the top is broken off.
[5]. For example it was stolen.

THE RABBI MICHAEL J ELJARRAT LEARNING PROGRAMME – CLASS NINETY THREE

CLASS 93 THE JEWISH CALENDAR

LAWS AND SIGNIFICANCE OF CHANUKAH PART ONE

In this lesson we will look at the significance of the festival of Chanukah. Chanukah is a festival instituted by the sages to commemorate the miracles which took place in the period before the destruction of the second Temple over 2000 years ago.

During the days of the second Temple, when the Greeks had authority over the Jews, the Greeks placed many decrees over the Jews. These decrees were designed to destroy the Jewish faith, and forbade Jewish people from studying Torah and performing Mitzvos. The Greeks oppressed the Jews with heavy taxes; they raped the Jewish women and desecrated the Temple. They placed them under great pressure to give up their Judaism. Until God had mercy and allowed the "Chashmonim" Priests to take control back from the Greeks. They then appointed a Jewish King, and they had relative peace for almost 200 years, until the destruction of the Second Temple.

The miracle of Chanukah was the last publicly open miracle in Jewish History, and tells the story of good triumphing over bad, of the oppressed triumphing over the oppressor and of the weak triumphing over the strong.

It was on the 25th day of the Jewish month of Kisliev, that the Jews regained control from their Greek oppressors. The word Chunukah in Hebrew is made up of two words "Chanu" – Meaning they rested (from their enemies) and "Kah" – Meaning 25 (The numerical value of Chaf - 20 and Hey – 5).

When the Kohanim went into the Temple to light the Menorah, they found that all the oil had been contaminated by the Greeks, and they were therefore unable to light the Menorah. Miraculously they found one container of oil which was still sealed with the seal of the High Priest, and with this oil they were able to light the Menorah. Miraculously the oil which was found lasted for eight days even though it should have lasted for just one day.

Therefore we commemorate these miracles and we celebrate eight days of Chanukah. On each day of Chanukah we light the Menorah, and we say Hallel. (We will look at the laws of lighting the Menorah in part two) In this lesson we will try and explore the deeper meaning behind these Miracles, and the lessons which we can learn from the story of Chanukah. We will soon see why the miracle of Chanukah was the last public miracle to occur in Jewish History, and why perseverance is such an important part of Judaism.

THE RABBI MICHAEL J ELJARRAT LEARNING PROGRAMME – CLASS NINETY THREE

The Greek Ideals:

Unlike the story of Purim, where Haman wanted to physically destroy the Jewish Nation, the Greeks on the other hand wanted to destroy Judaism, not the Jews. The Greeks were cultured, and were considered a superior race in their time. They viewed Judaism as being "out-dated" and "non-progressive". By contrast they viewed their own culture as being progressive and forward thinking; they celebrated physicality and fictionalized spirituality. The Greeks wanted the world to adopt their culture, and for the most part they were successful. In order for their ideals to gain acceptance in the world, other cultures and ideals had to be eliminated or at least suppressed. By making the lives of the Jews miserable, they hoped that the Jews would abandon their Judaism for the sake of comfort, and tranquillity and adopt the Greek culture. If they were successful, they could then show the world that their Greek culture was accepted by all with the claim "Even the Jews accept Greek Culture".

Judaism and Perseverance:

Since the Jewish Nation was liberated from Egypt, the Jewish nation was endowed with the trait of survival, and perseverance against the odds. The Jewish Nation was well aware that the life of a Jew and Judaism itself would be difficult. However they accepted the Torah by saying "Naseh Ve Nishma" (We will do and we will listen) or "We will do what ever it takes". When the Greek oppressors threatened the Jewish way of life, the Jews fought back with their trait "We will do what ever it takes" despite the hardship and suffering, they would remain true to their values under all conditions. The good Jew knows that he/she has a responsibility to bring "Light" (Godliness) into the world, in what ever state the world finds itself in.

The Menorah:

Our sages tell us, the purpose of the Menorah in the Temple was not for its physical light, but rather for its spiritual light. When the Menorah was lit, the "light" of Godliness was felt in the heart of every Human Being in the world. The physical lighting of the Menorah caused a spiritual lighting of the world.

Therefore it is no coincidence that the miracle of Chanukah revolved around the lighting of the Menorah. The Greek oppression was aimed at extinguishing the "Light" of Godliness in the world, and the Jewish revolt was aimed at restoring the "Light" of Godliness in the world. Thus the Jewish view and the Menorah have one in the same goal, namely to bring the "Light" of Godliness into the world. Thus the Miracle of the Menorah and the oil is also symbolic. The Jews wanted to light the Menorah, but could not find any oil, miraculously they found oil, but it was not enough; so they did their best and used what they had, and God did the rest, and miraculously made the little oil go a long way. The parallel to this is: The Jews wanted to bring the "Light" of Godliness into the world, but were prevented from doing so by the Greeks. They had a small group of fighters, so they did their best and God did the rest and allowed a little resource to go a long way.

THE RABBI MICHAEL J ELJARRAT LEARNING PROGRAMME – CLASS NINETY THREE

Do your best and God will do the rest:

We said earlier that the Miracle of Chanukah, was the last publicly open miracle to occur in Jewish History. Our sages tell us that this miracle occurred in preparation for the destruction of the Temple which would follow some 200 years later. God knew that a time would come when the Jewish people would not have a Menorah, and would be surrounded by people who were Anti-Semitic and wanted to extinguish the "Light" of Godliness in the world. Thus God wanted to show and reinforce the concept of perseverance. God wanted the Jewish people to know that despite the lack of resources and despite the lack of spirituality in the world, the job of a Jew to bring the "Light" of Godliness into the world remains constant. If we were to ask "How can we manage?" "How can we possibly bring the "Light" of Godliness into the world, when the world is so dark and void of spirituality?" or "How can we possibly bring the "Light" of Godliness into the world, when the main thrust of the world is directed against truth?" The answer is "Do your best and let God do the rest" Use what ever resources you have, no matter how limited it may seem, and God will do the rest.

Chanukah in Modern Times:

When we take a look at the story which unfolded in the war between the Chashmonim and the Greeks, we begin to appreciate the greatness of the miracle. The Greek soldiers were the most highly advanced army of their day; they were physically fit and underwent intensive training. By contrast the Chashmonim were a small group of untrained civilians, they were elderly men. By all laws of nature there is no way that the Chashmonim would have been able to defeat the Greek army. The Jews were less than the "Under – Dog" they were entirely hopeless. Therefore the miracle of Chanukah is in fact a miracle were the entirely hopeless gained victory, meaning even when "Our Best" is hardly good enough; still Hashem will do the rest.

Today we need to celebrate and remember the significance of Chanukah more than ever. If we look at the world today, and the spiritual darkness than has enveloped the world, where we desperately lack Torah leaders and people of pure heart, one may be inclined to feel that our chances of spreading the "Light" of Godliness in the world is entirely hopeless; Even so the story of Chanukah teaches us that, even when we are entirely hopeless we can still succeed, if we try our best to bring the 'Light" of Godliness into the world, God will take the little "Light" and make it go a long way.

This is what we say in the song of "Mo Otzore" (O Mighty Rock) the song of Chanukah, in the stanza:

"Bare your holy arm, and hasten the end of our salvation,
Avenge the vengeance of your servant's blood from the wicked nation. For the triumph is too long delayed for us,
And there is no end to the days of evil,
push aside Edom (Anti – Semites) into the deepest shadows and establish for us the seven Sheppard's"

(David, Adam, Seth, Methuselah, Avraham, Jacob and Moses -Talmud Succah 52b).

May we merit to see the building of the Beis Ha Mikdash and the lighting of the real Menorah speedily in our days, Amen.

THE RABBI MICHAEL J ELJARRAT LEARNING PROGRAMME – CLASS NINETY FOUR

CLASS 94
THE JEWISH CALENDAR

LAWS AND SIGNIFICANCE OF CHANUKAH PART TWO

In this lesson we will look at the laws of Chanukah, and concentrate on the Mitzvah of lighting the Menorah during the eight days of Chanukah.

Every Jew is obligated in the Mitzvah of Lighting the Menorah on Chanukah, this includes: Men, Women and Children above the age of "Chinuch" (the age where a child comprehends education), since all Jews were saved by the Miracle.

 With What to Light:

1. Unlike Shabbos candles, where one may only light with certain candles/oil, Chanukah candles can be lit with any candle/oil. The reason being: Shabbos candles are there for us to derive benefit, and if one were to use inferior candles/oils one may come to violate Shabbos by moving the candles/oils to improve the quality of the light, and violate the Melocho of "Aish" (Making a fire). Chanukah candles on the other hand are not there for us to have benefit from the light, therefore apart from the fact that Melocho is allowed on Chanukah, and subsequently one may move and touch the candles/oils to improve the quality of light nevertheless since Chanukah candles are there just for the Mitzvah all oils and candles are acceptable. It is however preferable to light with olive oil as this resembles the oil used in the Miracle of Chanukah.
2. One can also use wax candles, provided that their light is "Clean" (meaning it burns well).
3. It is preferable to light with candles/oil in a Menorah made from metal or glass as this beautifies the Mitzvah.

PAGE 1

Where to Light:

Since part of the Mitzvah is to publicize the miracle of Chanukah, the Chanukah Menorah must be lit in a time and place where people will be able to see.

1. In the times of the Talmud the custom was to light in the street in front of the house, this is still the custom in Israel. However outside of Israel, where Anti-Semitism is a concern, the custom is to light indoors. (The custom is to light near a window where the Menorah can be seen, in places that tolerate Jews.)
2. One should light on the left side of the door (If possible) in order to be surrounded by Mitzvos, with the Mezuza on the right and the Menorah on the left.
3. The Menorah should be placed near to the ground, between 3 -10 Tefachim (30 -100cm) from the ground. The reason why it is preferable to light close to the ground, is since the Menorah is not there for its light, lighting near the ground shows this purpose.
4. One who lives in an apartment building, may light the Menorah near the window, even though the Menorah will be placed above 10 Tefachim (100cm) from the ground. However if the Menorah will be placed 20 Amos (12m) from the ground, it is preferable to light downstairs.
5. When the Menorah is lit at Shul, it should be placed against the South wall. One cannot fulfill ones obligation with the Menorah which is lit at Shul, since the "Shul Menorah" is for display purposes only.

When to light:

Since part of the Mitzvah of lighting Chanukah candles is to publicize the miracle, we light at a time where people are likely to see the Menorah.

1. The time to light is at the end of sunset when the stars come out, and for the candles to burn half an hour after "Tzeitz" (The time when the stars come out)
2. In cases where one is unable to light at the above time (for example on Shabbos Chanukah), one may light from "Plag Ha Mincha" (which is, one and a quarter hours before the stars come out), provided that one places enough oil (or long enough candles) for the light to burn for half an hour after the stars come out (i.e. there must be sufficient burn time for one and three quarter hours in total).

THE RABBI MICHAEL J ELJARRAT LEARNING PROGRAMME – CLASS NINETY FOUR

 How to light:

On the first night of Chanukah one makes three blessings before the lighting of the Menorah. On the other nights one makes two blessings before the lighting of the Menorah, these blessings are:

1. "Le Hadlick Ner" – To Light the Chanukah Candles
2. "She Osoh Nisim" – Who performed miracles.
3. "Shechiyanu" – Who has kept us alive (This blessing is said only on the first night)

The custom is to set up the Menorah from right to left (i.e. on the first night to place the candle on the far right side, on the second night to place two candles, one on the far right and one on the left of the first etc.)

The custom is to light the newest candle first, so that one lights from left to right (If for what ever reason one confused the order of lighting, one has still fulfilled ones obligation.)

The main Mitzvah of lighting Chanukah Candles is to light one candle per night per household. All the additional candles are extra ways of enhancing the Mitzvah, and there are several customs in this regard.

THE RABBI MICHAEL J ELJARRAT LEARNING PROGRAMME – CLASS NINETY FIVE

CLASS 95 — THE JEWISH CALENDAR

LAWS AND SIGNIFICANCE OF PURIM
PART ONE

In this lesson we will look at the significance of the festival of Purim, the second of the two Festivals enacted by the sages. During the time between the destruction of the First Temple and the building of the Second Temple, a great Miracle took place and this is the story of Purim.

In this period in History, the world was ruled by a King named: "Achashverosh". Our sages tell us that there were four leaders in History that had dominion over the entire known world of their time, they were (In Historical Order)

1. Pharaoh – The King of Egypt (The Pharaoh that was involved in the exodus from Egypt in the days of Moses)
2. King Solomon (The son of King David)
3. Achashverosh (The Babylonian King involved in the story of Purim)
4. Alexander The Great (As documented in contemporary History)

Achashverosh had an advisor named Haman. Haman was a descendant of "Amalake", the root and source of Anti Semitism. Haman held a very powerful position, and a very extreme view towards Jews; thus he was a dangerous individual. Our sages tell us that due to the fact that the Jewish people of the time benefited from a "Sudas Reshoyim"[1] Haman was allowed to make a decree against the Jews.

The Decree of Haman:

Haman decreed that on the 14th day of the month of Adar, all Jews (Including: men, women and children) were to be killed. Haman arrived at the date "The 14th of Adar" through doing a lottery with potential dates, this lottery was called a "Pur". Although when we read the story of Purim in "Megilas Ester" we see the miraculous events very clearly, for the people living through that time the miracles were extremely hidden. The story of Purim unfolded over a number of years, and the Jews had no way of knowing what would transpire. This is one of the reasons that the Megila on Purim is called "Megilas Ester" which translates into "Revealing the Hidden". Through a series of miraculous events the Jews were ultimately saved, and Haman's decree was overturned, and Haman himself was killed. This is a summary of the events surrounding the miracle of Purim. In This lesson we will explore the concept of "Revealing the Hidden" and through this understand the festival of Purim.

---

[1]. Achashverosh invited the Jews to celebrate in a festive meal which lasted many days. Although the food served to the Jews was Kosher, nevertheless they should not have enjoyed the company of the wicked.

THE RABBI MICHAEL J ELJARRAT LEARNING PROGRAMME – CLASS NINETY FIVE

Revealing the Hidden:

The week before Purim we read the special Parsha of "Zachor"[2] (Remember) which contains the commandment to "Remember" that which Amalake did to the Jews when they came out of Egypt.

When the Jewish nation left Egypt, all the nations of the world saw the great miracles which God performed for the Jewish Nation, and were in awe of the Jewish Nation, as they realized that the hand of God was protecting them. Thus all the nations of the world did not wage war with the Jewish people as they feared the wrath of God. The Nation of Amalake on the other hand, refused to see "the hand of God" involved in the liberation of the Jewish people from Egypt. Instead they believed that the "Miraculous" events were nothing more than a coincidence, and with that attitude in mind they waged war against the Jewish Nation. This intern calmed the other nations, who subsequently also waged war with the Jews.

Our sages tell us that Amalake is the very opposite of a Jew. Where as Amalake believe in coincidence the Jew believes in the hand of God. Our sages also tell us that God rules the world with "Two Hands" the "Left Hand" is what we would call nature or the natural, and the "Right Hand" what we would call the Miraculous or the Super Natural. As the Ramchal explains; God created the world in such a way that events will occur in a predicable manner. This is a kindness of God as it allows Mankind the ability to plan and prepare. Thus when the seeds of an Orange tree are planted, an Orange tree will grow as ordained by Nature or the "Left Hand" of God. God can act miraculously and make an Apple tree grow when the seeds of an Orange are planted, but for the world to run with the "Right Hand" – By Super-nature, the world would be entirely random and chaotic.

The concept of God's "Left Hand" and "Right Hand" can be understood as follows: We can look at all events as being Miraculous, in the sense that whether it rains a "Natural" shower or whether the sea splits, both events have emanated from God. Such as one event from the "Left Hand" and the other event from the "Right Hand". Alternatively we can look at all events as being a part of Nature, whether it rains a "Natural" shower or whether the sea splits, both events have emanated from God the source of Nature. Such as one event from the "Left Hand" and the other event from the "Right Hand".

Therefore only one who acknowledges God in "Nature" (The "Left Hand") can appreciate God in a "Miracle" (The "Right Hand"). Since Amalake deny the existence of God altogether, all events which transpire in the world are attributed to random chaos and entropy. Once one denies the existence of God, one needs a concept to describe events which seem to carry a very specific purpose such as "The Splitting of the Sea", for this Amalake invented "Coincidence". The term coincidence is foreign to Judaism, since the mechanics of "Coincidence" ride on the premise that there is no God.

---

2. Devarim / Deuteronomy 25: 17-19

Amalake versus the Jew:

For many individuals a middle ground is held, meaning "Natural" events are viewed as transpiring from random chaos and entropy, whereas "Miraculous" events are viewed as transpiring from God. This of course cannot be true as we have explained above. Thus the war between Amalake and the Jews is centered around the very existence of God. This is one of the reasons that Amalake have tried to physically destroy the Jews many times in history, for the Jewish people spread the light of God in the world, where as Amalake seek to eliminate God altogether.

The Miracle of Purim:

The events which transpired around the story of Purim, brought to light the concept that even what happens appears to be "Natural" is in fact the "Hand of God" When God interacts with us through "Nature"/"The Natural" it is difficult to see the Hand of God, and thus we say God is "Hidden". When God interacts with us through "Miracles"/ "The Super-Natural" it is easy for everyone (except the hardened Atheist Amalake) to see the Hand of God. Thus the miracle of Purim did not contain open miracles like the miracles of Pesach, rather it contained a collection of "Natural" events, which when tied together create a full picture of a miraculous story. Therefore in a sense the miracle of Purim is the greatest of all miracles, since it demonstrates to all those "sitting on the fence" with regards to their belief in God, that all events, even those that appear to be "Natural" are governed by God.

The future festivals:

Our sages tell us that Purim is the only festival which will be maintained when Moshiach comes. One possible reason why this may be the case is owing to the nature of the miracle of Purim. In contrast to other festivals which celebrate open miracles such as Pesach and Chanukah for example, Purim on the other hand celebrates a hidden miracle. Our sages also tell us that the amount of open miracles that will occur when moshiach comes, will outweigh even the grand miracles that occurred in the exodus from Egypt. Thus when moshaich comes we will no longer need to celebrate open miracles of the past as we will have greater open miracles to celebrate in the present. However since we can only appreciate open miracles, when one has an appreciation for hidden miracles, Purim the ultimate hidden miracle will never be forgotten.

The significance of Purim for us is to appreciate that everything which happens in this world is from God. When situations appear to be unbearably difficult, the salvation may lie await around the corner. Although the presence of God may be hidden in "Nature" we have the ability through thought and analysis, and through awareness, understanding and wisdom to "Reveal the Hidden" and to find God. We can lead meaningful lives by appreciating the subtle nuances of our surroundings, and by recognizing the "Left Hand" of God in "Nature". If we succeed in the above, we will be able to appreciate open miracles, and we will be able to see the bad in good events as well as the good in bad events equally.

THE RABBI MICHAEL J ELJARRAT LEARNING PROGRAMME – CLASS NINETY SIX

CLASS 96 THE JEWISH CALENDAR

LAWS AND SIGNIFICANCE OF PURIM PART TWO

The days leading up to Purim:

Between Rosh Chodesh Adar and Nissan we read 4 unique Parshas they are

1. Shekalim
2. Zachor
3. Parah
4. Ha Chodesh

(There are those that say that Zachor and Parah are obligations from the torah)

- The 14th day of Adar is Purim and the 13th day of Adar is a fast day called Tanis Esther (the fast begins at sunrise and end at sunset)

Mitzvos of Purim:

- We wear Shabbos clothes for the reading of the Megilah
- There is a custom to give 3x "Machasis Ha Shekel" (a half of the standard coin) to charity before Purim.
- During all the prayers on Purim we add "Al Hanisim" (which is found in the Amidah after "Modim")
- Every man and woman is obligated to hear the reading of the Megilah both by day and by night.
- If one is weak from the fast one may have a snack such as coffee before the reading of the Megilah.
- The custom is to fold the Megilah one page over another because the Megilah is called the "letter" of Purim.

THE RABBI MICHAEL J ELJARRAT LEARNING PROGRAMME – CLASS NINETY SIX

Reading the Megilah:

- The one reading the Megilah makes three blessings before reading:

    1. "Al Mikra Megilah" (On the reading of the Megilah)
    2. "Sheh Osoh Nissim" (Who performed miracles)
    3. "Sheh Hechiyano" (Who has brought us to this time)

- When the chazzan makes the Blessing of "Sheh Hechiyano" one must have in mind that the Brocho covers the mitzvah of "Shlach Manos", "Matonos Le-Evyonim" and the Suda of Purim.

- If Purim falls on a Sunday one may not take the Migilah to Shul on Shabbos.

Mitzvos of Purim day:

- Every person is obligated to send 2 portions of food to one person.
- Every person is obligated to give 2 gifts to "Evyonim" (Poor individuals) (meaning 1 gift to 2 different people)
- Every person is obligated to eat a Sudas Purim and the main time is during the day.
- Men are obligated to get drunk on Purim to the extent that they don't know the difference between "Orroor Haman and Baruch Mordechai"
- One should refrain from doing work on Purim.

After Purim:

- The 15th of Adar is called "Shoshan Purim"
- On the 14th and 15th of Adar we do not say "Tachanoon" nor "El Erech Apyim" nor "Lamnasayach".(See Siddur for details)

THE RABBI MICHAEL J ELJARRAT LEARNING PROGRAMME – CLASS NINETY SEVEN

CLASS 97 THE JEWISH CALENDAR

LAWS AND SIGNIFICANCE OF PESACH PART ONE

In this lesson we will look at the significance of the festival of Pesach (Passover), and discover why this festival has become so well known in the world today.

The Month of Nissan is the first month (when we count the months of the year), and in it our Forefathers were redeemed from Egypt, and some say that even the future redemption (when Moshiach comes) will also take place in the month of Nissan. The festival of Pesach/Passover is the celebration of when the "Family of Israel" became the "Nation of Israel", when the Nation of Israel was liberated from slavery and openly saw the ("Right") hand of God.

In this lesson we will explore the concepts of "Mitzryim", "Slavery" and "Redemption". The story of Pesach, is the story which contains the two elements, which motivate a Jew namely: "Slavery" and "Redemption".

What is "Slavery"?

Today when we think about "Slavery" or "Slaves", we tend to think about a time in the distant past where slaves were traded and were forced into slave labor; a period in history which has long since past. We tend to think that slavery no longer exists today in our modern world.

However nothing could be further from the truth, slavery is a part of our "modern" world perhaps now more than ever before.

How so? There are many forms of "Slavery", physical "Slavery" that we referred to above is merely but one form of "Slavery".

As we are well aware the Human Being consists of a Body, Mind and Soul, therefore physical slavery is slavery of the "Body", hence the other two forms of "Slavery" are "Slavery of the Mind" and "Slavery of the Soul". We will now examine the three forms of slavery that we have mentioned above.

THE RABBI MICHAEL J ELJARRAT LEARNING PROGRAMME – CLASS NINETY SEVEN

Slavery of the Body:

Like all matters relating to physicality, simple observation is all that is required to gain an understanding of the concept (Unlike matters of a metaphysical or spiritual nature which require intelligence to gain an understanding of the concept). The essence of all forms of slavery is "Limitations and Restrictions", thus physical slavery can be defined as: A restriction of freedom of movement, which places limitations on the body. Hence one who is not free to move about without restrictions or limitations is in physical slavery. For example one who is in prison, or one who is an paralyzed, or one who lives in a country which restricts the travel of its citizens, or one who cannot move/travel due to a lack of means or/and resources, all of the above are forms of physical slavery.

Slavery of the Mind:

Slavery of the Mind also entails "Limitations and Restrictions". Slavery of the mind can be defined as a restriction of freedom of thought which places limitations on the mind. Hence one who is not free to think their own thoughts without restrictions or limitations is in "Mental Slavery". For example one who has been indoctrinated through a cult or belief system, or one who has a mental illness[1], or one who lacks self – awareness, or one who lacks critical thinking skills. All of the above are forms of Mental Slavery.

Slavery of the Soul:

Slavery of the Soul also entails "Limitations and Restrictions". Slavery of the Soul can be defined as a restriction of freedom of spirituality which places limitations on the Soul. Hence one who is not free to pursue spirituality without restrictions or limitations is in spiritual slavery. For example one who is living in a place where Anti Semitism restricts one from practicing Judaism freely, or one who is part of a cultural "System" (Such as the systems seen in class 86) or "Group"[2], or one who lacks the ability to integrate logic and emotion (so that all actions are guided by both logic and emotion simultaneously) or one who constantly uses "Heuristics and Schemas" or "Superficial Thinking". All of the above are forms of spiritual slavery.

Slavery Combinations:

As we have seen above, slavery takes on several forms, however very often these forms of slavery occur together in one individual. For example one who has been imprisoned and is thus in physical slavery, may then become depressed and thus develop mental slavery which may intern cause or be combined with spiritual slavery. The same can be said regarding any one form of "Slavery", namely that one form of "Slavery" can induce or be combined with any other form of "Slavery".

---

1. Mental illness as defined by Axis I and Axis II disorders in the DSM –IV- TR (and later)
2. Even systems and groups which are valid place limitations on spirituality.

THE RABBI MICHAEL J ELJARRAT LEARNING PROGRAMME – CLASS NINETY SEVEN

The three elements of Slavery:

Every form of "Slavery" contains within it three elements, namely:

1. The "Slave Master" – The one causing the "Slavery"
2. The "Slavery" – The limitations and restrictions.
3. The "Slave" – The one experiencing the "Slavery".

Hence the slave is enslaved by the slave master as such as described in the table below:

	Slave Master	Slavery	Slave
Physical Slavery	E.g.: Prison Warden	Restriction of Movement	"The Prisoner"
Mental Slavery	E.g.: Mental Illness	Restriction of Thought	"The Patient"
Spiritual Slavery	E.g.: Group Think	Restriction of Development	"The Member"

Modern day Slaves:

Now that we have a better understanding of Slavery, we can see that although one form of physical slavery was abolished many years ago, nevertheless the majority of forms of slavery still exist and are very common today.
Such as:

- "The Drug Addict" – Who is mentally enslaved to his/her addictions.
- "The Abused Employee" – Who is physically enslaved by financial difficulties, imposed by an unjust employer.
- "The Battered Wife" – Who is mentally enslaved by an abusive spouse.
- "The Discriminated" – Who is spiritually enslaved by the self-righteous bigot.
- "The Group Member" – Who is mentally/spiritually enslaved by beliefs imposed, by the group leader or group members.

These are just a few examples, there are of course many, many more. Thus it is clear that slavery is rampant in our times, across all peoples, places and cultures.

The "Slavery" of Mitzryim:

The word "Mitzryim" comes from the word "Maytzar" (meaning narrow). The Jews that were in Mitzryim were in a "Narrow" place, meaning they had limitations and restrictions imposed over them. The word "Maytzar" comes from the root "Tzar" meaning "Narrow".

When a Jew is in trouble he/she will say they are having "Tzoros" (Meaning trouble). The word "Tzoros" (Trouble) also comes from the root "Tzar" (Narrow), this is because the essence of "Tzoros" (Trouble) is having restrictions and limitations in regards to ones choices or possible solutions.

THE RABBI MICHAEL J ELJARRAT LEARNING PROGRAMME – CLASS NINETY SEVEN

This is also why we feel "Boxed In" or "Trapped" when we are experiencing "Tzoros" (Trouble). Having troubles is akin to slavery, as the problem/trouble at hand places limitations and restrictions on the one experiencing the problem/trouble.

The Jews, who were enslaved in Egypt, experienced all three forms of slavery simultaneously.

1. Physical Slavery in the form of physical work.
2. Mental Slavery in the form of abuse by the Egyptians.
3. Spiritual Slavery caused by the fact that they had no time to reflect (They fell spiritually because all their time was spent working).

Thus Pesach is not just the time where the Jews left Egypt; Pesach is the time that the Jewish Nation was released from all forms of Slavery.

Our Sages tell us that the Jewish calendar, contains within it inherent spirituality, and thus, if the Jewish Nation was released from Slavery on Pesach, we too can be released from our personal Slavery on Pesach. Thus Pesach is the time where a "Drug Addict" may find help, "The Abused Employer" finds liberation, and the "Hopeless" find hope etc.

It is for this reason that the festival of Pesach/Passover has become so well known and celebrated, as it is this festival which releases the "Slave" from his/her "Slavery", and when we trade in all forms of "Slavery" to become "Slaves" of God, who is infinite and posses no limitations on us.

THE RABBI MICHAEL J ELJARRAT LEARNING PROGRAMME – CLASS NINETY EIGHT

CLASS 98 — THE JEWISH CALENDAR

LAWS AND SIGNIFICANCE OF PESACH PART TWO

The days leading up to Pesach:

- During the month of Nissan we do not say "Tachanoon"
- One is forbidden to eat, or even to own any "Chometz" from the early morning before Pesach until the end of Pesach. (Latest time for owning Chometz 10:45am, latest time for eating 9:45am on the morning before Pesach)
- "Chometz" is any thing made out of the 5 types of grain,(wheat, barley, rye, spelt, oats) which has come into contact with water (some say any liquid) and left unattended for 18 minutes or longer.
- There is a separate prohibition to eat or own any leaven, which is any raising agent such as yeast.
- Since we may not own Chometz on Pesach, many people sell non perishable foods prior to Pesach (contact your local rabbi for details)
- Technically speaking, many grocery items may in actual fact not be Chometz (such as sugar for example) However since various products may have benign Chometz (such as salt which contains a free flowing agent which is Chometz) we only eat food products which are marked "Kosher for Passover"

The night before Pesach:

- One is obligated to search ones home for Chometz on the night prior to Pesach.
- The search begins as soon as it is night.
- Half an hour before the search it is forbidden to eat or do any work. (Since one may forget to do the search)
- The search is done using a wax candle with a single wick (One may not use a multi wicked candle since it hinders the search because of the fire hazard)
- One should check all the rooms of ones home where there is a possibility of there being Chometz. (Included in this, is pockets of clothes, school bags ect.)

- Before one begins the search one must make a Brocho "AL BEEOOR CHOMETZ" ("On destroying Chometz") one should refrain from speaking from the time of the Brocho until after the search has ended.
- Some have a custom to place pieces of bread around the house before the search, however one should insure that the search is done properly and is not just merely a collection of the pieces of bread.
- After the search we nullify the Chometz by saying "Kal Chamirah" which translated means "any Chometz which is in my possession whether or not I know about it, should be nullified and should be like the dust of the earth"
- One should make the above declaration in a language that one understands.

Erev Pesach (the morning before Pesach):

- The above declaration is made once again the following morning at the burning of the Chometz.
- If one finds Chometz in ones house during Pesach, one should cover it and burn it during Chol Ha Moed.
- It is forbidden to eat Matzah on Erev Pesach (some have a custom not to eat Matzah from Rosh Chodesh Nissan)
- During Pesach we do not use any utensils used through out the year. All cutlery and crockery is stored away in order to prevent us from using them.

Kashering and Cleaning for Pesach:

- Before Pesach one should clean all the rooms of ones home and insure that they are Chometz free.
- When cleaning the kitchen, one should clean all surfaces which come into contact with Chometz. The surface should then be covered or Kashered (preferably both)
- Kashering is done, by using a blowtorch over the surfaces. Surfaces, which can be damaged by the heat of the blowtorch, should be properly covered.
- The oven can be Kashered for Pesach in 2 stages
    1. First the oven should be thoroughly cleaned and
    2. Then the oven should be left on maximum temperature until the element glows red it should then be left like that with the oven door closed for 1 hour.
- Stovetops should be thoroughly cleaned, then covered with heavy-duty aluminium foil or similar.
- It is preferable not to use a microwave that is used though out the year since there are various opinions as to how to Kasher the microwave. A competent Rabbi should be consulted should you wish to use the microwave.

THE RABBI MICHAEL J ELJARRAT LEARNING PROGRAMME – CLASS NINETY EIGHT

 The Pesach Seder (Performed on the first two nights of Pesach)

1. **Kadaish:** (Kiddush) Unlike Shabbos and Yomtov on Pesach Seder night, everyone makes Kiddush on a cup of wine (or grape juice). This is the first of 4 cups, which we drink on Seder night.
2. **Oorchatz:** (Washing of the hands) Normally during the year we do not wash our hands before eating fruits and vegetables which are dipped into liquids, however on Pesach we wash our hands prior to eating the Karpas.(one of the reasons for this is to arouse curiosity among the children)
3. **Karpas:** (A vegetable) Karpas is any vegetable, which has the same Brocho as the Moror. Many people use a potato. We take a small peace of Karpas then we dip it into salt water and make a brocha then we eat it.
4. **Yachatz:** (Braking of the Matzah) The leader of the Seder brakes the middle Matzah in the Seder plate into two peaces, the bigger peace is separated and put aside for "Afikomon"
5. **Magid:** (Telling over the story of redemption from Egypt). This is one of the primary Mitzvos of the Night. It begins with the child asking the "Four Questions" and the leader of the Seder responding "Avodim Hayinu" ("We were slaves.")
6. **Rochtzah:** (Washing of the hands) Like during the year we wash our hands before eating bread, However since we do not eat bread on Pesach we wash before we eat Matzah.
7. **Motzie/ Matzah:** (Making "Ha Motzie" and eating the Matzah) On Seder night it is a Mitzvah from the torah to eat Matzah. We eat 2 olives worth's of Matzah. One should not talk until one has finished eating this amount of Matzah.
8. **Maror:** (Bitter herbs). We take an olives worth of bitter herbs (Many people use horse radish or Romain lettuce) and then we make a special Brocho and eat it.
9. **Koraich:** (Sandwich). We then take Matzah and Moror together; the Moror is first dipped into "Charoses".
10. **Shoolchan Oraich:** (Set table). We then go on to eat a Yomtov meal
11. **Tzafoon.** (Eating the"Afikomon") The afrikomon is Matzah; it was instituted after the destruction of the second temple when all sacrifices became prohibited. This Matzah is there to remind us of the sacrificial Lamb offering which was one the primary Mitzvos during the days of the Temple.
12. **Boraich:** (Blessing). We then make an after Brocho just as we would after any meal where we washed our hands for bread.
13. **Hallel:** (Praises). We then say the remainder of Hallel this is the same Hallel as we say during the year on special occasions.
14. **Nirtzah:** (Closing). We then go on to thank G-d for allowing us to complete the Seder and we pray that next year we will merit to the final and ultimate redemption, with the Temple being rebuild in Jerusalem.

THE RABBI MICHAEL J ELJARRAT LEARNING PROGRAMME – CLASS NINETY NINE

CLASS 99 — THE JEWISH CALENDAR

LAWS AND SIGNIFICANCE OF SHAVUOS PART ONE

In this lesson we will look at the significance of the festival of Shavuos. Shavuos is the festival which is celebrated 50 days after Pesach/Passover, and is known as "Zman Matan Torosaynu" (The time of the giving of our Torah). Shavuos marks the end of the counting the Omer, and thus Shavuos is known as the festival of "Weeks" (Shavuos in Hebrew – Week, and the plural Shavuos – Weeks). In this lesson we will explore the connection between "Zman" (Time), "Shavuah" (Week) and "Matan Torah" (The giving of the Torah); and through this exploration we will discover the significance of the festival.

The period between Pesach and Shavuos:

From the second night of Pesach until Shavuos, we count the Omer as it says in the verse:[1]

"And you shall count for yourselves from the morrow of the rest day......seven weeks they shall complete........fifty days............etc."

Our sages tell us that when the Jewish Nation left Egypt, they were on the lowest spiritual level (the 50th level of impurity). Each day the rose up one spiritual level so that by the time of "Matan Torah" (The giving of the Torah) they were on the highest spiritual level.

Why was the Jewish Nation on the lowest spiritual level when they left Egypt? As we saw previously,[2] the Jews who were in Egypt were subjected to all three forms of Slavery, and this caused their drop in spiritual level.

As the Ramchal explains[3]; Pharaoh devised a plan whereby the Jews had to work continuously all day, every day. As soon as one task ended the next task began. In this way the Jewish people had no free time, and thus they were unable to form groups or unions or plot schemes to over throw Pharaoh. Through this heavy work load Pharaoh was able to stifle any potential revolts or revolutions.

As a secondary consequence of this heavy work load system; the Jewish people had no time to think, and had to conduct their daily activities on "Auto Pilot" (meaning that they had no time to stop and think about what they were doing).

---

1. Vayikra / Leviticus 23:15-16
2. Class 97
3. Mesilas Yesharim – Chapter 2

The Jewish people had no time to monitor their spirituality, and were forced into a life of "survival and existence". They "existed" through life reacting to situations, and not "living" life, proactively making choices, and decisions.

Since the very essence of spirituality is making choices and decisions, and spiritual growth only comes from making good choices, and being challenged with difficult decisions; their lack of time to think directly influenced their spirituality.

Thus one of the greatest spiritual "Slave Masters" is the lack of time. We may therefore say, one who lacks adequate time to think about one's actions, is in "Spiritual Slavery". Shavuos is therefore the time, where the Jewish Nation receives the final step in emancipation from slavery, namely the gift of "Time".

The Modern Day Problem:

Ever since the industrial revolution, Mankind as a whole has become progressively more productive. With the invention of the "Automobile" Man was able to travel further, with the invention of the "Telephone" Man was able to communicate quicker, with the invention of the "Airplane" Man was able to travel the world.

More recent inventions have allowed Man to do even more; with the invention of "Computers" Man was able to handle complex tasks, with the invention of the "Internet" Man was able to access information with ease, with the invention of the "Cell-Phone" Man was able to communicate with the entire world from any location.

Even more recent inventions have allowed Man to do more, such as Video Calling, Collaborating Projects with team members around the world, and communicating with the entire world simultaneously with "Webinars" and the like, to name but a few.

However despite Mankind's achievements in technology, Mankind has not achieved tranquillity, in fact quite the opposite is true. With each technological advancement; Mankind has become increasingly "Busy". As Mankind has gained the ability to be more productive, so too have the demands increased on Mankind to be as productive as technology allows for.

Thus Mankind was expected to travel by automobile or airplane and to pick up the phone and call. Later Mankind was expected to handle complex tasks, access all the information and communicate with the entire world. More recently Mankind was expected to be available all the time, for the entire world simultaneously. Thus although the "Cell-Phone", "Note-Pad" and "Tablet" are great tools in terms of productivity, at the same time we become enslaved to these devices, and are expected to use them. One cannot simply ignore a phone call, e-mail, text or instant message.

Egypt again today:

As was the case in Egypt, thousands of years ago; Today we face a similar problem. Just as the Jewish Nation fell spiritually in Egypt because they had no time to think, so too today the Jewish Nation is falling spiritually for the very same reason, a lack of time.

THE RABBI MICHAEL J ELJARRAT LEARNING PROGRAMME – CLASS NINETY NINE

It now becomes very clear to us why the sages compared Egypt with the era before the coming of Moshiach, and the redemption with the coming of Moshiach; As both these periods in History are periods of "Spiritual Slavery", followed by "Spiritual Liberation".

In Egypt the "Spiritual Slavery" was brought about through the decrees of Pharaoh, and in the modern era the "Spiritual Slavery" was brought about through complex interactions between society and technology. In a sense the "Spiritual Slavery" of today is worse than that which was found in Egypt, for two reasons;

1. Firstly from the time of the giving of the Torah, each generation is spiritually weaker than the preceding generation, thus spiritual slavery imposed on one who is spiritually weak to start with, has far greater ramifications.
2. Secondly the "Spiritual Slavery" which occurred in Egypt, was limited to the inhabitants of Egypt, today however "Spiritual Slavery" has become a part of world culture, and is entrenched throughout the entire world. It could be for this reason that the miracles which will take place in the time of Moshiach will be greater, since the slavery itself is greater than in Egypt.

Matan Torah – The giving of the Torah:

As we have said above, Shavuos is the festival which celebrates the giving of the Torah, and the final step in the liberation from slavery. Thus we may conclude that the key to freedom from "Spiritual Slavery" is the Torah itself. Phrased differently, we may say the Torah contains within it, the key to distance oneself from the elements which bring about spiritual enslavement; namely "The lack of time". This means to say that locked away somewhere in the Torah, is the tool to make more Time. Let us try and understand how this is so.

Torah and Time:

In the Braisa[4] of Rebbe Pinchas Ben Yair, which describes the steps of spiritual elevation and forms the basis of the work called the Mesilas Yesharim (Path of the Just) written by the Ramchal (Rabbi Moshe Chaim Luzzato) it states as follows:

1. Torah brings one to carefulness
2. Carefulness brings one to Hastiness
3. Hastiness brings one to Cleanliness ect..

Thus we see that the first step in spiritual elevation is Torah. The Ramchal explains[5] that one who wants to enlighten him/her self needs to maintain two perspectives:

1. One needs to contemplate the true definitions of "Good" and "Bad".
2. One needs to introspect about one's actions to see whether they fall into the category of "Good" or "Bad"

---

4. A Braisa is a teaching similar to a Mishna.
5. Mesilas Yesharim Chapter 3

THE RABBI MICHAEL J ELJARRAT LEARNING PROGRAMME – CLASS NINETY NINE

Thus the process of counting the days leading up to Shavuos, is not merely about counting the days but:

"Making the days count"

Meaning that the route to emancipation from "Spiritual Slavery" caused by the lack of time is as follows:

1. First one needs to set aside time, (As minimal as it may be) to learn Torah.
2. This Torah study will open the door to contemplation and introspection. (As mentioned in the two steps above)
3. Apart from the mechanical dynamic, there is also the aspect of "Heavenly Assistance". As our sages tell us: "One who comes to purify himself, receives heavenly assistance"
4. If one accepts upon him/her self the yolk of heaven, God removes from him/her the yolk of worldly responsibilities, and the yolk of government.[6]

My own method for accepting the yolk of heaven upon myself is through saying the "Shema" with the following intention:

- "Shema Yisroel" – Listen all Jews,
- "YHVH Elokaynu" – YHVH not money, people or cultures etc is our God.
- "YHVH Echad" – YHVH is number one in my list of priorities, and not anything else.

---

6. Ovos Chapter 3 Mishna 6

THE RABBI MICHAEL J ELJARRAT LEARNING PROGRAMME – CLASS ONE HUNDRED

CLASS 100 — THE JEWISH CALENDAR

LAWS AND SIGNIFICANCE OF SHAVUOS PART TWO

Please Read:

In this lesson we will look at some of the laws and customs of the festival of Shavuos. This lesson is the final lesson in the section dealing with the "Jewish Calendar", as well as being the final lesson in the course entitled "Fundamentals of Judaism" Although we have not covered the laws and significance of the "Three Weeks" and "Tisha B'Av", the mourning period in the Jewish calendar starting on the 17th of the month of Tamuz and ending on the 9th/10th day of the month of Av. I have deliberately not included it in this course, for two reasons:

1. Firstly I did not want to end the course on a "Bad Note" dealing with mourning.
2. Secondly I only wanted to include "Festivals" and not periods of mourning. Our sages tell us that when Moshiach comes, and the Third Beis Ha Mikdash is rebuilt, the mourning day of Tisha B'Av will become a festival to be celebrated. Thus class 101 is reserved for the "Festival of Tisha B'Av", I look forward to writing class 101 very soon God willing.

Laws of Shavuos:

Unlike the other festivals such as Rosh Ha Shana, which has the special Mitzvah of Shofar, or Succos which has the special Mitzvah of Succah, and the Four Species, and Pesach which has the special Mitzvah of Matzah amongst others, Shavuos on the other hand has no special Mitzvos associated with it. (The reason for this has been explained in another class).

There is however several laws and customs associated with this festival.

- In the times of the Beis Ha Mikdash, there was a special sacrifice brought called "Shetei Ha Lechem" – The Two Loaves.

From this a custom developed, where we remember the two loaves of bread.

THE RABBI MICHAEL J ELJARRAT LEARNING PROGRAMME – CLASS ONE HUNDRED

This is accomplished by:

1. Having a "Milky" meal, followed by a "Meaty" meal at the same sitting, thus requiring two loaves of bread. As the bread which is placed at the first meal (The "Milky" meal) must be removed, and replaced with a new loaf for the second course (The "Meaty" meal).
2. In order to follow this custom, care must be taken not to God Forbid mix Meat and Milk.
3. Since many individuals are not fluent in the laws of "Meat and Milk", the custom amongst non-learned individuals is to serve a "Milky" meal only. Although this does not necessitate two loaves of bread, and hence the "Shetei Ha Lechem" is not remembered, nevertheless it is acceptable to have a "Milky" meal on Yom-Tov (or even Shabbos), as one is not obligated to eat meat on Shabbos or Yom-Tov.[1]
4. However having a meat meal, is more honorable to the festival, and certainly one who is Lactose Intolerant should have a meat meal on Shavuos.

Davenning on Shavuos:

- The custom is to wait until "Tzaitz Ha Kochavim" (When the stars come out) to Daven Mariv, the reason being: The Omer consists of 49 complete days, and the day does not end until nightfall.
- The Zohar[2] writes that one who stays up all night on the first night of Shavuos, and does not sleep at all, but learns Torah through the night, is guaranteed that he will finish the year (i.e. from Shavuos until Rosh Ha Shana) and nothing will happen to harm him.
- One who stays up all night learning, should have someone else say the morning Brochos for him, as there are several doubts regarding which blessings may be said by the individual who stays up all night.
- There is a custom to recite "Akdomos" after the Kohen has been called to the Torah, but before he recites his blessing. (This Piyut speaks about the value of Torah amongst other things)
- On the first day of Shavuos we read the "Ten Commandments" in a special tune.
- On both days of Shavuos we say the full Hallel.
- On both days of Shavuos we do "Birkas Kohanim" (The Priestly blessing) in the prayer of Musaf.
- On the second day of Shavuos we read "Megilas Rus" (The Megilah of Ruth)
- On the second day of Shavuos we do Yiskor (The prayer remembering those who have passed away).

---

1. See Mishna Berura – Siman 552 Halacha 10 – Mishna Berura 23 "Even though one is not obligated to eat meat on Shabbos."
2. See the Mishna Berura – Siman 494 Halacha 1 Mishna Berura 1. It seems to me that, learning on Shavuos through the night protects one from damage that may occur in the month of Av, a period of "Bad Mazel".

Other Customs of Shavuos:

- There is a custom to decorate the Shul with flowers on Shavuos, the reason for this custom is to remember Mount Sinai (The mountain on which the Torah was given) which sprouted forth with beautiful flowers in honor of receiving the Torah.
- We do not say Tachanun from Rosh Chodesh Sivan until the eighth day of Sivan.
- King David passed away on the festival of Shavuos, and was also born on the festival of Shavuos (As it says: God fills the life of the righteous – Meaning that righteous people die on the same date as their birth, thus having a complete life.) According to some this is the reason we read "Megilas Rus" (The Megilah of Ruth) on Shavuos since King David, descended through Ruth.
- The Sharei Teshuvah brings in the name of the "Birchei Yosef" who himself brings in the name of the "Olelos Ephryim" that one who gives a new Sefer Torah (Torah Scroll) to a Shul just prior to the festival of Shavuos, is as if he has brought a "Mincha" sacrifice to Hashem in the right time.

May we soon merit the rebuilding of the Beis Ha Mikdash, Amen.

www.ingramcontent.com/pod-product-compliance
Lightning Source LLC
Chambersburg PA
CBHW080332170426
43194CB00014B/2530